9E

crossroads
Cooking

Other Books by Elisabeth Rozin

The Universal Kitchen

The Primal Cheeseburger

Blue Corn and Chocolate

Ethnic Cuisine

The Flavor-Principle Cookbook

ELISABETH ROZIN

crossroads Cooking

*The Meeting and Mating
of Ethnic Cuisines—
from Burma to Texas
in 200 Recipes*

VIKING

VIKING
Published by the Penguin Group
Penguin Putnam Inc., 375 Hudson Street,
New York, New York 10014, U.S.A.
Penguin Books Ltd, 27 Wrights Lane, London W8 5TZ, England
Penguin Books Australia Ltd, Ringwood, Victoria, Australia
Penguin Books Canada Ltd, 10 Alcorn Avenue,
Toronto, Ontario, Canada M4V 3B2
Penguin Books (N.Z.) Ltd, 182–190 Wairau Road,
Auckland, 10, New Zealand

Penguin Books Ltd, Registered Offices:
Harmondsworth, Middlesex, England

First published in 1999 by Viking Penguin,
a member of Penguin Putnam Inc.

10 9 8 7 6 5 4 3 2 1

LIBRARY OF CONGRESS CATALOGING-IN-PUBLICATION DATA
Rozin, Elisabeth.
    Crossroads cooking/by Elisabeth Rozin.
        p. cm.
    Includes index.
    ISBN 0-670-87338-1
    1. Cookery, International.   I. Title.
TX725.A1R684   1999
  641.59—dc21   98–53226

This book is printed on acid-free paper. ∞

Printed in the United States of America
Set in New Baskerville
Designed by Kathryn Parise

The discovery of a new dish is more beneficial to humanity than the discovery of a new star.

JEAN ANTHELME BRILLAT-SAVARIN

acknowledgments

To my editor, Dawn Drzal, whose belief in the work was steadfast and uplifting. I thank her for her support, her creative input, and her friendship.

To Jariya Wanapun, editorial assistant, who was unfailingly helpful, competent, and courteous.

To my children, a constant loving presence in my life, who kept the faith, ate the experiments, and never let me off the hook.

To my friends and colleagues who tasted and tested with skill and generosity: Reid Bodek, Claire Dudley, Laurie Dudley, Helena Grady, Constance Horwitz, Liz Lempert and Ken Norman, Ruth Loewen, Arden Neisser, Rod Pelchat, Irene Pleasure, Patricia Pliner, Lex Rozin, Lillian Rozin, Judy Stern, Marcy Stricker, Karoline Wallace, and the Culture and Foods Class of Cazenovia High School (B. J. Palmer, Instructor).

contents

introduction

In the contemporary language of cuisine, "fusion" and "melting pot" are buzzwords, denoting novel, innovative, and sometimes bizarre marriages and meldings of different ethnic traditions. "Melting pot" is a generally accepted term for the gradual, inevitable, and, to the food purist, unfortunate blurring of culinary contours that occurs when many different people come together and contribute their traditions to the common pot. Fusion, on the other hand, is the specific coinage of trendy young chefs in fashionable restaurants who deliberately set about to design unprecedented combinations of ingredients, self-consciously creating stylish new dishes in which the world's foods and techniques are brought together in unique presentations. Both fusion and melting-pot cookery bubbled up to gastronomic attention from the fermentative, multiethnic cauldron of twentieth-century America.

But in fact this kind of cooking is nothing new. For as long as can be remembered or recorded, people have been exchanging goods, ideas, and technology—swapping an interesting new herb for a handful of seeds, copying the design of a neighbor's pot, recreating a delicious dish eaten at someone else's table. Wherever and whenever groups of people came together, by reason of travel or migration, commerce, or war, for social, communal, or religious purposes, they inevitably affected one another's food practices, sometimes slowly and subtly, occasionally with astonishing swiftness and force. And sometimes when it happened, a new tradition was created, one that would itself be subject in time to other influences and innovations.

There are throughout the world hundreds of places where the distinctive elements of different cultures have come together to form a host of vital new culinary traditions; indeed, there are few places on earth, if any, that remain genuinely pristine and unaffected by outside influences of some kind. But there are some areas, some cuisines, that show more dramatically than others the mergings, the collaborations, the innovations that have resulted in the evolution of exciting and viable new practices and products. Many of these cuisines, which developed at different times and at various rates throughout human history, have achieved with time and tradition their own identity and integrity, even though they are composed of a number of diverse elements. They are true Crossroads Cuisines, the happenstance meeting and successful mating of the different foods of different people.

Many of us know something about the food blendings that have occurred here on our own shores as a part of our unique history: the Creole cooking of New Orleans, the Tex-Mex traditions of the Southwest, the lively "nuevo Latino" food of south Florida and the Caribbean. But how many of us realize that the cuisine of Burma, an unusual and distinctive tradition, is a mélange of many Asian cultures—Chinese, Indian, Southeast Asian? That much of the food of South Africa is an unlikely blend of Dutch, Malaysian, Indian, and native African? That Turkey, for untold centuries the natural gateway between the East and the West, shows in its kitchens the long-accumulated influences of Asia and Europe, the Mediterranean, and the Middle East?

The formation of stable culinary traditions from a successful integration of different cultural elements raises some interesting issues. How does culinary change take place? Why and under what circumstances are people more or less receptive to new ideas and new experiences? Why did the New World peanuts and chile peppers have such a profound impact on Thai cooking, yet little, if any, on French, while at the same time the French enthusiastically embraced chocolate and potatoes, two foods largely ignored by the Thais? By looking at a number of areas where different culinary traditions have merged to form happy and productive alliances, we can perhaps gain some insight into the current explosion of fusion cuisine and melting-pot meals, their value and meaning for ourselves and, ultimately, our children.

Cuisine, like other cultural forms, is both conservative and dynamic, reflecting the nature of the beings who create it. For we humans are creatures who take pleasure in the safety and reassurance of the known and familiar even as we search for excitement and novelty, always looking for a new spin on things, something unusual and a little—but not too much—out of the ordinary. It is this tension between the novel and the familiar that shapes much of our culinary practice, enabling us to retain what is valuable and good while at the same time encouraging our inclination to elaborate, to innovate, to tinker, to play. Tradition provides a necessary foundation, but change is the name of the game: We may cherish a nostalgia for Grandma's meat loaf, but it is changing right under our noses, and we are the ones who are changing it—substituting ground turkey or soy protein for the beef, using salsa rather than canned tomato soup, seasoning with herbs and spices that Grandma would not have recognized, much less used.

The food we eat is much more than mere nutrition and is intimately bound up with other aspects of our lives—our history, our politics, our religious and social beliefs. But in the end it is the universal desire for nutritious, pleasurable, gratifying food that shapes our culinary practice and often overrides other issues. The Germans and the French, traditional ancient enemies, have in some real sense collaborated to produce the unique and delicious contours of Alsatian cuisine; the glory of Southern cooking evolved from the merging of African slaves and their upper-class English masters; the flavorful food of Afghanistan is a multiethnic tapestry woven by conquerors, merchants, and marauding armies. If we humans are consistently imperfect and unkind, our food frequently tells another story—one that reveals the best in us, come together to make something new and better.

fusion or folly?

When we look at the many instances of crossroads cooking throughout the world, we may well wonder why cuisines accept certain new
elements while rejecting others. How does an innovation—whether
an ingredient, a technique, or a presentation—find its way to become a part of an already established tradition?

Proximity is one obvious factor: Cuisines that share some common ground tend to be open to one another because their culinary
structure of basic foods, cooking techniques, and seasoning practices are similar. Vietnamese cuisine is likely to be more receptive to
Thai cooking than to Swedish, because it already shares much that is
familiar in both form and function; stir-fried noodles and coconut
milk, lemongrass and fish sauce provide a commonality of experience that is wholly different from that afforded by boiled beets and
potatoes, herring and sour cream.

But other factors are at work. Cuisines tend in general to maintain
and perpetuate the foods, practices, and beliefs on which they are
based. People everywhere are inclined to enjoy what is known and familiar, food that is perceived as comforting, safe, appropriate, good.
It is the reason why in our travels to foreign and exotic places many
of even the most adventurous eaters among us slip furtively from
time to time into a McDonald's for a little taste of home, why orbit-
ing astronauts return to earth craving pizza and burgers, why we eat
turkey and cranberry sauce on Thanksgiving, hot dogs and peanuts
at the ballpark. Familiar traditional food defines us as members of

families, communities, and cultures; it comforts and reassures us, and so we value it and perpetuate it as a stabilizing and pleasurable part of our lives.

Curiously, it is this very conservatism that allows us to accept new elements into our traditions, cautiously adding them to or fitting them into already existing patterns. When the tomato arrived in southern Italy, for example, it did not replace or eliminate familiar ingredients but, rather, merged with them, adding exciting new dimensions of color, flavor, and texture to the olive oil, the garlic, the anchovies, and the pasta that were an established part of the cuisine. The familiar old patterns were retained, but heightened and made even more attractive by the addition of this saucy newcomer. Similarly, when the Spanish introduced wheat flour into Mexico, it did not replace the limed cornmeal (masa harina) long used by native cooks to make tortillas, but was itself adapted to fit into the pattern of a flat griddle-cooked bread that served as a base or wrapper for other foods. The old was retained, but the tradition became more elaborate.

These examples lead us to the issue of suitability, the factors involved in making a new element acceptable or appropriate for inclusion in another tradition. Suitability functions on many levels and in different domains of the food experience: It involves issues of health and nutrition; economic factors such as cost, availability, and ease of production; aesthetic concerns involving flavor, texture, color, and the ways that they are produced and experienced; social or religious beliefs concerning the culturally determined value or danger of various food substances. All these considerations, and many more, come into play when a cuisine comes face-to-face with a novel element.

As a general rule, a new culinary element is likely to be accepted and incorporated if it enhances or adds something of value and does not challenge or detract from the familiar parameters of the established tradition. The enhancement can be nutritional, providing valuable nutrients that may be scarce or lacking; the enhancement can be gustatory, adding heightened flavor or richer color or textural variety to systems that are already sensitive to those qualities or perhaps in need of added stimulation. The chile peppers are a case in point: Unknown anywhere outside the New World before the sixteenth century, they found a welcome new home in cuisines throughout the world that were already using intense and powerful seasoning ingredients as a characteristic part of their culinary practice—in India, Southeast Asia, North Africa. The pungent chiles reinforced these traditions, enriching and heightening the ginger and the garlic, the onions and the spices, without detracting from what was already in place. And they were easy to grow, cheap, and readily available.

Peanuts are another interesting example. Although they look like nuts and act like nuts, they are actually legumes, more closely related to peas and beans than to true nuts. They grow well in warm, sandy, coastal areas and are a rich and concentrated source of vegetable protein and oil. Introduced to the Old World after the Spanish conquest, they were enthusiastically accepted into cuisines that were in need of inexpensive, easily produced protein and fat and that responded positively to their unique flavor and texture. Ground into rich, oily pastes or chopped into crunchy toppings and garnishes, they enriched and embellished the food of China, Malaysia, and sub-Saharan Africa. The cuisines of Western Europe, on the other hand, were wholly unreceptive to peanuts because their protein and fat needs were already amply filled by red meats and dairy products, their palates unaccustomed to the distinctive flavor and texture of this nutty little newcomer. So peanuts were largely rejected except, ultimately, by the French, who embraced peanut oil as a superior cooking oil because of its clean flavor and high smoke point. Frying and sautéing are important techniques for the French, and so they took from the peanut what was valuable and enhancing for their culinary practice.

All these examples come from stable, established traditions that evolved slowly over generations, if not centuries. But innovation begins somewhere, usually with a single cook who dares to try something new (or is forced into it by circumstances beyond her control). Whether the innovation is a deliberate experiment or an act of desperation, its ultimate success will depend on its acceptance by a community of people who choose to repeat and perpetuate it. There follows a number of examples from the contemporary fusion repertoire, some serious, some silly. Will they survive and endure as our legacy to the future, or will they wind up, like so many before them, on the garbage dump of history? We are the ones to decide; between fusion and folly, the choice is ours.

The Fusion Follies: An informal and wholly personal selection of quirky couplings and combinations from all over the world:

From Yunan, China: Yak-cheese pizza

From a supermarket take-out counter: Moshe's falafel burritos

From Australia: Kangaroo and goat cheese calzone

From a Philadelphia restaurant: Siberian nachos (deep-fried wonton skins layered with caviar, sour cream, and smoked salmon)

From Venezuela: Trout-flavored ice cream

From California: Breakfast bagel with ham, cream cheese, and Italian olive salsa

From an English fish-and-chips emporium: Battered deep-fried Milky Way bars

From Taos, New Mexico: Battered kabobs of western diamond-back rattlesnake, served with a tomatillo rémoulade

From Lapland: Szechuan reindeer

From a D.C. pizza parlor: Hawaiian pizza with green peppers, pineapple, and Spam

From the Net: Bangkok-style ostrich hamburgers

From a Philadelphia restaurant: Siamese tacos (fried corn tortillas stuffed with Thai barbecue pork and served with mango salsa)

From south Florida: Tri-color ravioli stuffed with jerked venison and served with a sweet and spicy chile sauce

From Dijon, France: Goat-cheese ice cream

From Baton Rouge, Louisiana: Matzo Ball Gumbo (if you'd like to try it yourself, see recipe on page 245)

crossroads Cooking

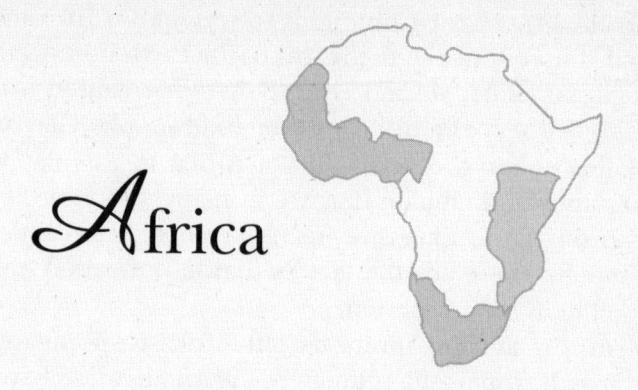

Africa

If we wanted to find a place where the food of our kind was unmuddled, pristine, we should have to travel back in time more than a million years to the land that brought us forth, nudged us to walk upright on two spindly legs, and so set us on the long hard road to the business of being human. Africa is the home of our species, the mother of us all, and while some of her children stayed close to the ancestral hearth, others walked out and away to become the many people of the world.

We don't know much about the foodways of our earliest ancestors, just as we have little evidence of the spirits they feared, the lullabies they crooned, the stories they told in the darkening night. We believe that they nourished themselves on a wide variety of foodstuffs: fruits and vegetables, roots and tubers, nuts and seeds, as well as wild game, birds, fish and mollusks, insects and reptiles, pilfered eggs and stolen honeycombs. And it is fairly certain that by the time those ancient ones were ready to leave Africa, probably not yet fully modern humans, they had developed a sure taste for meat and had mastered the use of fire.

What impelled these early hominids to trek out of Africa was almost surely a consequence of the forces of the earth itself—climatic upheavals, glacial shifts, volcanic eruptions—that caused a reduction of resources and a diminishing of the food supply. They are the very forces that shape the landscape of Africa to this day with a unique geography and climate that are in many ways not the most hospitable to our kind. Excessive heat, barren soil, too little rainfall or too much—these are the factors that have formed much of Africa's subsequent food experience.

As some of our ancient forebears left Africa to populate Asia, the Middle East, Europe, and, ultimately, the Americas, so have their descendants, all the people of the world, returned to Africa at various times in the unrecorded centuries since that first migration. The people of Africa are wide-ranging and diverse, from the Nilotic groups of the north to the Bushmen of the southern Kalahari desert, from the pastoral Masai of the eastern highlands to the Bantu of the steaming equatorial center. There exists on the ancestral continent an extraordinary assortment of people and cultures, with a corresponding variety of languages and lifestyles.

Despite this striking physical and cultural diversity, however, there is a tenacious underlying unity of culinary expression. This may well be due in part to difficult climatic conditions, which restrict the kinds of plants and animals that can be successfully grown or domesticated. Whatever the reasons, and whatever their origins, certain features are uniquely characteristic of the sub-Saharan African table.

First is the use of a wide variety of roots, tubers, grains, and starchy fruits to produce thick pastes or porridges that form the mainstay of the diet. Bananas and plantains, sweet potatoes and yams, cassava (manioc), corn, and millet all function similarly, frequently boiled and mashed, sometimes formed into balls or fried into fritters and croquettes. Rice has become an important staple in more recent times, as a more expensive but highly esteemed base for other foods or cooked together with many different ingredients to make attractive one-dish meals. (Wheat, the grain that feeds so many elsewhere in the world, is of little importance in Africa, where neither traditional breads nor pasta products have ever played a significant role.)

The second crucial feature of pan-African cuisine is the savory sauce or stew, designed as an essential gastronomic and nutritional complement to the bland starchy base. These dishes are composed of a wide variety of ingredients—meat, poultry, fish, seafood, vegetables. They are typically highly seasoned and demonstrate the African dedication to leafy greens, okra, beans, and legumes cooked into peppery, flavorful sauces.

The starchy base and the embellishing sauce or stew are pervasive themes throughout Africa, played out in dozens of regional variations, many strongly shaped by outside influences that have become assimilated into the African experience. But of the many cultures that have had a part—Arab, Indian, Malay, Chinese, Dutch, English, Portuguese, French—perhaps none has had so powerful an impact as the Americas. Much today that we regard as fundamentally African came from the New World only in the last several hundred years, introduced by traders, slavers, sailors, and merchants who plied the coasts of Africa, exchanging the goods of the world for human cargo. Of the starchy tubers and grains so widely used today, sweet potatoes, manioc, and corn are of American origin; a multitude of spicy sauces owe their characteristic flavors to the American tomato, the peanut, and the all-important chile pepper.

To investigate the culinary crossroads of Africa, we leave behind the north, which belongs both geographically and culturally more to the Mediterranean and the Arab world of the Middle East, and dive below the Sahara to three regions—the west coast, the east, and the south. Each area retains its own unique Africanness while revealing some strange and delicious cultural mixes.

The land that nurtured and sent forth those unknown ancestors who would become a thousand versions of ourselves has received us all back, our complexities, our similarities, and our differences made palpable and fragrant in a thousand thousand simmering pots.

west africa

The Atlantic coast of Africa—the west coast—is the part of the continent closest to the Americas, and it is here that the indigenous products of the New World seem to have had their most vivid impact. It is in West Africa that maize and manioc were first transformed into the ever-present foo foo—the stiff, filling mushes eaten at almost every meal. Here the red, ripe tomato is cooked into vibrant sauces fragrant with onions and garlic and peppers. Here the peanut (called groundnut) has its heaviest production and most intense use, ground into savory sauces and stews filled with distinctive flavor and rich creamy texture, providing an invaluable source of vegetable protein. Peanuts are also a rich source of oil, used throughout Africa for cooking and frying, along with the more traditional red palm oil.

In addition to onions and garlic, the most common seasoning ingredient is the chile pepper, another American import; it is used fresh, dried, and ground into hot red pepper powders that enliven almost all cooked foods. Thyme is a familiar herb, as are a number of melon seeds and aromatic leaves. Another characteristic flavoring ingredient is dried or smoked fish or shrimp, cooked whole, in pieces, or ground into powders. These products are not noticeably fishy in flavor but add depth and complexity to the seasoning profile.

Besides the ingredients introduced to the African larder from the Americas are influences from a number of other cultures. Wherever they settled or built their railroads, the British brought sweetened tea and curries from India, in the typical and widely popular form of premixed spice powders. The French introduced a more generous assortment of vegetables and, from their colonies in North Africa, such traditional preparations as couscous and bouillabaisse-like seafood stews. And, of course, French bread!

Whatever it may once have been, the West African table has evolved into an appealing mix—spicy, colorful, earthy—not only incorporating a number of outside elements into its own design, but also sending forth many of its traditions to contribute to the culinary style of the Caribbean and the American South.

RECIPES

Spicy Grilled Peanut Shrimp

Senegalese Fish with Mixed Vegetables

Jollof Rice with Crawfish

Chicken Groundnut Stew

Chicken with Okra and Corn

Mixed Vegetable Mafé

Spinach and Peanut Sauce

Fried Plantains with Peppery Dipping Sauce

Roasted Corn and Banana Fritters

Spicy Grilled Peanut Shrimp

Ground peanuts, more typically used as a component of savory stews and sauces, here combine with coconut milk in a spicy marinade/coating for grilled shrimp. The marinade is quite thick and should be fairly spicy, but you can adjust the hot pepper to suit your palate. These shrimp are best served as an hors d'oeuvre or appetizer, hot off the grill.

¼ cup unsweetened coconut
    milk
2 tablespoons peanut butter
1 tablespoon fresh lemon juice
3 or 4 cloves garlic, crushed
½ to 1 teaspoon cayenne or
    other ground hot red
    pepper

1 pound large shrimp or
    prawns, peeled and
    deveined
Coarse salt to taste

1. In a small bowl, combine the coconut milk, peanut butter, lemon juice, garlic, and cayenne and mix thoroughly.

2. Add the shrimp to the marinade, making sure all sides of the shrimp are coated. Cover with plastic wrap and refrigerate for 1 to 2 hours. Soak the skewers if using bamboo.

3. Put 3 or 4 shrimp on each skewer, keeping as much of the marinade on as possible. Grill over hot charcoal, turning once, just until the shrimp turn pink on each side. Do not overcook. (Or the shrimp can be broiled in the oven for a minute or two on each side.)

4. Sprinkle the shrimp with the coarse salt before serving.

Serves 4 to 6

Senegalese Fish with Mixed Vegetables

The French influence on Senegalese cuisine is reflected in this dish in the herbs, the vinegar, and the lavish assortment of vegetables, but the tomatoes, chiles, okra, and dried shrimp are typically African. There are many versions of this popular dish; in some the fish is stewed along with the vegetables, but in this somewhat more elegant presentation, the fish is separately sautéed and served on top.

2 tablespoons peanut oil or vegetable oil
1 large onion, thinly sliced
1 red bell pepper, seeded and cut into thin strips
2 to 3 fresh long green chiles, seeded and cut into julienne strips
4 or 5 cloves garlic, crushed
1 medium sweet potato, peeled and sliced
2 to 3 carrots, sliced
10 to 12 small whole okra, trimmed
2 medium zucchini, thickly sliced
2 large tomatoes, coarsely chopped

2 tablespoons red wine vinegar
1 teaspoon whole dried shrimp (see Note)
2 bay leaves
½ teaspoon dried thyme
1 teaspoon salt
Several good grinds of black pepper
Good handful of finely chopped parsley leaves
1 pound fish fillets (red snapper, cod, flounder, bluefish, etc.)
Flour for dredging
Oil for frying
Cayenne pepper
Hot cooked rice or couscous

1. Heat the oil in a large heavy pot or Dutch oven and sauté the onion, bell pepper, chiles, and garlic over moderate heat, stirring, until the onion wilts and the mixture becomes aromatic.

2. Add the sweet potato, carrots, okra, zucchini, tomatoes, vinegar, shrimp, bay leaves, thyme, salt, and black pepper. Mix gently, bring to a simmer, then cover and cook over low heat for 30 to 40 minutes. When all the vegetables are tender, stir in the parsley; taste for salt and hotness.

3. Dredge the fish fillets lightly in flour, then fry in oil over moderate to high heat until they are golden brown on both sides. Salt the fried fish lightly and dust with the cayenne pepper.

4. To serve, spoon the hot cooked rice or couscous into a large shallow bowl or a rimmed platter. Make a slight well in the rice, then spoon the vegetables over the rice. Place the fish fillets over the rice and vegetables.

Serves 4

NOTE: Dried shrimp, whole and sometimes ground, can be purchased in African, Asian, and Latin American groceries.

Jollof Rice with Crawfish

Recipes for Jollof rice abound throughout West Africa, spicy dishes flavored and colored with tomatoes, chile, and sometimes red palm oil, and cooked or garnished with meat, poultry, or shellfish. The Jollof rice tradition undoubtedly contributed a great deal to the New Orleans jambalaya as well as to a variety of Caribbean rice-and-bean combinations. This version makes an attractive presentation, garnished with the whole cooked Louisiana crawfish now widely available in fish markets.

2 tablespoons peanut oil
1 medium onion, finely chopped
4 or 5 cloves garlic, minced
1 medium green bell pepper, seeded and diced
½ to 1 teaspoon cayenne or other ground hot red pepper
1 cup long-grain rice
2 medium tomatoes, coarsely chopped

2 cups chicken broth (African cooks frequently use bouillon cubes dissolved in water)
2 tablespoons tomato paste
Several good grinds of black pepper
1 cup cooked or canned kidney beans or black-eyed peas, drained
1 pound whole cooked crawfish

1. Heat the oil in a medium, heavy saucepan and sauté the onion, garlic, and bell pepper over moderate heat, stirring, until the onion softens and just begins to turn golden. Add the cayenne and the rice and stir them in the oil for a minute or two.

2. Add the tomatoes, broth, tomato paste, and black pepper. Mix well, bring to a simmer, then cover and cook over low heat for about 20 minutes, until the rice is tender and all the liquid has been absorbed.

3. Stir in the beans, mix well, then cover and let stand for about 5 minutes. Taste for salt and add a bit if necessary.

4. Turn the rice out onto a serving platter and garnish with the crawfish.

Serves 4

Chicken Groundnut Stew

It is in West Africa that peanut stews and sauces achieve their special eminence, with a host of regional variations on the theme. Almost any meat, poultry, or fish can form the basis of the dish; some add the traditional dried shrimp powder as a seasoning ingredient, while the Senegalese mafé includes a more varied assortment of vegetables. Note that peanut oil is the cooking oil of choice for these groundnut stews; the popular red palm oil is generally not used for peanut-based dishes. Here is a simple and delicious chicken dish from Nigeria.

2 tablespoons peanut oil
2 to 2½ pounds chicken parts (breast quarters, thighs, drumsticks)
1 large onion, finely chopped
1 medium green bell pepper, seeded and diced
1 medium red bell pepper, seeded and diced
4 large cloves garlic, minced

½ to 1 teaspoon cayenne pepper (or other ground hot red pepper)
1 teaspoon salt
Several good grinds of black pepper
4 to 5 medium tomatoes, coarsely chopped
¼ cup peanut butter

1. Heat the oil in a large skillet or heavy pot and brown the chicken parts over moderate heat, turning to brown evenly on all sides. While the chicken is browning, add the onion, peppers, garlic, and cayenne and sauté, stirring.

2. Sprinkle the browned chicken with the salt and black pepper, then add the tomatoes. Bring to a simmer, then cover and cook over low heat for about 30 minutes. Uncover and cook for another 15 to 20 minutes, until the chicken is tender and the sauce is reduced by about one half.

3. Stir in the peanut butter and mix until well blended. Taste for salt and hotness. Serve the stew with hot cooked rice.

Serves 4

Chicken with Okra and Corn

This long-simmered stew is undoubtedly the model for the famous gumbos of Louisiana, thick, highly seasoned, soupy stews that almost always contain okra, as well as a variety of meats, seafood, and poultry. The long, slow cooking reduces the gumminess of the okra, and the vegetables and chicken exude enough liquid to produce a thick, flavorful sauce. While the Louisiana gumbo is always eaten with rice, the West African original is more typically served with a stiff foo foo made from plantain, cassava, cornmeal, or yams.

2 tablespoons peanut oil or vegetable oil
2 to 2½ pounds chicken thighs, or a mix of thighs and drumsticks
½ to 1 teaspoon salt
Freshly ground black pepper
1 onion, coarsely chopped
1 green bell pepper, seeded and coarsely chopped
2 to 3 fresh hot red or green chiles, seeded and minced, or ½ to 1 teaspoon crushed dried hot pepper

3 or 4 cloves garlic, minced
½ pound okra, trimmed and cut into ½-inch pieces
2 medium tomatoes, coarsely chopped
½ teaspoon dried thyme
1 cup fresh or frozen corn kernels
Cayenne pepper to taste (optional)

1. In a large, heavy pot or Dutch oven, heat the oil over moderate to high heat; brown the chicken parts, turning them to brown on all sides. When the chicken is browned, sprinkle it with about ½ teaspoon of the salt and add black pepper to taste. Remove from the pot and set aside.

2. Add the onion, bell pepper, chiles, and garlic to the pot and cook, stirring, until the onions begin to turn golden and the mixture is aromatic.

3. Add the okra and fry it briefly, then add the tomatoes and thyme. Return the chicken to the pot, cover, and cook over low heat for 1 to 1½ hours, until the chicken is very tender and the sauce is thick.

4. Stir in the corn and cook for another 10 minutes. Taste for salt and add some if necessary. If additional pungency is desired, add some cayenne pepper to taste.

Serves 4

Mixed Vegetable Mafé

The popular groundnut stew is known in Senegal as mafé, and, as elsewhere in West Africa, it can be made with meat, chicken, or seafood. In this purely vegetable version, French influence is evident in the use of turnips and zucchini. Other vegetables—such as diced eggplant, chopped cabbage, and okra—are also frequently used. Serve this hearty, colorful dish with rice, couscous, or cornmeal mush.

2 tablespoons peanut oil
1 large onion, coarsely
   chopped
4 or 5 cloves garlic, minced
1 teaspoon (or more to taste)
   crushed dried hot pepper
1 large sweet potato, peeled
   and cut into small cubes
2 medium white turnips, sliced
2 carrots, sliced
1 medium green bell pepper,
   seeded and cut into small
   chunks

1 red bell pepper, seeded and
   cut into small chunks
2 medium zucchini, cut into
   small chunks
2 cups canned Italian-style
   tomatoes, with juice,
   coarsely chopped
1 teaspoon salt
¼ teaspoon freshly ground
   black pepper
2 to 3 tablespoons peanut
   butter

1. Heat the oil in a large, deep skillet or large, heavy pot and sauté the onion, garlic, and crushed hot pepper over moderate heat, stirring, until the onion wilts and just begins to turn golden.

2. Add the sweet potato, turnips, carrots, bell peppers, zucchini, tomatoes, salt, and black pepper and mix thoroughly. Bring to a simmer, then cover and cook over low heat, stirring from time to time, for 40 to 50 minutes, until the sweet potato and turnips are tender.

3. Stir in the peanut butter and mix gently until well blended. Taste and adjust for salt and hotness.

Serves 4 to 6

Spinach and Peanut Sauce

A popular and traditional dish, this richly flavored sauce reveals the West African dedication to cooked greens, peanuts, and zesty seasonings. Eaten with rice or cornmeal mush or mashed plantain foo foo, it makes a very appealing and highly nutritious meal.

2 tablespoons peanut oil
1 medium onion, coarsely chopped
2 large cloves garlic, crushed
2 to 3 small fresh hot chiles, seeded and minced, or ½ to 1 teaspoon crushed dried hot pepper

2 tomatoes, coarsely chopped
1 pound fresh spinach or 1 box (10 ounces) frozen chopped spinach
1 teaspoon salt
About ¼ cup peanut butter

1. Heat the oil in a medium, heavy saucepan or deep, heavy skillet and sauté the onion, garlic, and chiles over moderate heat, stirring, until the onion wilts and the mixture becomes aromatic.

2. Add the tomatoes and cook over moderate heat, stirring occasionally, until the tomatoes are soft and most of the liquid has cooked away.

3. While the tomatoes are cooking, trim the spinach, wash it thoroughly, and drain it. Chop the spinach coarsely. (If using frozen spinach, defrost prior to cooking, then squeeze out as much water as possible.)

4. Add the spinach to the pot and cook, stirring, until it is wilted and soft. If there is a lot of liquid, cook it down quickly over high heat until only a small amount of liquid remains.

5. Stir in the salt and enough peanut butter to make a thick sauce. Mix thoroughly, then taste for salt and hotness and adjust seasoning, if necessary. Serve the sauce with plain rice, cornmeal mush, or mashed plantain foo foo.

Serves 4

Fried Plantains with Peppery Dipping Sauce

West Africa's entry into the salsa sweepstakes is a wonderfully pungent and flavorful mixture that functions as a relish or condiment for starchy or fried foods. It is an excellent accompaniment to fried chicken, fish, shrimp, and all kinds of fritters. Africans typically add a lot more chile than I have used; you can adjust the pungency to suit your own palate. Note that this is a cooked relish; it can be stored, covered, in the refrigerator for a couple of weeks.

4 to 5 tablespoons peanut oil or vegetable oil
1 large onion, finely chopped
3 cloves garlic, minced
1 large red bell pepper, seeded and finely chopped
2 to 3 small fresh hot chiles, seeded and minced, or ½ teaspoon cayenne or other ground hot red pepper

2 large, very ripe tomatoes, finely chopped
1 teaspoon dried shrimp powder (see Note)
1 teaspoon salt, plus additional for sprinkling plantain
⅛ teaspoon nutmeg
2 to 3 large, medium-ripe plantains (see NOTE, page 237)

1. In a heavy saucepan or skillet, heat 2 tablespoons of the oil over moderate heat and sauté the onion, garlic, bell pepper, and hot pepper, stirring, until the vegetables become soft and aromatic.

2. Add the tomatoes, shrimp powder, salt, and nutmeg. Mix well, then simmer, uncovered, over low to moderate heat for 15 to 20 minutes, until the sauce is soft and thick and most of the liquid has cooked away. Taste for salt and hotness.

3. Peel the plantains and cut them in half lengthwise and crosswise.

4. Heat the remaining 2 or 3 tablespoons oil in a clean heavy skillet over moderately high heat. Fry the plantain slices, turning once, until nicely browned on both sides. Drain the fried plantains on paper towels; sprinkle lightly with salt. Pass the sauce with the plantains.

Makes 2 cups sauce,
serving 4 to 6

NOTE: Dried shrimp, whole and sometimes ground, can be purchased in African, Asian, and Latin American groceries. The whole shrimp can easily be ground in a food processor or spice mill, or crushed to a powder with a mortar and pestle.

Roasted Corn and Banana Fritters

Introduced from its aboriginal American home, corn became a valuable dietary staple in Africa, used primarily in the form of a dried ground meal. But it is also enjoyed as a fresh vegetable, cooked in stews or roasted on the cob in hot ashes. In these savory little fritters, the unique flavor of corn roasted in its own husk combines with sweet banana for a delicious snack or vegetable side dish.

2 ears fresh sweet corn, unhusked
2 medium very ripe bananas
1 large clove garlic, crushed
½ teaspoon salt, plus more to taste

2 tablespoons stone-ground yellow cornmeal
3 to 4 tablespoons vegetable oil, for frying

1. Roast the unhusked corn in a hot (450°F) oven for about 50 minutes. Let the corn cool, then remove the husks and all the silk. Cut the kernels off the cobs.

2. In a medium bowl, mash the bananas, then stir in the garlic, ½ teaspoon salt, and cornmeal, and mix thoroughly. Stir in the corn kernels, then let the mixture stand for about 1 hour.

3. Heat a heavy skillet over moderately high heat. Swirl in enough oil to generously film the bottom of the pan. Drop the banana mixture by rounded tablespoons into the hot oil, and fry, turning once, until nicely browned on both sides. Drain on paper towels. Sprinkle with salt to taste.

Makes 10 to 12 small fritters

east africa

As West African cuisine was most heavily influenced by traditions from the West, so East Africa, not surprisingly, shows a more intense impact from the East, from Asia. The basic African theme of starch base and savory sauce remains constant, as do such fundamentals as cooked greens, beans, peanuts, and chile peppers. But the emphasis shifts subtly to a heavier dependence on coconut and bananas, as well as a more varied assortment of herbs and aromatics.

In the north, the ancient kingdom of Ethiopia maintains long-held traditions that seem more related to the Arab world and the Middle East than to the rest of Africa. The most widely used starch product, besides rice, is injera—large, spongy, griddle-cooked, pancake-like bread made from fermented millet. There is a heavier use of beef and dairy products and of such Middle Eastern staples as lentils and chickpeas. Sauces are frequently fiery with hot chiles, and there is an old tradition of spiced butters and oils with flavors reminiscent of the seasonings of southern Arabia and the Gulf states.

From the mountains of Ethiopia to the coastal flats of Mozambique, there is a great distance, in both miles and flavor. Here in the south, dishes are seasoned with many of the ingredients typical of Malaysia and Indonesia—lemongrass, gingerroot, coconut, coriander. Mozambique is the home of piripiri, the tiny red-hot chile introduced from the Americas by the Portuguese in the sixteenth century. Portugal also left her mark with such traditional foods as olive oil, salt cod (bacalhau), and a variety of mixed rice and seafood dishes; she is also the agent responsible for the intense and creative culinary exchange between Africa and Brazil.

Between Ethiopia in the north and Mozambique in the south is what once was known as British East Africa, the legendary land of wildlife safaris and the Serengeti, of the Great Rift Valley and the Mountains of the Moon. The food here is blander, with a less intense use of chile peppers but with a distinctive tradition of spices and curries, brought in by Arab traders, British colonials, and immigrants from India. This is the Africa of our romantic imaginings; if you can't afford to go on safari, you can at least evoke a part of the experience with a flavorful curry or a hearty bean-and-coconut stew!

RECIPES

Fresh Cod and Spinach in Coconut Sauce

Shrimp with Cashews in Spicy Coconut Sauce

Piripiri Wings

Spicy Chicken with Tomatoes, Coconut, and
   Coriander

Spiced Pepper Beef

Lamb and Peanut Curry

Curried Eggplant and Potatoes

Spiced Lentils and Collard Greens

Black-Eyed Peas in Coconut-Peanut Sauce

Baked Banana Pudding with Coconut

Fresh Cod and Spinach in Coconut Sauce

The Portuguese love for codfish, both fresh and dried salted (bacalhau), cooked in savory sauces, was revitalized in Mozambique, where it joined forces with the chiles and cooked greens so dear to the African palate and a variety of seasoning ingredients from Southeast Asia. This dish is traditionally eaten with rice.

2 tablespoons olive oil
1 medium onion, finely
     chopped
1 tablespoon finely minced
     gingerroot
3 to 4 fresh green chiles, seeded
     and minced
2 medium tomatoes, coarsely
     chopped
1 pound fresh spinach,
     trimmed, washed, and
     coarsely chopped
1 (5 to 6 ounces) can
     unsweetened coconut milk

1 teaspoon salt
Several good grinds of black
     pepper
2 teaspoons finely minced
     lemongrass, or
     1 teaspoon dried powdered
1 pound fresh cod fillets, cut
     into large chunks
2 tablespoons fresh lemon juice
3 to 4 tablespoons finely
     chopped fresh coriander
     leaves

1. In a deep heavy skillet or a heavy pot, heat the oil over moderate heat and sauté the onion, gingerroot, and chiles, stirring, until the onion wilts and the mixture becomes aromatic.

2. Add the tomatoes, spinach, and coconut milk and bring to a simmer. Stir in the salt, pepper, and lemongrass and cook for a few minutes, until the spinach is wilted.

3. Add the fish and cook, turning once, for about 10 minutes, until the fish flakes easily. Stir in the lemon juice and the coriander.

Serves 4

Shrimp with Cashews in Spicy Coconut Sauce

Traditional Indian spices, Portuguese olive oil, and cashews introduced by the Portuguese from Brazil combine in this lively dish with the familiar East African complex of coconut, tomatoes, and hot pepper. It is always served with rice.

2 tablespoons olive oil
1 medium onion, finely
    chopped
1 tablespoon finely minced
    gingerroot
3 or 4 large cloves garlic,
    minced
1 to 2 teaspoons cayenne
    pepper
2 tomatoes, coarsely chopped
½ teaspoon salt, or more to
    taste
Several good grinds of black
    pepper

1 teaspoon ground cumin
1 teaspoon ground coriander
1 small can (5 to 6 ounces)
    unsweetened coconut milk
1 pound shrimp, peeled and
    deveined
½ cup roasted cashews, whole
    or halves
1 tablespoon fresh lemon juice
Chopped fresh coriander leaves,
    for garnish

1. Heat the oil in a medium skillet and sauté the onion, gingerroot, garlic, and cayenne over moderate heat, stirring, until the onion wilts and the mixture becomes aromatic.

2. Add the tomatoes and cook over moderate heat, stirring occasionally, until the mixture is soft and thick and most of the liquid has cooked away.

3. Add the salt, black pepper, cumin, and coriander and mix well, then stir in the coconut milk. Simmer, uncovered, for about 5 minutes.

4. Add the shrimp and cashews and cook, stirring, just until the shrimp turn pink. Add the lemon juice, then taste for salt and hotness. Serve hot, garnished with a bit of the chopped coriander.

Serves 4

Piripiri Wings

In East Africa, piripiri is the name of a fiery little red chile; throughout Africa, it refers to any food that is seasoned primarily by hot red pepper. In Portugal, it has come to signify olive oil infused with the peppers and used as a condiment, much as we use Tabasco. Even if you're an aficionado of Buffalo wings, try this mouth-popping East African version—and lose the blue cheese!

2 to 2½ pounds chicken wings
or wing drumettes
3 tablespoons olive oil
3 or 4 large cloves garlic,
crushed
½ teaspoon crumbled dried
thyme

1 teaspoon ground cumin
1 to 2 teaspoons cayenne or
other ground hot red
pepper, or more to taste
Coarse salt
Lemon wedges, for serving

1. If using whole wings, remove the wing tips and discard or reserve for stock.

2. In a small bowl or measuring cup, combine the oil, garlic, thyme, cumin, and hot pepper and blend thoroughly. Pour the mixture over the wings and mix well. Cover and refrigerate for 3 to 4 hours.

3. Preheat the oven to 400°F. Line a baking tray with foil.

4. Place the wings on the tray, using every bit of the marinade. Bake for 50 to 60 minutes, until the wings are crisp and golden. Sprinkle generously with the coarse salt. Serve warm or at room temperature, with lemon wedges.

Makes 8 to 10 wings

Spicy Chicken with Tomatoes, Coconut, and Coriander

Some of East Africa's most familiar and pervasive ingredients—onion, chiles, tomatoes, coconut—give character to this simple but intensely seasoned dish. The flavor of the sauce is reminiscent of both Southeast Asia and the Caribbean, which is not at all surprising, as both Africa and Asia contributed heavily to the island cuisine of the Americas. Serve the chicken hot with rice, and perhaps some fried bananas.

2 tablespoons peanut oil
2 to 3 pounds chicken thighs, on the bone, skin removed
1 medium onion, coarsely chopped
1 medium green or red bell pepper, seeded and coarsely chopped
2 to 3 small fresh hot chiles, seeded and minced, or ½ to 1 teaspoon crushed dried hot pepper

3 or 4 cloves garlic, crushed
1 teaspoon salt
2 large tomatoes, coarsely chopped
¼ cup unsweetened coconut milk
Juice of ½ lime
½ cup finely chopped fresh coriander leaves

1. Heat the oil in a large skillet and brown the chicken thighs lightly over moderate heat, turning once to brown on both sides.

2. While the chicken is browning, add the onion, bell pepper, chiles, and garlic and sauté along with the chicken. Sprinkle the chicken with the salt.

3. Add the tomatoes and the coconut milk, bring to a simmer, then cover and cook over low heat for about 30 to 40 minutes.

4. Uncover the pan and continue to cook, stirring occasionally, until the chicken is very tender and the sauce is quite thick.

5. Stir in the lime juice and the coriander. Taste for salt and hotness and adjust seasoning if necessary. Serve hot with rice.

Serves 4 to 6

Spiced Pepper Beef

This classic of the Ethiopian kitchen owes its unique flavor to the combination of a complex array of spices, with the distinctive flavor of green peppers and fresh green chiles. It is sometimes accompanied by yogurt as a cooling agent and is typically served with injera or another flat bread, used to scoop up the stew with the hands. It can also be served with rice or couscous.

2 tablespoons butter or vegetable oil
1 medium onion, finely chopped
2 cloves garlic, minced
2 fresh long green chiles, seeded and minced
1 pound boneless beef, cut into ½-inch cubes or thin strips
1 teaspoon ground cumin
1 teaspoon ground coriander
1 teaspoon ground ginger
1 teaspoon ground fenugreek

1 teaspoon paprika
½ to 1 teaspoon cayenne pepper
½ teaspoon cinnamon
½ teaspoon ground cardamom
⅛ teaspoon ground nutmeg
⅛ teaspoon ground cloves
½ to 1 teaspoon salt
2 large green bell peppers, seeded and finely chopped
½ cup water
Plain yogurt, for serving (optional)

1. Heat the butter in a heavy skillet or heavy pot and sauté the onion, garlic, and chiles over moderate heat, stirring, just until the onion begins to turn golden.

2. Add the beef and stir to brown on all sides. While the beef is browning, add the cumin, coriander, ginger, fenugreek, paprika, cayenne, cinnamon, cardamom, nutmeg, cloves, and salt and mix to coat the beef thoroughly. Continue to cook, stirring, until the beef is browned.

3. Stir in the bell peppers and the water. Bring to a simmer, then cover and cook over low heat for 1½ to 2 hours, until the beef is very tender. If too much liquid cooks away during the cooking, add a little more water. Cook the sauce down at the end until it is fairly thick. Taste for salt.

4. Serve hot, with yogurt to pass, if desired, and bread for scooping.

Serves 4 to 6

Lamb and Peanut Curry

The curry powders brought in by the British took a particularly firm hold in East Africa, where they have become a familiar and valued part of the seasoning repertoire. This tasty lamb dish is given added flavor and richness with ground peanuts, another import that has had a lasting impact on the African table. Serve the curry with rice and a tangy chutney.

2 tablespoons peanut oil
1 medium onion, coarsely chopped
1 tablespoon minced gingerroot
1 to 2 fresh hot chiles, seeded and minced, or ½ to 1 teaspoon crushed dried hot pepper
1½ pounds boneless lamb, cut into ½-inch cubes
3 large cloves garlic, minced
2 teaspoons curry powder, preferably Madras
½ teaspoon salt, or more to taste

Several good grinds of black pepper
1 green or red bell pepper, seeded and cut into small chunks
1 medium potato, peeled and cut into small cubes
1 cup canned Italian-style tomatoes, coarsely chopped, with juice, or 3 to 4 fresh tomatoes, coarsely chopped
1 tablespoon fresh lemon juice
3 tablespoons peanut butter

1. Heat the oil in a heavy pot or Dutch oven and sauté the onion, gingerroot, and chiles over moderate heat, stirring, until the onion just begins to turn golden.

2. Add the lamb cubes in small batches, so as not to crowd the pan, and brown on all sides. When some of the cubes have browned, push them to the side of the pot and add more cubes to brown.

3. While the meat is browning, add the garlic, curry powder, ½ teaspoon salt, and black pepper.

4. When all the meat is browned, add the bell pepper, potato, and tomatoes. Mix well, bring to a simmer, then cover and cook over low heat for 1½ to 2 hours, until the meat is very tender. If the stew becomes too dry while cooking, add some water.

5. Stir in the lemon juice and peanut butter and mix until the sauce is well blended and smooth. Taste for salt and hotness and adjust the seasoning, if necessary.

Serves 4 to 6

Curried Eggplant and Potatoes

Unlike the curry dishes introduced into East Africa by the British, which featured premixed spice powders and focused on meat, fish, or poultry, this dish reflects a more direct influence of the Indians who settled in the region, bringing a complex tradition of purely vegetarian cookery. The eggplant and potatoes are more typical of India than of Africa, but the heavy use of tomatoes is probably an expression of the African palate.

¼ cup vegetable oil
1 medium onion, finely
  chopped
1 tablespoon finely minced
  gingerroot
3 or 4 cloves garlic, minced
3 to 4 small fresh hot chiles,
  seeded and minced, or 1
  teaspoon crushed dried
  hot pepper
2 medium eggplants, peeled
  and diced
2 teaspoons ground cumin
2 teaspoons ground coriander
1 teaspoon turmeric
½ teaspoon ground cardamom

¼ teaspoon cinnamon
1 teaspoon salt
Several good grinds of black
  pepper
2 medium potatoes, peeled and
  cut into ½-inch cubes
3 to 4 medium tomatoes,
  coarsely chopped
2 tablespoons tomato
  paste
⅓ to ½ cup water
1 teaspoon garam masala
  (see Note)
Good handful of chopped fresh
  coriander leaves

1. Heat the oil in a large, deep skillet or heavy pot and sauté the onion, gingerroot, garlic, and chiles over moderate heat until the onion wilts and the mixture becomes aromatic.
2. Add the diced eggplant and fry, stirring, for a few minutes.

While the eggplant is frying, sprinkle it with the cumin, coriander, turmeric, cardamom, cinnamon, salt, and pepper.

3. When the eggplant is just lightly browned, add the potatoes, tomatoes, tomato paste, and water. Mix well, then cover and cook over low heat, stirring occasionally, for 40 to 50 minutes, until the eggplant is soft and the potatoes are tender. If the mixture becomes too dry during the cooking, add a bit more water. When it is finished, it should be soft and thick.

4. Stir in the garam masala and the chopped coriander. Mix well and taste for salt; you may need a bit more at this point. Serve the curry with chapatis or rice.

Serves 4 to 6

NOTE: Garam masala is a spice mixture typically added toward the end of the cooking process. The combination of cumin, coriander, cardamom, and cinnamon is common, but there are many masala mixtures available at Indian groceries.

Spiced Lentils and Collard Greens

The lentils of the Middle East and the collard greens of Africa come together here in a well-flavored, pungent stew. This tasty and nutritious dish is sometimes served with buttermilk curds; you can substitute plain yogurt if you wish. It is traditionally eaten with injera or another flat bread for scooping.

2 tablespoons vegetable oil or butter
1 medium onion, finely chopped
1 tablespoon finely minced gingerroot
4 cloves garlic, minced
2 to 3 fresh hot green chiles, seeded and minced
1 cup lentils, rinsed and drained

2 cups water
8 ounces trimmed collard greens, shredded or chopped
1 teaspoon ground cardamom
1 to 1¼ teaspoons salt
Several good grinds of black pepper
Plain yogurt, for serving (optional)

1. Heat the oil in a medium saucepan and sauté the onion, gingerroot, garlic, and chiles over moderate heat, stirring, until the vegetables soften and become aromatic.

2. Add the lentils, water, and collards. Bring to a simmer, then cook over low to moderate heat, stirring occasionally, for about 20 minutes, until the lentils are tender but still slightly firm and most of the liquid has cooked away.

3. Stir in the cardamom, salt, and pepper. Taste for salt and hotness; add some ground hot red pepper if more pungency is needed. Serve hot—with yogurt to pass, if desired.

Serves 4 to 6

Black-Eyed Peas in Coconut-Peanut Sauce

This substantial and nourishing bean dish contains no meat or dairy products; its richness, body, and creamy texture come from coconut milk and ground peanuts. For a satisfying vegetarian meal, serve the beans with rice and a cooked green vegetable or salad.

2 tablespoons peanut oil or vegetable oil

1 medium onion, finely chopped

1 medium red bell pepper, seeded and diced

3 or 4 cloves garlic, crushed

2 teaspoons curry powder (preferably Madras)

1 can (5 to 6 ounces) unsweetened coconut milk

1 teaspoon salt

4 cups cooked or canned black-eyed peas, drained

2 tablespoons peanut butter

Several good squeezes of lemon juice

1. Heat the oil in a medium, heavy saucepan and sauté the onion, bell pepper, and garlic over moderate heat, stirring, just until the onion wilts and the mixture becomes aromatic.

2. Add the curry powder and cook, stirring, for a minute or two.

3. Add the coconut milk and salt and bring to a simmer. Cook over low heat for about 5 minutes.

4. Add the black-eyed peas and peanut butter and cook, stirring, until the peanut butter is well blended in. Continue to cook over low heat for 10 minutes or so; add a bit of water if the mixture becomes too thick.

5. Stir in the lemon juice and serve hot.

Serves 4 to 6

Baked Banana Pudding with Coconut

Elaborate sweets are not a significant part of the native African tradition; where they turn up, they are almost always indicative of an influence from Europe, with its passion for cookies, cakes, puddings, and pies. This hearty pudding is probably of English inspiration, although its primary ingredients, bananas and coconut, are staples of the East African larder. Serve it well chilled, with a dollop of whipped cream if desired.

4 medium overripe bananas	½ cup sugar
1 teaspoon vanilla	Butter for pie plate
1 can (5 to 6 ounces) unsweetened coconut milk	¼ cup dry, shredded, sweetened coconut
¾ cup milk	3 tablespoons finely chopped salted peanuts
1 teaspoon cinnamon	Whipped cream, for garnish
¼ teaspoon nutmeg	(optional)
3 eggs	

1. In a medium bowl, mash the bananas thoroughly, then stir in the vanilla, coconut milk, milk, cinnamon, and nutmeg. Mix well and set aside.

2. In another medium bowl, beat the eggs with an electric mixer until foamy, then add in the sugar and beat until the mixture is thick and pale. Preheat the oven to 375°F.

3. Stir the banana mixture into the eggs and mix gently but thoroughly.

4. Generously butter a deep 9- or 10-inch pie plate or shallow casserole. Pour the banana mixture into the dish. Sprinkle the coconut and peanuts evenly over the top.

5. Bake the pudding for 45 to 50 minutes, or until it is set and nicely browned. Let cool, then refrigerate. Serve chilled—with whipped cream, if desired.

Serves 6 to 8

south africa

There is perhaps no place in Africa—or in the world, for that matter—that illustrates more vividly than South Africa the power of food to transcend cultural barriers. As effective as apartheid may have been in protecting white settlers politically and socially, it had little power over the cuisine, an eclectic and unlikely mixture of Dutch, Malay, Indian, and native African traditions.

The Dutch colonized South Africa in the seventeenth century; those self-styled Afrikaners brought slaves from their colonies in Malaysia, and later workers from India, to provide the labor to build their rich new country. And while these sturdy Dutchmen remained fundamentally European in their outlook and their biases, their cuisine would be forever changed.

From Malaysia came the chile peppers, not yet much known in this southernmost part of Africa, as well as coconut and a strong tradition of sweet and spicy marinated foods. India contributed her ancient wealth of spices and spice mixtures and traditional preparations like curries and biryanis. From both Malay and Indian cuisines came a rich legacy of preserved fruits, relishes, sambals, and sweet and tangy chutneys. And the native Bantu people provided the basic African theme of starch base served with stews and sauces.

Dutch food gone native! Hearty bean and split pea soups, now flavored with exotic spices rather than smoked pork. Robust stews of lamb, poultry, and vegetables newly invigorated with garlic and ginger and plenty of fresh hot chiles. A traditional favorite, pickled fish, redone in tangy marinades laced with aromatic herbs and spices. And all of it served up with rice or corn bread or cornmeal mush.

Contemporary South African cooks, like their colleagues all over the world, are involved today in creating a complex and eclectic new cuisine based on a myriad of local products and a burgeoning wine industry. But the old unlikely alliance of Europe, Malaysia, Africa, and India provides a solid and familiar foundation.

RECIPES

Spiced Split Pea Soup with Mint and Coriander

Spiced Pickled Fish

Spicy Chicken with Potatoes and Green Chiles

Curried Lamb and Bean Stew

Sweet and Spicy Grilled Lamb

Vegetable Biryani

Date and Onion Salad

Peach Chutney

Spiced Split Pea Soup with Mint and Coriander

The traditional Dutch split pea soup, with its familiar flavor of ham or bacon, gets a lively new twist with a variety of typical Indian spices, herbs, and aromatics. For the best flavor, the spices should be toasted and ground before cooking, but you can substitute pre-ground spices if you are short on time.

2 teaspoons cumin seeds
2 teaspoons coriander seeds
1 teaspoon cardamom pods
2 tablespoons vegetable oil
1 medium onion, finely chopped
1 tablespoon finely minced gingerroot
3 or 4 cloves garlic, minced
1 to 2 fresh hot green chiles, seeded and minced, or ½ to 1 teaspoon crushed dried hot pepper

1 teaspoon turmeric
1 cup green split peas
6 cups chicken broth
Several good grinds of black pepper
1 tablespoon fresh lime juice
3 to 4 tablespoons finely chopped fresh mint leaves
3 to 4 tablespoons finely chopped fresh coriander leaves

1. In a small skillet, toast the cumin, coriander seeds, and cardamom over moderate heat, shaking the pan, until the seeds are just beginning to brown and become aromatic. Do not overbrown. Let cool slightly, then grind in a spice mill.

2. Heat the oil in a large, heavy pot and sauté the onion, gingerroot, garlic, and chiles over moderate heat, stirring, until the onion wilts and the mixture becomes aromatic. Stir in the turmeric and the ground spices and cook for a minute or two.

3. Add the split peas, chicken broth, and black pepper. Bring to a simmer, then cook, uncovered, over low heat, stirring occasionally, for 35 to 45 minutes, until the split peas are very tender.

4. Remove the split peas from the broth and purée in a blender or food processor. Return the purée to the pot.

5. Bring the soup to a simmer again, then stir in the lime juice, mint, and coriander leaves. Taste for salt. Serve hot.

Serves 4 to 6

Spiced Pickled Fish

The venerable Dutch practice of pickling fish, particularly herring, traveled to South Africa, where it was refashioned by the Malay tradition of sweet and spicy marinated dishes (see, for example, the recipe for marinated fish on page 52). Unlike the European practice, where the fish is pickled raw, the fish here is first fried and then marinated in its pungent golden sauce for one to three days. It makes an excellent appetizer or first course, served chilled in small portions with greens and sliced cucumber, and perhaps some potato salad, another Dutch favorite.

Vegetable oil for frying
1 to 1¼ pounds firm white fish
    fillets
Flour for dredging
1 large onion, thinly sliced
1 carrot, thinly sliced
1 to 2 fresh hot chiles, seeded
    and cut into julienne strips
1 tablespoon finely minced
    gingerroot

1 teaspoon curry powder
    (preferably Madras)
½ teaspoon turmeric
½ cup white or cider vinegar
1 bay leaf
½ teaspoon salt
Several good grinds of black
    pepper
1 tablespoon sugar

1. Heat 2 to 3 tablespoons of oil in a large skillet. Dredge the fish fillets lightly in flour, then fry over moderate to high heat, turning once, until nicely browned on both sides. As the fillets are browned, remove them from the pan and place in a glass, enamel, or other nonreactive container.

2. Add the onion, carrot, chile, and gingerroot to the oil remaining in the pan (add a tablespoon or so more if necessary) and sauté, stirring, until the onions wilt and the mixture becomes aromatic.

3. Stir in the curry powder and turmeric and mix well, then add the vinegar, bay leaf, salt, black pepper, and sugar. Bring to a simmer, then cook for a minute or two, stirring.

4. Pour the marinade over the fish, cover, and refrigerate for 1 to 3 days. Serve chilled in small portions, with a little of the sauce spooned over each serving.

Serves 4 to 6

Spicy Chicken with Potatoes and Green Chiles

A hearty chicken-and-potato stew, made pungent with the fresh green chiles favored in South Africa and spiced with both curry powder and a number of aromatic spices that have gained wide popularity with Europeans. Serve this dish with a sweet-and-sour salad, sambal, or chutney.

2 tablespoons vegetable oil

2 to 2½ pounds chicken thighs (for a leaner dish, remove the skin)

1 medium onion, coarsely chopped

1 tablespoon finely minced gingerroot

3 to 4 fresh long green chiles, seeded and slivered

½ to 1 teaspoon salt

¼ teaspoon freshly ground black pepper

1 teaspoon curry powder (preferably Madras)

¼ teaspoon cinnamon

¼ teaspoon nutmeg

¼ teaspoon ground allspice

2 medium-to-large potatoes, peeled and thickly sliced

1 bay leaf

⅓ to ½ cup water

1. Heat the oil in a large, heavy skillet or Dutch oven and brown the chicken thighs over moderate heat, turning the parts to brown evenly on all sides. While the chicken is browning, add the onion, gingerroot, and chiles, stirring them to sauté.

2. When the chicken is browned, sprinkle it with about ½ teaspoon of the salt and the black pepper, curry powder, cinnamon, nutmeg, and allspice.

3. Add the potatoes and turn them briefly in the pot. Add the bay leaf and water, bring to a simmer, then cover and cook over low heat for about 1 hour, until the chicken and the potatoes are tender.

4. Uncover, and if the sauce is too liquid, cook it down rapidly. Remove the bay leaf. Taste for salt and adjust the seasoning if necessary.

Serves 4 to 6

Curried Lamb and Bean Stew

A heart- and mouth-warming stew, a kind of Afro-Asian chili. The curry powder and the subtle hint of sweet-and-sour point to a Malay rather than an Indian influence. This dish belongs to a characteristic group of South African meat and vegetable stews called bredies.

2 tablespoons vegetable oil
1 large onion, finely chopped
1 to 2 fresh long green chiles, seeded and minced, or ½ to 1 teaspoon crushed dried hot pepper
2 cloves garlic, crushed
1 pound boneless lamb, cut into ½-inch pieces
1 teaspoon salt
2 teaspoons curry powder (preferably Madras)

1 large potato, peeled and diced
½ to 1 cup water
2 bay leaves
2 cups cooked or canned white kidney beans or black-eyed peas
2 tablespoons fresh lemon juice
2 teaspoons sugar

1. Heat the oil in a large skillet and sauté the onion and chiles over moderate heat, stirring, until the onions begin to wilt.

2. Add the garlic and the lamb and continue to cook, stirring, until the lamb is lightly browned on all sides.

3. Sprinkle the lamb with the salt and curry powder, then add the potato, water (start with ½ cup), and bay leaves. Bring to a simmer, then cover and cook over low heat for about 1 hour, or until the lamb is tender. Add more water if needed during cooking.

4. Stir in the beans, lemon juice, and sugar, mix well, and cook for about 15 to 20 minutes. Remove the bay leaves. Serve hot with rice and chutney.

Serves 4

Sweet and Spicy Grilled Lamb (Sosaties)

This dish is the South African adaptation of the Malaysian satay, evident in both the name and the seasonings. The Afrikaner version always uses lamb, however, and the marinade is more assertively sweet-and-sour; the addition of dried apricots lends a tangy, fruity note that is very appealing with the lamb. Try this as a delicious change of pace for your summer barbecue menu.

1 medium onion, grated or very finely chopped
2 cloves garlic, crushed
1 tablespoon vegetable oil
1 bay leaf, finely crumbled
2 tablespoons cider vinegar
1 tablespoon firmly packed dark brown sugar
1 tablespoon curry powder (preferably Madras)
Several good grinds of black pepper
½ teaspoon turmeric
1 pound lean boneless lamb, cut into 1-inch chunks
10 to 12 plump dried apricots (avoid the dry, leathery ones)
Salt to taste

1. In a glass or ceramic dish, combine the onion, garlic, oil, bay leaf, vinegar, brown sugar, curry powder, black pepper, and turmeric. Mix well.

2. Add the lamb and apricots and mix well. Cover and refrigerate for at least 6 to 8 hours, preferably overnight.

3. Thread the lamb and the apricots on skewers, keeping on as much of the marinade as possible. Grill over hot charcoal, turning

once, 3 to 4 minutes each side. (Or broil under the broiler, turning once, until nicely browned on each side.) Sprinkle with salt to taste. Good with pan-fried potatoes or potato salad.

Serves 4

Vegetable Biryani

Afrikaners, true to their Dutch heritage, enjoyed a diet rich in meat and fish but were exposed in their new home to a more elaborate vegetable cookery from both native and Asian traditions. This lavish rice-and-vegetable dish, straight from the Indian kitchen, has become a favorite on the South African table. For best flavor, the cumin, coriander, and cardamom seeds should be toasted and ground fresh, but preground spices can be used if necessary.

2 tablespoons butter or ghee
   (see Note)
1 teaspoon turmeric
1 cup basmati rice
2 cups water
2½ teaspoons salt
⅓ cup golden raisins
2 teaspoons cumin seeds
2 teaspoons coriander seeds
1 teaspoon cardamom pods
2 tablespoons vegetable oil
1 medium onion, finely
   chopped
2 cloves garlic, minced
1 tablespoon finely minced
   gingerroot
2 to 3 small fresh hot chiles,
   seeded and minced, or
   1 teaspoon crushed dried
   hot pepper

½ teaspoon cinnamon
⅛ teaspoon ground cloves
1 red bell pepper, seeded and
   cut into small chunks
2 carrots, sliced
2 medium potatoes, peeled and
   cut into small cubes
8 ounces green beans, trimmed
   and cut into 1-inch pieces
¼ teaspoon freshly ground
   black pepper
4 medium tomatoes, coarsely
   chopped
½ small head cauliflower,
   separated into small florets
1 cup fresh or frozen peas
Good squeeze of lime juice
Chopped fresh mint leaves or
   coriander leaves, for
   garnish (optional)

1. In a medium saucepan, melt the butter or ghee over moderate heat. Stir in the turmeric and rice and mix until all the butter has been absorbed by the rice.

2. Add the water, 1 teaspoon of the salt, and the raisins, bring to a simmer, then cover and cook over low heat for about 20 minutes, until all the liquid has been absorbed. Set aside and let stand, covered.

3. In a small skillet, toast the cumin, coriander, and cardamom over moderate heat, shaking the pan, until the seeds are just lightly browned and aromatic. Let cool slightly, then grind in a spice mill.

4. Heat the oil in a large pot or deep skillet and sauté the onion, garlic, gingerroot, and chiles over moderate heat, stirring, until the vegetables become aromatic. Stir in the ground spices, the cinnamon, and the cloves.

5. Add the bell pepper, carrots, potatoes, and green beans. Add the remaining 1½ teaspoons of salt and the black pepper and mix well. Add the tomatoes, then bring to a simmer, cover, and cook over low heat for 30 to 40 minutes, until the potatoes and green beans are just tender.

6. Add the cauliflower and peas for the last 10 minutes of cooking. Stir in the lime juice, then taste for salt. Preheat the oven to 350°F.

7. Layer the rice into a lightly buttered casserole; spoon the vegetable mixture over the rice. Cover and bake for about 15 to 20 minutes. Garnish with some chopped fresh mint or coriander, if desired.

Serves 4 to 6

NOTE: Ghee, cooked clarified butter, adds a distinctive nutty flavor to many Indian dishes. It is available in jars in Indian groceries, and stores well in the refrigerator.

Date and Onion Salad

Although this is called a salad, it functions more appropriately as a kind of relish or chutney, with its intense sweet-and-sour flavor. It's an interesting example of how the simple substitution of one ingredient, dates, for the more typical Dutch cucumber can produce a wholly different effect. This is good with curries, kebabs, and grilled or roasted meat.

8 to 10 ounces pitted dates, thinly sliced
1 large onion, cut into quarters and thinly sliced
¼ cup cider vinegar
¼ teaspoon salt
½ teaspoon sugar
2 tablespoons chopped fresh mint leaves

Combine all the ingredients except the mint and mix thoroughly. Let stand for 1 to 2 hours at room temperature, stirring occasionally, before serving. Stir in the mint at the last minute.

Makes about 2 cups

Peach Chutney

The European love for highly sweetened preserved fruit found full realization in the Afrikaner kitchen with a number of jams, preserves, and conserves and was further expanded and elaborated by the sweet-and-spicy chutney tradition from India. This delicious chutney, best made when summer fruit is at its peak, is excellent with curries and spiced foods, as well as roasted, grilled, or smoked meats.

12 fully ripe peaches, pitted and coarsely chopped (no need to peel)
1 large onion, coarsely chopped
1 tablespoon finely chopped garlic
1 tablespoon finely chopped gingerroot

1 teaspoon crushed dried hot pepper
1 teaspoon cinnamon
1 teaspoon ground coriander
1 teaspoon salt
1 cup sugar
1 cup cider vinegar

1. Combine all the ingredients in an enamel or stainless-steel pot. Mix thoroughly and bring to a boil.

2. Boil gently over moderate heat, uncovered, stirring from time to time, for 1 to 1¼ hours, until the mixture is soft and thick. Mash the fruit gently with the back of a spoon while stirring.

3. Spoon the chutney into clean glass jars. Cover and let cool, then store in the refrigerator. It will keep almost indefinitely.

Makes about 1 quart

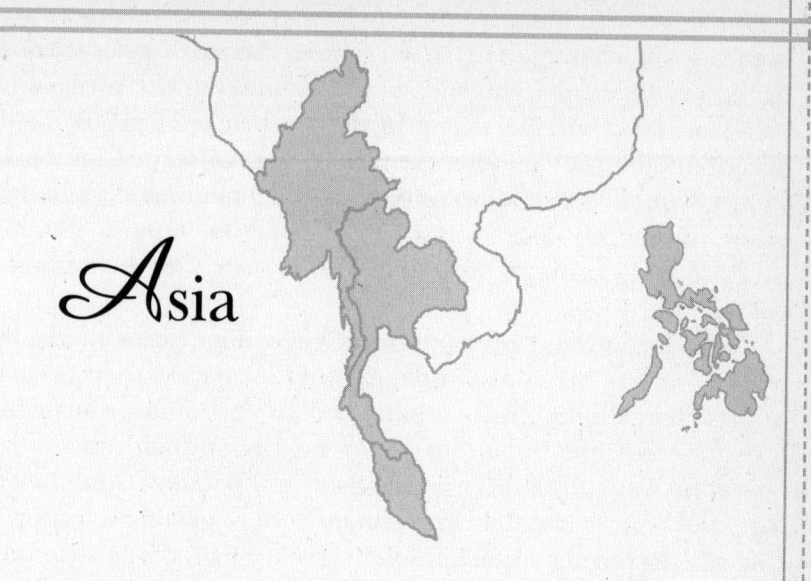

Asia

Two colossi dominate the culinary landscape of Asia, two ancient and enduring cultures that have shaped and colored all the food of the Eastern world. Both are complex, deep-rooted, and utterly distinctive; neither influenced the other in any great measure. Yet between them, in a myriad of subtle shifts of power and accommodation, they left their unmistakable mark on all the kitchens of Southeast Asia—and beyond.

The cuisines of China and India share a number of important features. Both are based on rice and, to a lesser extent, on wheat; both maintain strong vegetarian traditions and show a heavy and imaginative use of vegetable foods; both use the same aromatics—garlic and gingerroot—fried in oil or fat, as a prelude to the seasoning process. But here the likeness ends, and even the apparent similarities are illusory, for they are expressed very differently by each tradition.

India's use of wheat is reflected in an extensive repertoire of breads—roti, chapatis, puri, naan—fried, baked, or griddle-cooked. China produces some breads, mostly steamed in the form of buns and pancakes, but the major focus of wheat cookery is directed toward noodles, in an impressive variety. So great is the Chinese dedication to noodles that it has resulted in the ingenious exploitation of other substances—rice, beans, sweet potatoes, tapioca starch—to produce an assortment of noodle products that serve a number of culinary purposes.

The selection and preparation of vegetables differ markedly in both cuisines. China opts for delicacy of flavor and variety of texture in succulent shoots, crisp sprouts, and an enormous assortment of leafy greens, while India relies more heavily on such robust vegetables as carrots and cauliflower, cabbage and potatoes. And the cooking styles generally reflect and enhance the vegetable selection, the Chinese preferring a quick, high-heat stir-fry or gentle steaming to preserve flavor and retain texture, while the Indian cook favors a long, slow braising in seasoned liquids.

It is, however, in the seasoning enterprise that the two cuisines most clearly differentiate themselves, not only in the choice of flavoring ingredients but also in the manner of their production. China consistently uses a number of fermented products—soy sauce, soy pastes, rice wine, rice vinegar, fermented soybeans—as well as a large variety of preprocessed seasoning substances: hoisin sauce, oyster sauce, meat stocks, toasted sesame oil.

India's seasoning practice rests almost completely on an unparalleled array of aromatics and spices, an ancient and complex assortment of seeds, barks, and leaves used in constantly shifting and subtle combinations. Cumin, coriander, cardamom, fenugreek, mustard seed, cinnamon, bay leaves, pepper, asafetida, turmeric, cloves . . . and the list goes on. In traditional practice, the seeds are toasted and the spices freshly ground and combined for each individual preparation. Few processed or fermented products are used; the notable exception is yogurt, a cultured dairy product introduced into India by Aryan immigrants from central Asia, and an elaborate complex of condiments, chutneys, relishes, and pickles.

The basic seasoning profile of Indian food is savory and spicy, with sweetness typically provided separately as an option by accompanying condiments. In Chinese food, sweetness is more commonly an element balanced with the savory within the flavor of the individual dish or sauce.

A few short pages are hardly adequate to describe two of the world's most ancient and influential cuisines, but they highlight the issues that will come up when we look at the impact that China and India have had on the kitchens of Burma and Thailand, Malaysia, and the Philippines. We will see how each culture dips into the common Asian pot and fashions something unique and distinctive; it is a fascinating dance with intricate steps and changing patterns, some basic themes with a multitude of variations that transform endlessly into something wholly different and yet curiously alike.

For although the influence of China and India is clear and unmistakable, the cuisines of Southeast Asia are not merely immature offspring, thoughtlessly aping the practices of their elders. They are, all of them, rich and full traditions, with their own identity and integrity. They bring to the culinary experience their own unique elements—coconut and lemongrass, fish sauce and shrimp paste, galangal, peanuts, and sweet aromatic herbs. A whole set of characteristic dishes is typical of the region: sweet-and-spicy marinated satays, pungent sambals lavish with fresh hot chiles, complex salads constructed of seafood, vegetables, meat, and fruit, with textures succulent and crisp, flavors aromatic, citrusy, and bold.

The giants have become grist for the neighbors' mills: Indian spices meet with Chinese noodles in sweet and savory coconut sauces; soy sauce and bean curd make their way into curries; a variety of fresh herbs and unexpected aromatics turn up in stir-fried dishes. Is this really a melting pot, where distinctive traditions and tastes lose their identity in an undistinguishable mush, or is it, rather, a cauldron at the crossroads of Asia, bubbling over with creative new life?

malaysia

Malaysia is often called the Crossroads of Asia, a commercial and cultural center in which every Asian ethnic tradition and religious belief has a presence and an impact on the culinary scene. In the bustling food courts of Singapore and Kuala Lumpur, where vendors hawk ready-made food for the hungry traveler or the hurried businessman, one risks the delicious danger of sensory overload; all the colors, the aromas, and the flavors of Asia, separate and mingling, create a riot for the senses and an unprecedented salivary rush.

Here are noodles from China, glistening with a hundred sauces, succulent pork, and crispy glazed duck; here are spicy curries from India, rich with layers of complex flavor; and everywhere the fragrant smoke from charcoal braziers holding bamboo skewers of marinated satays, served with sweet-and-pungent peanut sauces. And everywhere the fresh red chiles, transplanted from the New World to take firm root as a beloved seasoning in the Malaysian repertoire.

But whatever Malaysia took from Asia and the rest of the world was assimilated into a rich trove of her own. The South China Sea yields a bounty of fish and seafood, with such typical dishes as spicy chile-fried crabs, delicate fish marinated and steamed in banana leaves, stir-fried squid, and grilled giant prawns. From the sea comes as well a variety of seasoning products based on dry or fermented shellfish. Tropical fruits like mango, tamarind, pineapple, and banana are unparalleled for flavor and sweetness, used in both sweet and savory dishes. And central to everything is the coconut, its sweet white flesh grated and squeezed for the rich, creamy milk that forms the basis of so many soups and sauces.

There are in Malaysia a number of distinct regional and ethnic traditions, each with its own style and character. But there is throughout an exuberant sense of give-and-take, a joyful participation in a multitude of ingredients and cooking styles, and a creative energy that comes from sharing the best that Asia has to offer.

RECIPES

Seafood Noodles in Coconut Broth

Banana-Shrimp Dumplings

Shrimp Sambal

Steamed Mussels in Spicy Red Sauce

Crispy Crab and Sweet Potato Cakes with
    Tamarind Dipping Sauce

Baked Marinated Fish

Chile-Fried Rice with Chicken and Shrimp

Straits Chicken Salad

Sweet-and-Sour Lamb Satay with Coconut-
    Peanut Dipping Sauce

Spicy Fried Steak Strips

Eggplant with Basil and Chile

Pineapple and Cucumber Salad

Frozen Pumpkin and Sweet Corn Custard

Seafood Noodles in Coconut Broth
(Laksa Lemak)

This delicious dish of fish, shrimp, and noodles in a richly seasoned, spicy coconut broth is popular throughout Malaysia. Laksa, the traditional rice-flour noodles, are round rather than flat and about the same diameter as, or just slightly larger than, spaghetti. Note the use of such typical seasonings as galangal, an aromatic rhizome related to gingerroot, and shrimp paste, a concentrated mixture of salted ground shrimp and oil. Laksa Lemak is a souplike dish that is almost a meal in itself.

2 tablespoons peanut oil
6 ounces dried round rice noodles (spaghetti size or slightly thicker)
3 to 4 shallots, minced
2 cloves garlic, minced
3 to 4 small fresh hot red chiles, seeded and minced, or ½ to 1 teaspoon crushed dried hot pepper
2 teaspoons finely minced gingerroot
1 teaspoon turmeric
2 teaspoons minced lemongrass, or 1 teaspoon dried powdered
2 teaspoons minced fresh galangal, or 1 teaspoon dried powdered (Laos powder)

1 cup unsweetened coconut milk
2 cups water
2 tablespoons fish sauce
1 teaspoon shrimp paste
½ teaspoon sugar
8 to 12 ounces boneless firm white fish, cut into small chunks
8 ounces shrimp, peeled and deveined
6 to 8 ounces fresh bean sprouts
1 medium cucumber, peeled, seeded, and diced; finely shredded or chopped fresh mint; and additional fresh red chiles, seeded and cut into julienne strips, for serving

1. Cover the noodles with warm water and let soften for 15 to 20 minutes.

2. Heat the oil in a medium, heavy pot and sauté the shallots, garlic, chiles, and gingerroot over moderate heat, stirring, until the mixture becomes aromatic.

3. Stir in the turmeric, lemongrass, and galangal, then add the coconut milk, water, fish sauce, shrimp paste, and sugar. Mix well, then bring to a simmer and cook over low heat for about 5 minutes.

4. Bring a medium saucepan of water to a boil; drain the softened noodles and cook in the boiling water for just a minute or two, until tender but still firm. Drain.

5. Add the fish and shrimp to the coconut broth and cook for a few minutes, just until the fish turns opaque and the shrimp turn pink.

6. Distribute the noodles and the bean sprouts into individual bowls; ladle the hot broth and fish over them.

7. Arrange the cucumber, mint, and chiles on a plate and pass separately.

Serves 4 to 6

Banana-Shrimp Dumplings

China is an ancient and esteemed center of dumpling cookery and has sent forth the savory stuffed little pockets of dough throughout Southeast Asia and the Pacific and as far west as Afghanistan and Turkey. Boiled, steamed, or fried, wherever it went the dumpling incorporated the ingredients and flavors of its new homes. This Malaysian version combines sweet banana, shrimp, and shallots for a delicious variation.

1 large, very ripe banana
6 to 8 ounces shrimp, peeled, deveined, and coarsely chopped
2 or 3 cloves garlic, crushed
2 shallots, minced
½ teaspoon sugar
½ teaspoon salt

2 teaspoons plus 2 tablespoons Asian sesame oil
24–30 wonton wrappers or potsticker wrappers
2 tablespoons soy sauce
Few sprigs of fresh coriander, for garnish

1. In a small bowl, mash the banana thoroughly, then add the chopped shrimp, garlic, shallots, sugar, and salt and 2 teaspoons of the sesame oil. Mix well.

2. Have a small cup of cold water at hand. Place a teaspoonful of the banana filling in the center of a wrapper. With your finger, moisten the four edges of the wrapper with some water. Fold the dumpling in half to form a triangle or semicircle, and pinch the edges to seal.

3. Cook the dumplings in boiling water, in several batches if necessary, for about 2 to 3 minutes. Remove from the water with a slotted spoon.

4. Place the cooked dumplings on a warm serving dish. Drizzle the soy sauce and the 2 remaining tablespoons of sesame oil over the dumplings and garnish with the coriander sprigs.

Makes about 24 dumplings, serving 4 to 6
(Unless you're Lex and Wendy,
in which case it's enough for just Lex and Wendy.)

Shrimp Sambal

Sambals are pungent, highly seasoned dishes meant to serve as accompaniments or condiments to curries and other dishes in the meal. They can range from the simplest of preparations—such as fresh chopped chiles fried in oil—to rather more complex recipes, like this one for shrimp in a spicy coconut sauce. The level of hotness from the chiles can be adjusted to suit your own palate.

3 to 4 small shallots
5 large cloves garlic
2 to 4 fresh hot red chile
    peppers, seeded, or
    ½ to 1 teaspoon
    crushed dried hot
    pepper

2 teaspoons finely minced fresh
    galangal (if not available,
    substitute an equivalent
    amount of fresh
    gingerroot)
2 tablespoons peanut oil
2 teaspoons ground coriander

1 teaspoon ground cumin	1 teaspoon shrimp paste
½ teaspoon turmeric	½ teaspoon salt
1 medium tomato, finely chopped	Several good grinds of black pepper
1 tablespoon firmly packed brown sugar	1 pound shrimp, peeled and deveined
½ cup unsweetened coconut milk	1 tablespoon fresh lime juice

1. Combine the shallots, garlic, chiles, and galangal and pound or process into a coarse paste.

2. Heat the oil in a skillet and sauté the paste over moderate heat until the mixture becomes aromatic.

3. Add the coriander, cumin, and turmeric and stir for a few minutes. Stir in the tomato and cook for a few minutes more.

4. Add the sugar, coconut milk, shrimp paste, salt, and black pepper. Mix well, then simmer over low heat, stirring occasionally, for about 10 minutes. The sauce should be fairly thick.

5. Add the shrimp and cook just long enough for them to turn pink. Stir in the lime juice. Taste for salt and hotness and adjust the seasoning if necessary.

Serves 4 to 6 if served with other foods

Steamed Mussels in Spicy Red Sauce

Southern Italy is deservedly famous for mussels in red sauce, but they show up as well in Malaysia in a complex, aromatic sauce that enhances the subtle briny flavor of the mollusks in a very different way. The large, plump green-shelled mussels are an excellent choice for this preparation, if you can get them, but almost any variety will work well. Serve the mussels as an appetizer or first course, warm or at room temperature, in shallow dishes with the sauce spooned over them.

2 to 2½ pounds fresh mussels
1 tablespoon peanut oil
2 shallots, minced
4 or 5 cloves garlic, minced
2 teaspoons finely minced or grated gingerroot
1 teaspoon crushed dried hot pepper

½ cup tomato sauce
2 tablespoons oyster sauce
1 tablespoon soy sauce
2 teaspoons finely minced lemongrass, or 1 teaspoon dried powdered
Good handful of finely chopped fresh coriander leaves

1. Scrub and debeard the mussels; discard any that are open or damaged.
2. Heat the oil in a large, heavy pot and sauté the shallots, garlic, gingerroot, and hot pepper until the vegetables wilt and the mixture becomes aromatic.
3. Stir in the tomato sauce, oyster sauce, soy sauce, and lemongrass. Simmer, stirring, for a few minutes.
4. Place the mussels in the pot, cover, and cook over low heat for about 10 minutes, until the mussels have opened. Stir in the chopped coriander leaves.
5. Serve the mussels warm or at room temperature—on the half shell, if desired—with the sauce spooned generously over them.

Serves 4 to 6 as an appetizer

Crispy Crab and Sweet Potato Cakes
with Tamarind Dipping Sauce

The white potato, imported from the Americas, did not have a significant impact on the cuisines of Southeast Asia, except in dishes heavily influenced by Indian tradition. The sweet potato, however, with its higher protein and sugar content, has fared much more successfully and is used in a variety of sweet and savory dishes. These delicately seasoned, crisp little fritters make an excellent appetizer or hors d'oeuvre, served hot with a sweet-and-spicy dipping sauce.

2 eggs
½ teaspoon salt
½ teaspoon sugar
Several good grinds of black pepper
¼ teaspoon crushed dried hot pepper
1 medium shallot, minced
2 teaspoons grated or finely minced gingerroot
2 teaspoons finely minced lemongrass, or ½ teaspoon dried powdered

2 teaspoons minced fresh galangal, or ½ teaspoon dried powdered (Laos powder)
2 to 2½ cups grated peeled sweet potato (1 medium to large, about 8 to 10 ounces)
8 ounces fresh crabmeat, picked over to remove any cartilage
Peanut oil, for frying

1. In a medium bowl, whisk the eggs, then stir in the salt, sugar, black pepper, hot pepper, shallot, gingerroot, lemongrass, and galangal and mix well.

2. Stir in the grated sweet potato and mix thoroughly, then fold in the crabmeat. Cover the mixture and refrigerate for 1 hour.

3. Heat about 3 to 4 tablespoons of the oil in a heavy skillet over high heat. Drop the sweet potato mixture by small tablespoons into the hot oil. Fry, turning once, until golden brown on each side. Drain the cakes on paper towels. Serve warm with tamarind dipping sauce (recipe follows).

Makes about 18 to 24 small cakes

1 tablespoon tamarind
    concentrate (see Note)
1/2 cup water
2 tablespoons firmly packed
    brown sugar
1 teaspoon grated or very finely
    minced gingerroot

1 clove garlic, crushed
1/2 teaspoon garam masala
1/4 teaspoon crushed dried hot
    pepper

Combine all the ingredients in a small saucepan and simmer over low heat, stirring occasionally, for about 10 minutes, or until slightly thickened and syrupy. Let cool before serving. The sauce will keep well, covered, in the refrigerator.

Makes about 1/2 cup

NOTE: Tamarind is available dried and pressed, with the pits still in it, or as a strained concentrate in small jars. It will keep almost indefinitely in the refrigerator.

Baked Marinated Fish

These little packets of marinated fish are filled with delightful flavor and very easy to prepare. In Malaysia, banana leaves are typically used as the wrappers, adding a subtle herbal note, but heavy-duty foil or baking parchment can serve as well. The fish packets can also be grilled over hot charcoal.

2 shallots, finely chopped
2 cloves garlic, minced
1 tablespoon finely minced
    gingerroot

2 to 3 small fresh hot red chiles,
    seeded and minced, or
    1/2 to 1 teaspoon crushed
    dried hot pepper

1 tablespoon finely minced
    lemongrass, or 1 teaspoon
    dry powdered
2 teaspoons soy sauce
1 teaspoon sugar
1 teaspoon shrimp paste

1 teaspoon Asian
    sesame oil
1 to 1½ pounds fish fillets
    (snapper, mackerel,
    pompano,
    bluefish, etc.)

1. In a small bowl, combine the shallots, garlic, gingerroot, chiles, lemongrass, and soy sauce. Pound into a paste or process into a paste in the food processor. Add the sugar, shrimp paste, and sesame oil and mix well.

2. Coat or rub all sides of the fish fillets with the paste. Refrigerate, covered, for 1 to 2 hours.

3. Preheat the oven to 400°F. Wrap the fish in banana leaves or heavy-duty foil, using 1 or 2 small fillets per package. Fold up all the sides to make a secure envelope. Place the packets seam side down on a baking tray and bake for 10 to 12 minutes, or until the fish just flakes easily with a fork.

Serves 4 to 6

Chile-Fried Rice with Chicken and Shrimp

Colorful and filled with tasty tidbits, this dish is clearly of Chinese origin, but demonstrates the characteristic Malaysian generosity with fresh hot chiles. For best results, the rice should be cooked and completely cold or it will stick in the pan.

6 to 8 scallions
2 tablespoons oyster sauce
2 tablespoons soy sauce
½ teaspoon sugar
3 to 4 tablespoons peanut oil
4 large cloves garlic, minced
1 tablespoon finely minced
    gingerroot
2 to 3 small fresh red chiles,
    seeded and minced
6 to 8 ounces small-to-medium
    shrimp, peeled and
    deveined (or large shrimp,
    coarsely chopped)

2 cups diced bok choy or other
    cabbage, coarsely chopped
2 cups cooked short- or
    medium-grain rice, cold
1 cup diced cooked chicken
½ cup frozen or fresh peas
2 to 3 small fresh red chiles,
    seeded and cut into slivers,
    for garnish

1. Separate the scallions into white and green parts. Chop the green parts and reserve for garnish. Coarsely chop the white parts.

2. Combine the oyster sauce, soy sauce, and sugar and set aside.

3. Heat a wok or large skillet over high heat. Swirl in the oil and heat until very hot. Add the chopped white parts of the scallions and the garlic, gingerroot, and minced chiles and stir-fry for a few minutes.

4. Add the shrimp and bok choy and stir-fry just until the shrimp turn pink.

5. Add the rice and stir-fry, breaking up the clumps of rice as you cook it. Add the chicken and peas and continue to stir-fry until everything is well mixed.

6. Drizzle in the reserved sauce and cook, stirring, until all is well mixed and hot. Garnish the rice with the chopped green scallion tops and the slivers of red chile.

Serves 4, more if served with other foods

Straits Chicken Salad

An intriguing mixture of flavors characterizes this complex salad, with sweet, sour, pungent, and fruity blending in a sauce that shows its Chinese origins with soy sauce, plum sauce, and sesame oil. It makes a light but satisfying summer meal or an exotic addition to the buffet table.

2 tablespoons peanut oil
2 shallots, minced
4 large cloves garlic, minced
1 tablespoon finely minced gingerroot
2 to 3 small fresh hot red chiles, seeded and minced, or 1 to 2 teaspoons crushed dried hot pepper
6 tablespoons Chinese plum sauce
2 tablespoons soy sauce
1 tablespoon fresh lime juice
1 tablespoon rice vinegar
1 teaspoon sugar

2 teaspoons Asian sesame oil
2 cups shredded cooked chicken
2 cups shredded napa cabbage
3 to 4 scallions, sliced on the diagonal into 1-inch pieces
Small lettuce leaves or torn greens
Slices of cucumber, carrot, and daikon, for garnish
2 to 3 tablespoons finely chopped peanuts, for garnish

1. Heat the oil in a small, heavy nonreactive saucepan and sauté the shallots, garlic, gingerroot, and chiles over moderate heat, stirring, until the vegetables wilt and the mixture becomes aromatic.

2. Add the plum sauce, soy sauce, lime juice, vinegar, and sugar. Simmer for a few minutes, stirring, then remove from the heat and stir in the sesame oil.

3. In a bowl, combine the chicken, cabbage, and scallions. Reserve 3 to 4 tablespoons of the sauce, then mix the rest with the chicken.

4. Mound the chicken salad on the lettuce leaves on a serving plate. Surround the salad with the sliced cucumber, carrot, and daikon.

5. Drizzle the remaining sauce over the salad, then sprinkle with the chopped peanuts.

Serves 4 to 6

Sweet-and-Sour Lamb Satay with Coconut-Peanut Dipping Sauce

Although pork is the favored meat of most Asians, lamb is a delicious alternative for the many Malaysian Muslims whose religion forbids the meat of the pig. The sweet-and-sour marinade works particularly well with the full flavor of lamb. The coconut-peanut dipping sauce is but one variety of a host of sweet-and-spicy satay sauces.

1 pound lean boneless lamb, cut into ½-inch cubes
3 tablespoons regular soy sauce
2 tablespoons firmly packed dark brown sugar
1 teaspoon tamarind concentrate
4 cloves garlic, crushed
2 tablespoons peanut oil
2 shallots, minced
1 tablespoon minced gingerroot

1 teaspoon crushed dried hot pepper
½ cup unsweetened coconut milk
2 tablespoons black soy sauce
1 tablespoon fresh lemon juice
2 teaspoons finely minced lemongrass, or 1 teaspoon powdered dry
⅓ cup peanut butter

1. If you are using bamboo skewers, soak them in water for an hour or two before you need them.

2. Combine the lamb with 2 tablespoons of the regular soy sauce, 1 tablespoon of the brown sugar, and the tamarind and garlic. Mix well, then let stand, covered, in the refrigerator for 2 to 4 hours.

3. Heat the oil in a small, heavy saucepan and sauté the shallots, gingerroot, and hot pepper over moderate heat, stirring, for a few minutes, until the mixture becomes aromatic.

4. Add the coconut milk, the remaining tablespoon of regular soy sauce, the black soy sauce, the lemon juice, the lemon grass, and the remaining tablespoon of dark brown sugar. Mix well and bring to a simmer. Simmer, stirring, for a few minutes. Add the peanut butter and mix until the sauce is well blended and smooth. Remove from the heat.

5. Thread the marinated lamb onto skewers. Grill over hot charcoal, turning once, about 4 to 5 minutes on each side. Serve the satay with the coconut-peanut sauce for dipping.

Serves 4, more if served as an
appetizer or with other foods

NOTE: Any leftover dipping sauce can be stored in a covered jar in the refrigerator for a couple of weeks. Heat the sauce to a simmer before serving again.

Spicy Fried Steak Strips

Many diverse elements from the broad Asian spectrum—Indian, Indonesian, Chinese—blend to produce the complex intriguing flavor of the marinade/sauce for this stir-fried beef dish. In Southeast Asia, the beef is sometimes tough and of poor quality and is frequently boiled before it is stir-fried, but the dish is quickly done here with the excellent beef available to most of us.

1 teaspoon coriander seeds
½ teaspoon caraway seeds
2 tablespoons soy sauce
1 tablespoon firmly packed
    brown sugar
1 teaspoon tamarind
    concentrate
4 cloves garlic, crushed
2 teaspoons grated gingerroot
1 teaspoon finely minced
    lemongrass, or ½ teaspoon
    dried powdered
1 teaspoon finely minced fresh
    galangal, or ½ teaspoon
    dried powdered (Laos
    powder)

¾ to 1 pound boneless beef
    steak (filet mignon, etc.),
    cut in strips about ¼ to
    ⅜ inch thick
2 tablespoons peanut oil
1 large onion, cut in half and
    thinly sliced
2 to 3 fresh long hot red or
    green chiles, seeded and
    cut into thin strips
Salt to taste

1. In a small skillet, toast the coriander and caraway seeds over moderate heat, shaking the pan, until the seeds are just lightly browned and aromatic. Let cool slightly, then grind in a spice mill.

2. In a shallow baking dish or pie plate, combine the soy sauce, brown sugar, tamarind, gingerroot, garlic, lemongrass, galangal, and ground spices. Mix well. Add the beef strips to the marinade and mix thoroughly. Let stand for 30 minutes to 1 hour.

3. Heat a wok or skillet over high heat. Swirl in the oil, then add the sliced onion and the chiles and stir-fry for a few minutes.

4. Add the marinated beef strips and stir-fry just long enough to brown the beef on all sides. Sprinkle with salt to taste; serve with rice.

Serves 3 to 4

Eggplant with Basil and Chile

The Malaysian rempeh—a mixture of pounded chiles, shallots, garlic, and gingerroot fried in oil—provides the underlying flavor for this delightfully piquant dish, further enhanced by a touch of sweet-and-sour and plenty of fresh basil. The flavor and the pungency of fresh red chiles are critical, as is the soft, velvety texture of the long, slender Asian eggplant. Serve the dish at room temperature as part of a buffet or a larger Asian meal.

3 to 4 (or more to taste) fresh red chiles (the 2- to 3-inch finger hots are a good choice), seeded and coarsely chopped

2 medium shallots, coarsely chopped

4 to 5 cloves garlic

1 tablespoon chopped gingerroot

3 tablespoons chili sauce (the American bottled tomato variety)

1 tablespoon fish sauce

1 tablespoon fresh lime juice

½ teaspoon sugar

1 pound long, slender Asian eggplants

3 to 4 tablespoons peanut oil

½ cup fresh basil leaves, finely chopped or shredded

Additional chopped basil leaves, for garnish (optional)

1. Combine the chiles, shallots, garlic, and gingerroot and pound or process into a coarse paste.

2. Combine the chili sauce, fish sauce, lime juice, and sugar. Mix well and set aside.

3. Trim the stem ends off the eggplants, then cut each eggplant in half lengthwise. Cut each half into two or three pieces.

4. Heat the oil in a large skillet over moderately high heat. Add the eggplant pieces and fry on one side, then turn to brown on the other. While the eggplant is frying, add the pounded chile-shallot paste and fry along with the eggplant.

5. When the eggplant pieces are browned on both sides and the mixture is aromatic, stir in the reserved chili sauce mixture. Continue to cook, stirring gently, until the eggplant is soft and the sauce thick.

6. Remove from the heat and stir in the basil. Serve at room temperature, garnished with more basil, if desired.

Serves 4 to 6

Pineapple and Cucumber Salad
(Rojak)

It is hard to imagine the cuisines of the Pacific and Southeast Asia without the pineapple, the sweet and tangy tropical American fruit that fits so well the spicy, sweet, and fruity preference of the Malaysian palate. The combination of sweet/tart pineapple with crisp, cool cucumber in a spicy sweet-and-sour dressing is both exciting and refreshing, a wonderful foil for savory curries or grilled meat.

½ small pineapple, peeled, cored, and diced
2 medium cucumbers, peeled, seeded, and diced
1 small red onion, finely chopped
2 to 3 fresh hot red chiles, seeded and pounded into a paste, or ½ to 1 teaspoon cayenne or other ground hot red pepper

Juice of 2 limes
1 teaspoon sugar
1 teaspoon shrimp paste
Fish sauce or salt, to taste

1. In a bowl, combine the pineapple, cucumbers, and onion.
2. In another small nonreactive bowl or measuring cup, combine the chile paste or ground chile with the lime juice, sugar, and shrimp paste. Mix thoroughly.
3. Just before serving, pour the dressing over the salad and mix well. Add fish sauce or salt to taste.

Serves 4 to 6

Frozen Pumpkin and Sweet Corn Custard

Asians value native American corn as a sweet vegetable, rather than as a grain milled into flour or meal, and use it as an ingredient in sweet as well as savory dishes. This unusual frozen custard combines canned cream-style corn with puréed pumpkin for a delicately flavored, velvety treat. The mixture can also be spooned into a prepared crumb piecrust and chilled.

2 egg yolks
½ cup sugar
1 cup canned cream-style corn
½ cup pumpkin purée (canned or homemade)

1 teaspoon vanilla
Good pinch of salt
1 cup heavy cream
⅓ cup toasted shredded sweetened coconut

1. In the top of a double boiler, whisk the egg yolks lightly, then add the sugar and corn and mix well. Cook over simmering water, stirring constantly, for 7 to 10 minutes, until the mixture is slightly thickened and smooth. Do not overcook or you will get scrambled eggs.

2. Remove from the heat and stir in the pumpkin, vanilla, and salt. Let cool completely.

3. Whip the cream until stiff. Fold the whipped cream gently into the cooled custard.

4. Line a cupcake tin with foil liners. Spoon the custard into the cups. Sprinkle the tops with the toasted coconut.

5. Cover the tin tightly with plastic wrap, then freeze (3 to 4 hours). Remove the custard cups from the freezer 10 to 15 minutes before serving.

Serves 8 to 10

burma

Lying just across the Bay of Bengal from India, and with China on her northernmost border, the ancient kingdom of Burma (now called Myanmar) shows perhaps more clearly than any other cuisine of Southeast Asia the creative tension between those two great cuisines. The ultimate resolution favors neither one side nor the other but balances the two in a savory equilibrium that is uniquely Burmese.

Curries are central to the Burmese table, and they are modeled on the Indian tradition of spiced sauced dishes, built on an aromatic base of onions, garlic, gingerroot, and chiles, then slow-simmered in spiced liquids. The spice mixtures are somewhat less complex than the typical Indian, however, and novel flavor elements enter the brew: soy sauce and toasted sesame oil from China; the lemongrass, fish sauce, and shrimp paste shared with Thailand and Malaysia; a variety of pungent fresh green herbs. Coconut milk is a familiar ingredient but is used somewhat less intensively than in other areas of Southeast Asia. The resulting flavor profile tends, like the Indian, toward the savory, with a slight acidic cast and with sweet accents provided by accompanying dips and relishes.

While rice is the fundamental focus of the Burmese meal, noodles are also extremely popular, in soups and in pan-fried dishes, and bean curd (tofu) is widely used. Burma shares the Chinese appreciation of crisp vegetables and leafy greens quickly cooked, as well as such Indian favorites as potatoes, tomatoes, lentils, and split peas.

Although most meats, including pork, beef, and mutton, are enjoyed, fish, seafood, and chicken are the more typical foods of nonvegetarian dishes.

Savory soups, rich curries, hearty salads, with flavors bold and subtle, frequently spicy, sometimes delicate—all contribute to a complex cuisine that has absorbed both India and China and refashioned them in a distinctive and individual mix.

RECIPES

Tiny Spiced Shrimp Fritters

Sesame Eggplant with Shrimp

Fragrant Chicken Curry

Chicken Noodles

Golden Pork Coins

Burmese-Style Curried Lamb

Aromatic Coconut Rice

Potato Curry with Spinach

Asparagus Burmese-Style

Tangy Bean Curd and Bean Sprout Salad

Tiny Spiced Shrimp Fritters

Indian cooks use chickpea flour to make crunchy coatings and spiced fritters and croquettes. These crispy little fritters come directly from that tradition but are further embellished from the Chinese side with sesame oil, shrimp, and bean sprouts. They make a nice appetizer or cocktail tidbit, served hot with a fresh mint chutney.

½ cup chickpea flour (besan)
½ cup all-purpose flour
1 teaspoon salt
1 teaspoon baking powder
½ to 1 teaspoon cayenne or other ground hot red pepper
1 teaspoon ground cumin
1 teaspoon ground coriander
½ teaspoon turmeric
½ teaspoon ground ginger

1 egg
½ cup water
1 teaspoon Asian sesame oil
8 ounces shrimp, peeled, deveined, and coarsely chopped
1 small onion, finely minced
1 clove garlic, crushed
1 cup fresh bean sprouts
Vegetable oil for frying

1. In a medium bowl, combine the chickpea flour, all-purpose flour, salt, baking powder, cayenne, cumin, coriander, turmeric, and ginger. Mix thoroughly.

2. In a small bowl, whisk the egg, then mix in the water and the sesame oil.

3. Add the egg mixture to the flour mixture and stir until just blended. Gently fold in the shrimp, onion, garlic, and bean sprouts.

4. Heat 3 to 4 tablespoons of oil in a skillet over high heat. Drop the batter by small spoonfuls into the oil. Fry the fritters, turning once, until nicely browned on both sides. Drain on paper towels.

Makes 16 to 20 small fritters

Sesame Eggplant with Shrimp

A fascinating blend from the Asian seasoning repertoire characterizes this highly flavored and texturally exciting dish. In typical Burmese fashion it tends to the savory and pungent, with a heavy dependence on onions and garlic, fragrant Asian sesame oil, and fish-based seasoning ingredients. Fish sauce is a pervasive flavoring agent throughout Southeast Asia, a strained liquid made from salted fermented fish. It is known as nuoc mam in Vietnam, nam pla in Thailand, patis in the Philippines, and ngan-pya-ye in Burma. One variety will serve most needs. Serve this dish with plain cooked rice.

4 to 5 long, slender Asian
   eggplants
3 tablespoons peanut oil
1 large onion, finely chopped
4 or 5 large cloves garlic,
   minced
1 tablespoon finely minced
   gingerroot
2 to 3 small fresh hot chiles,
   seeded and minced,
   or ½ to 1 teaspoon
   crushed dried hot
   pepper
2 medium tomatoes, coarsely
   chopped

1 tablespoon fish sauce
1 teaspoon shrimp paste
1 teaspoon turmeric
8 ounces shrimp, peeled
   and deveined (if
   large, cut in half
   lengthwise)
2 teaspoons Asian sesame oil
2 to 3 tablespoons chopped
   fresh coriander leaves
1 tablespoon sesame seeds,
   lightly toasted

1. Cut off the stem ends of the eggplants, then cut the eggplants on the diagonal into ½-inch-thick slices.

2. Heat the peanut oil in a large skillet and sauté the onion, garlic, gingerroot, and chiles over moderate heat, stirring, until the onions are wilted and the mixture is aromatic.

3. Add the eggplant slices and fry, turning once, until lightly browned on each side. Stir in the tomatoes, fish sauce, shrimp paste, and turmeric and cook, stirring, until the tomatoes are soft and most of the liquid has cooked away.

4. Add the shrimp and cook just until the shrimp turn pink. Stir in the sesame oil and mix well. Stir in the chopped coriander and sprinkle the sesame seeds over the top.

Serves 4, more if other foods are served

Fragrant Chicken Curry

Like many others from the Southeast Asian repertoire, this dish is called a curry, although its flavor is very different from the more familiar Indian varieties. The turmeric, potatoes, and slow cooking are typically Indian elements, while the fish sauce and the heavier dependence on aromatics rather than spices bring it closer to Thai and Malaysian models. In any case, it is very good and worth a try, especially if you think you don't like curry.

2 tablespoons peanut oil
2 large onions, finely chopped
4 or 5 large cloves garlic, minced
1 tablespoon finely minced gingerroot
1 teaspoon crushed dried hot pepper
2 to 2½ pounds chicken thighs, on the bone, skin removed
About ½ teaspoon salt
Several good grinds of black pepper

2 teaspoons finely minced lemongrass, or 1 teaspoon dried powdered
1 teaspoon turmeric
½ teaspoon ground coriander
1 large tomato, coarsely chopped
1 tablespoon fish sauce
2 medium potatoes, peeled and cut into small cubes
Good handful of fresh coriander leaves, finely chopped

1. Heat the oil in a heavy pot or deep skillet and sauté the onion, garlic, gingerroot, and hot pepper over moderate heat, stirring, until the vegetables soften and become aromatic.

2. Add the chicken thighs and turn them briefly in the mixture. Sprinkle the chicken with the salt and pepper.

3. Add the lemongrass, turmeric, ground coriander, tomato, and fish sauce. Mix well, bring to a simmer, then cover and cook over low heat for about 30 minutes.

4. Add the potatoes, mix well, cover, and continue to cook, turning the chicken in the sauce once or twice, for about 1 hour, until the chicken is very tender and the sauce is thick. If the sauce is too liquid, cook it down quickly. Stir in the chopped coriander leaves. Serve the curry with rice.

Serves 4 to 6

Chicken Noodles

Who doesn't love chicken and noodles? The Burmese certainly do, using the techniques of stir-frying, pan-frying, and braising for this satisfying dish filled with robust flavor. Although you will need two pans, one for the noodles and one for the chicken-and-vegetable mixture, it is quite easy to prepare and a wonderful way to stretch a cupful or so of leftover cooked chicken.

8 ounces fresh Chinese wheat-flour noodles
1 to 2 tablespoons Asian sesame oil
3 to 4 tablespoons peanut oil or vegetable oil
1 large onion, finely chopped
6 to 8 large cloves garlic, finely chopped
1 teaspoon crushed dried hot pepper
1 teaspoon turmeric
1 teaspoon shrimp paste

2 cups shredded or thinly sliced napa cabbage
1 large carrot, shredded
2 medium tomatoes, coarsely chopped
1 cup diced or shredded cooked chicken
½ cup chicken broth
1 tablespoon fish sauce
1 cup fresh bean sprouts
2 to 3 scallions, thinly sliced, for garnish

1. Cook the noodles in boiling water for just a few minutes (depending on thickness), until they are just tender but still quite firm. Drain the noodles, rinse thoroughly in cold water, and drain again. Mix the noodles with the sesame oil.

2. Pour 1 to 2 tablespoons of the peanut oil into a medium, heavy skillet and swirl to film the bottom of the pan. Spoon the noodles into the pan in an even layer and set aside.

3. Heat a large skillet or wok over high heat. Swirl in the 2 remaining tablespoons of peanut oil. Add the onion, garlic, and hot pepper and stir-fry until the mixture becomes aromatic.

4. Stir in the turmeric and shrimp paste and mix well.

5. Add the cabbage, carrot, and tomatoes and stir-fry for a few minutes.

6. Place the pan with noodles over moderate heat.

7. Add the chicken, broth, and fish sauce to the stir-fried vegetables. Mix well, bring to a simmer, and cook for a few minutes.

8. Turn the heat under the noodles to high, and when the noodles are just beginning to get crisp on the bottom, carefully pour the stir-fried mixture and sauce over them. Add the bean sprouts, mix slightly, then garnish with the sliced scallions. Serve hot.

Serves 4

Golden Pork Coins

This is a simple and delicious Burmese dish in which small round slices—"coins"—of tender pork fillet are braised in a savory sauce with a moderate pungency and a hint of sour. The golden color is supplied by turmeric, a dried powdered rhizome related to ginger-root, and heavily used in Indian cuisine. Serve the dish with rice and a simple green vegetable or salad.

2 tablespoons peanut oil
1 pound pork fillet, cut into
  ½-inch slices
1 large onion, cut in half and
  thinly sliced
1 tablespoon finely minced
  gingerroot

4 large cloves garlic, minced
½ teaspoon crushed dried hot
  pepper
1 teaspoon turmeric
2 tablespoons soy sauce
1 tablespoon cider vinegar
1 teaspoon shrimp paste

1. Heat the oil in a skillet and sauté the onion, gingerroot, garlic, and hot pepper over moderate heat, stirring, until the onion wilts and the mixture becomes aromatic. Stir in the turmeric.

2. Add the pork slices and turn them briefly in the onion mixture (no need to brown). Add the soy sauce, vinegar, and shrimp paste, mix gently, and bring to a simmer. Cover and cook over low heat for 30 to 40 minutes, until the meat is very tender.

Serves 4

Burmese-Style Curried Lamb

Lamb was introduced into India from the northern meat-and-dairy cultures of central Asia, and for Hindus, who worship the sacred cow, it replaces beef as an esteemed red meat. Although not widely used in most of the cuisines of Southeast Asia, lamb has found its way into the Burmese kitchen via the Indian tradition. In this richly flavored dish, a typical Indian curry gets a uniquely Burmese twist with soy sauce and plenty of onions and garlic.

2 tablespoons vegetable oil
1 very large onion, finely chopped
1 tablespoon finely minced gingerroot
4 or 5 large cloves garlic, minced
½ to 1 teaspoon crushed dried hot pepper
1 to 1¼ pounds boneless lamb, cut into ½-inch cubes
1 teaspoon turmeric
2 teaspoons curry powder (preferably Madras)

4 to 5 medium tomatoes, coarsely chopped, or 1 can (1 pound) Italian-style tomatoes, with juice, coarsely chopped
2 bay leaves
1 tablespoon soy sauce
Several good grinds of black pepper
Chopped fresh coriander leaves or chopped fresh mint leaves, for garnish (optional)

1. Heat the oil in a large, heavy skillet or pot and sauté the onion, gingerroot, garlic, and hot peppers over moderate heat, stirring, until the onion just turns golden and the mixture becomes aromatic.

2. Push the vegetables to the side of the pan and add the lamb. Brown the meat lightly, turning the pieces to brown on all sides. While the lamb is browning, sprinkle it with the turmeric and curry powder.

3. When the meat is browned, add the tomatoes, bay leaves, soy sauce, and black pepper. Mix well, then bring to a simmer. Cover and cook over low heat for about 1 hour, or until the lamb is quite tender. Uncover and cook until the sauce is thick. Taste for salt and hotness; garnish with some chopped coriander or mint, if desired. Serve the curry with rice and a green vegetable or salad.

Serves 4

Aromatic Coconut Rice

Like other Asian people, the Burmese are connoisseurs of rice, which serves as the focus of almost every meal. Many varieties are cultivated and appreciated for their distinctive flavor, aroma, and texture. This delicate coconut rice has clear affinities to the Indian tradition of flavored rice pilaus, with the addition of some typical Southeast Asian ingredients.

2 tablespoons peanut oil or
    vegetable oil
1 medium onion, finely
    chopped
½ teaspoon turmeric
1 cup basmati rice
1 can (5 to 6 ounces)
    unsweetened coconut milk

1½ cups water
1 teaspoon salt
6 cardamom pods
1 cinnamon stick
1 stalk lemongrass, bruised and
    cut into 2 or 3 pieces

1. Heat the oil in a medium, heavy saucepan and sauté the onion over moderate heat, stirring, just until the onion wilts.

2. Add the turmeric and rice and stir just until well blended.

3. Add the coconut milk, water, salt, cardamom, cinnamon stick, and lemongrass. Mix well, bring to a simmer, then cover and cook over very low heat for 15 to 20 minutes. Turn off the heat and let stand, covered, for 10 minutes. Before serving, remove the cinnamon stick and the pieces of lemon grass.

Serves 4 to 6

Potato Curry with Spinach

Although Burma is largely Buddhist, most Burmese do not adhere strictly to the rigorous vegetarian precepts of the Buddha. Even dishes that contain no meat are frequently seasoned with products made from dried or fermented fish and seafood, which add depth and richness of flavor. This mellow Indian-style curry of slow-cooked vegetables gets its characteristic flavor from spices and aromatics, as well as the pervasive fish sauce; if your vegetarianism is more orthodox than that of the Burmese, you can substitute a teaspoon or so of salt for the fish sauce.

2 tablespoons peanut oil
1 large onion, finely chopped
4 cloves garlic, minced
1 tablespoon finely minced
  gingerroot
½ teaspoon crushed dried hot
  pepper
2 teaspoons ground cumin
1 teaspoon ground coriander
1 teaspoon turmeric
2 medium potatoes, cut into
  small cubes

2 medium tomatoes, coarsely
  chopped
1 tablespoon fish sauce
1 pound fresh spinach,
  trimmed, washed, and
  coarsely chopped, or
  1 box (10 ounces) frozen
  chopped spinach
1 teaspoon Asian sesame oil

1. Heat the peanut oil in a skillet or heavy pot and sauté the onion, garlic, gingerroot, and hot pepper over moderate heat, stirring, until the onion wilts and the mixture becomes aromatic.

2. Add the cumin, coriander, and turmeric and stir for a minute or two.

3. Add the potatoes, tomatoes, fish sauce, and spinach. Cover and cook over low heat, stirring from time to time, for about 30 to 40 minutes, until the potatoes are tender and the mixture is thick.

4. Stir in the sesame oil. Taste for salt. Serve hot, with rice.

Serves 4

Asparagus Burmese-Style

Asparagus is not a common part of the Burmese vegetable repertoire, but works beautifully in this dish that might more typically feature green beans, Chinese long beans, or Chinese broccoli. It is a quick and simple preparation that amply demonstrates the Burmese love for the flavor and texture of fresh vegetables, stir-fried in the classic Chinese fashion.

1 pound medium asparagus
2 tablespoons peanut oil
1 large onion, cut in half and
    thinly sliced
4 large cloves garlic, very thinly
    sliced
1 tablespoon fish sauce
2 teaspoons Asian sesame oil

1. Trim the tough ends off the asparagus, then cut the stalks, on the sharp diagonal, into 1½-inch pieces.

2. Heat a wok or skillet over high heat. Swirl in the peanut oil, then add the onion and garlic and stir-fry for a few minutes, just until the onion wilts.

3. Add the asparagus and stir-fry for a couple of minutes.

4. Sprinkle in the fish sauce and stir-fry for a minute or so, until the asparagus is nicely glazed.

5. Remove from the heat and stir in the sesame oil. Serve the dish hot or at room temperature.

Serves 4

Tangy Bean Curd and Bean Sprout Salad

A variety of textures make this hearty salad very appealing, along with the sour, salty, slightly pungent flavor so typical of Burmese vegetable dishes. Serve it with another dish or two and plenty of rice as part of a larger Burmese meal.

8 ounces firm or extra-firm bean curd, cut into ½-inch cubes, or prefried bean curd squares (see introduction to recipe on page 87)
2 tablespoons peanut or vegetable oil
1 medium onion, finely chopped
6 cloves garlic, minced
1 tablespoon Asian sesame oil

3 tablespoons white or cider vinegar
¼ teaspoon cayenne pepper, or more or less, to taste
1 teaspoon salt
2 cups very crisp fresh bean sprouts
2 to 3 scallions, thinly sliced
Small handful of fresh coriander leaves, finely chopped

1. Pat the bean curd cubes thoroughly dry with paper towels. Heat the peanut oil in a medium skillet over high heat and fry the bean curd cubes, turning carefully, until they are lightly browned. Place the fried bean curd in a nonreactive mixing bowl.

2. Add the onion and garlic to the oil remaining in the pan and sauté over moderate heat, stirring, until the onion and the garlic are just beginning to turn golden.

3. Stir in the sesame oil, vinegar, cayenne, and salt and mix well. Remove from the heat and pour over the bean curd.

4. Just before serving, add the bean sprouts, scallions, and coriander and toss lightly but thoroughly (easiest to do with the hands).

Serves 4 to 6

thailand

Thailand is Burma's closest neighbor to the east and is thus one step removed from India and one step closer to Malaysia, a geographic fact amply reflected in the cuisine. Thai cooking, like Burmese, makes choices and combinations from the broad Asian spectrum, and comes up with a characteristic style that is highly individual.

The Thai flavoring system is complex and many-layered, but it is firmly rooted in a selection of herbs and aromatics that is unparalleled in Southeast Asia. Garlic, shallots, lemongrass, gingerroot, galangal, coriander (both leaf and root), basil, kaffir lime leaves, and the hottest little chiles in all of Asia—these are the ingredients that inform Thai food with its unique flavor and perfume. The ingredients are pervasive throughout the region, of course, but used in Thailand with a particular intensity and emphasis. The result is a wide range of dishes that play endlessly with sweet, sour, spicy, citrusy, and aromatic.

Thai curries are renowned, some closer to the typical Indian, with their use of such spices as cumin and coriander, cardamom and turmeric, others closer to the Malaysian types that rely so heavily on fish sauce, shrimp paste, and coconut. Curry mixtures, designated by the color of the primary ingredients, are traditionally made from the appropriate seasonings, ground or pounded into pastes with one or more of the favored aromatics.

In addition to these characteristic features of Thai cuisine, Chinese influence is evident in a love of noodles, with a preference for the more delicate bean threads and rice noodles, a taste for soy and oyster sauces, and a frequent use of stir-frying—all combining to produce food that is texturally exciting. Reinforcing the interest in texture is a selection of crisp, crunchy, chewy vegetables, nuts, and sprouts.

Not Chinese or Indian or Malaysian but these three and more, Thai food is imaginative and intriguing, expressing a playful deftness with the complexities of flavor and texture.

RECIPES

Thai Pumpkin Soup

Many-Flavored Soup with Mushrooms and
    Shrimp

Appetizer Rollups with Hoisin Dipping Sauce

Crispy Crab and Pork Balls

Salmon Poached in Coconut-Basil Sauce

Mango and Chicken Salad

Ginger Chicken with Cashews

Chiles Stuffed with Pork and Peanuts

Masaman Beef Curry with Peanuts and Potatoes

Sweet-and-Spicy Bean Curd with Peanuts

Thai Pumpkin Soup

This delicious soup, with its intense flavor and rich, creamy texture, shows how successfully the native American chiles, peanuts, and pumpkin were assimilated into the kitchens of Southeast Asia. If you are looking for shortcuts, you can substitute canned pumpkin purée, but the caramelized home-baked pumpkin provides additional sweetness and depth to the final flavor of the soup.

1 small pie pumpkin or dumpling squash (about 2 pounds)

2 tablespoons peanut oil, plus additional for brushing pumpkin

2 shallots, minced

2 teaspoons finely minced gingerroot

1 to 2 small fresh hot chiles, seeded and minced, or ½ teaspoon crushed dried hot pepper

4 cups chicken stock

1 can (5 to 6 ounces) unsweetened coconut milk

2 teaspoons finely chopped lemongrass, or ½ teaspoon dried powdered

2 tablespoons fish sauce

About 1 tablespoon fresh lime juice

Good handful of fresh coriander leaves, coarsely chopped

2 to 3 tablespoons coarsely chopped roasted peanuts, for garnish

1. Preheat the oven to 400°F. Cut the pumpkin or squash in half crosswise and scoop out the seeds. Brush the cut sides lightly with oil, then place cut side down on a baking sheet. Bake the pumpkin for 45 to 50 minutes, until it is quite soft and the cut sides are nicely caramelized.

2. Let the pumpkin cool, then scoop out the pulp and purée it. You should have about 2 cups of purée. (Or substitute 2 cups of canned purée.)

3. Heat the 2 tablespoons oil in a medium saucepan and sauté the shallots, gingerroot, and chiles over moderate heat, stirring, until the mixture becomes aromatic.

4. Add the stock, coconut milk, lemongrass, fish sauce, and pumpkin purée. Bring to a simmer, then cook, uncovered, over low heat, stirring occasionally, for about 10 minutes.

5. Stir in the lime juice and chopped coriander. Taste for salt and sweetness. (If you used canned pumpkin purée, you may need to add ½ teaspoon or so of sugar.) Serve the soup hot, and garnish each portion with a sprinkle of chopped peanuts.

Serves 6 to 8

Many-Flavored Soup with Mushrooms and Shrimp

The favored seasonings of the Thai kitchen are deftly orchestrated in this clear, clean soup, intensely flavored and highly aromatic. Coconut milk is sometimes added for a richer, creamier broth, and chicken can be substituted for the shrimp. Kaffir lime leaves are an essential ingredient, providing not only a lime flavor but also an intense perfume that is a large part of the soup's appeal (see Tip).

8 to 10 ounces medium shrimp
4 cups clear chicken stock
1 cup water
1 tablespoon fish sauce
1 stalk lemongrass, coarsely chopped, or ½ teaspoon dried powdered
2 cloves garlic, finely chopped
2 kaffir lime leaves (if not available, substitute 2 teaspoons grated lime zest)
2 quarter-size slices fresh galangal or gingerroot
1 to 2 small whole dried chile peppers

1 cup thinly sliced mushrooms or enoki mushrooms
4 scallions, thinly sliced on the sharp diagonal
Juice of ½ lime (about 1 tablespoon)
Several good grinds of black pepper
1 teaspoon sugar
¼ cup finely chopped fresh coriander leaves
4 to 6 additional lime leaves, for garnish (optional)

1. Peel and devein the shrimp, reserving the shells.
2. In a medium saucepan, combine the shrimp shells with the

stock, water, fish sauce, lemongrass, garlic, lime leaves, galangal, and chile pepper. Simmer, uncovered, over low heat for 15 to 20 minutes.

3. Strain out all the solids from the broth and discard them.

4. Add the mushrooms, scallions, lime juice, black pepper, and sugar to the broth. Mix well and simmer for a few minutes. Add the peeled shrimp and cook just until the shrimp turn pink. Stir in the coriander leaves and serve hot. Garnish each portion with an additional lime leaf, if desired.

Serves 4 to 6

TIP: If you find yourself with some extra lime leaves, put them in a bottle or jar and cover them with rice vinegar. Let stand, covered, at room temperature for a couple of days; the flavor and fragrance of the lime leaves will infuse the vinegar and you will have a useful ingredient for salads, sauces, etc.

Appetizer Rollups with Hoisin Dipping Sauce

These delightful little lettuce-wrapped rolls combine all the most valued flavor and texture components of Thai cuisine. A popular restaurant appetizer, they are a fun-filled and easy dish for the home cook, a do-it-yourself hand-held snack with exciting sensations of sweetness, spiciness, and crunch in every bite.

8 ounces cooked and peeled
   small shrimp
1 cup shredded cooked chicken
½ cup finely chopped roasted
   peanuts
½ cup sliced or shredded
   toasted unsweetened
   coconut
2 cups crisp bean sprouts
2 limes, finely chopped (rind
   and all)

4 to 6 small fresh hot chiles,
   seeded and finely slivered
   or chopped
4 to 6 scallions, slivered
1 cup fresh coriander sprigs
12 to 16 leaves Boston lettuce
   (the smaller, more tender
   inner leaves are best)
¾ cup Hoisin Dipping Sauce
   (recipe follows)

Arrange all the ingredients separately on a large serving platter. Provide each guest with a small individual dish of dipping sauce. Instruct guests to take a leaf of lettuce, sprinkle it with small amounts of the filling ingredients, then roll it up and eat with dipping sauce.

Serves 6

HOISIN DIPPING SAUCE

¼ cup hoisin sauce
¼ cup rice vinegar
2 tablespoons fish sauce

2 teaspoons grated gingerroot
1 teaspoon sugar

Combine all the ingredients and mix thoroughly.

Makes about ¾ cup

Crispy Crab and Pork Balls

A variety of Indian and Southeast Asian ingredients flavor these tasty little tidbits, but the golden-fried crab-and-pork mixture is more closely related to Chinese tradition. Serve these as an hors d'oeuvre, with toothpicks, if desired, on a platter with small crisp lettuce leaves and thin slices of cucumber, carrot, and daikon. The sauce can be passed separately as a dip, or simply drizzled just before serving directly over the crab and pork balls.

1 large shallot or 2 small, chopped
1 large clove garlic
2 teaspoons finely chopped lemongrass, or 1 teaspoon dried powdered
2 teaspoons minced gingerroot
1 tablespoon fish sauce
¼ cup fresh coriander leaves
4 ounces ground or finely chopped pork
1 egg white
½ teaspoon sugar
¼ teaspoon crushed dried hot pepper

¼ teaspoon ground cumin
¼ teaspoon ground coriander
⅛ teaspoon salt
Good dash of white pepper
8 ounces fresh crabmeat, picked over to remove any cartilage
3 to 4 tablespoons peanut oil, for frying
Lettuce leaves, sliced cucumber, carrot, and daikon, for garnish
½ cup dipping sauce (recipe follows)

1. In a food processor, combine the shallot, garlic, lemongrass, gingerroot, fish sauce, and coriander leaves and process into a paste.

2. Add the pork, egg white, sugar, dried hot pepper, cumin, ground coriander, salt, and white pepper, and process into a coarse purée.

3. Turn out the mixture into a bowl and carefully fold in the crabmeat. Cover and refrigerate for 1 to 2 hours.

4. Form the mixture by rounded teaspoonfuls into small balls. Fry in the oil over moderate heat, turning carefully once or twice, until browned on all sides. Drain on paper towels and serve on a platter with vegetables and dipping sauce.

Makes 20 to 24 balls

2 tablespoons fish sauce
2 tablespoons fresh lime juice
2 teaspoons sugar
½ teaspoon crushed dried hot
   pepper

2 tablespoons finely chopped
   roasted peanuts

Combine all the ingredients in a nonreactive bowl and mix well.

Makes ½ cup

Salmon Poached in Coconut-Basil Sauce

Salmon is not typically found in the Southeast Asian repertoire, but it turns up frequently on the menus of Thai restaurants in America, where it is a plentiful and popular fish. Its fine flavor and firm texture make it particularly appropriate for poaching in this characteristic aromatic Thai sauce, a richly seasoned coconut broth.

1 tablespoon peanut oil
2 shallots, minced
2 to 3 small fresh green chiles,
   seeded and minced
2 teaspoons finely minced
   gingerroot
½ teaspoon ground cumin
½ teaspoon ground coriander
1 can (5 to 6 ounces)
   unsweetened coconut
   milk

1 tablespoon fish sauce
1 teaspoon shrimp paste
1 teaspoon grated lime zest
¼ teaspoon sugar
1 to 1¼ pounds fresh salmon,
   in small steaks or fillets
¼ cup finely chopped or
   shredded fresh basil leaves

1. In a skillet large enough to accommodate the fish in a single layer, heat the oil and sauté the shallots, chiles, and gingerroot over

moderate heat, stirring, until the shallots wilt and the mixture becomes aromatic.

2. Stir in the cumin and coriander, then add the coconut milk,
fish sauce, shrimp paste, lime zest, and sugar. Mix well and bring to a
simmer.

3. Place the salmon in the sauce, then bring to a simmer and
cook over low heat, turning once, until just cooked through—about
12 minutes total for fish ½ inch thick.

4. Stir in the basil and bring just to a simmer.

Serves 4

Mango and Chicken Salad

Thai cooks are masterful at creating salads, which range from simple
mixtures of crisp vegetables to heartier dishes built around sliced
grilled beef, fish, or seafood. These composed salads almost always
offer pleasing textural contrasts, as well as the spirited play of complex flavors. This delightful chicken salad, with bits of sweet mango
and crunchy cabbage, makes an appealing light summer meal.

1 cup (firmly packed) diced
    cooked chicken
1 mango, ripe but firm, peeled
    and diced
1 cup finely chopped napa or
    savoy cabbage
3 to 4 scallions, finely
    chopped
1 small fresh red chile, seeded
    and finely chopped
2 tablespoons fish sauce
1 tablespoon fresh lime juice
2 teaspoons sugar
2 cloves garlic, crushed

2 teaspoons finely minced
    lemongrass, or 1 teaspoon
    dried powdered
Several good grinds of black
    pepper
About ⅓ cup coarsely
    chopped fresh coriander
    leaves
Lettuce cups or torn greens
Cucumber slices, tomato
    wedges, and hard-boiled
    egg slices, for garnish
    (optional)

1. In a large bowl, combine the chicken, mango, cabbage, scallions, and chile.

2. In a small bowl, combine the fish sauce, lime juice, sugar, garlic, lemongrass, and black pepper. Whisk to blend thoroughly.

3. Pour the dressing over the salad and mix gently but thoroughly. Stir in the chopped coriander. Serve the salad in lettuce cups or over greens, and garnish with cucumber, tomato, and hard-boiled egg, if desired.

Serves 4

Ginger Chicken with Cashews

This popular Thai dish—full of color, flavor, and textural variety—takes its cooking technique directly from the Chinese. Note also that a number of the ingredients—the sweet and hot peppers, the corn, and the cashews—are imports from the Americas. Serve the chicken with a fragrant steamed jasmine rice.

¼ cup oyster sauce
1 tablespoon soy sauce
1 tablespoon fish sauce
1 teaspoon cornstarch
2 tablespoons peanut oil or vegetable oil
1 shallot, minced
3 or 4 large cloves garlic, minced
1 tablespoon finely minced gingerroot
2 to 3 small whole dried hot peppers, or ½ to 1 teaspoon crushed dried hot pepper

¾ to 1 pound boneless, skinless chicken breast, cut into ½-inch cubes
½ cup sugar snap peas
½ cup canned baby corn
1 medium red bell pepper, seeded and cut into ½-inch pieces
½ cup whole roasted cashews
2 to 3 scallions, thinly sliced on the diagonal

1. In a small bowl or measuring cup, combine the oyster sauce, soy sauce, fish sauce, and cornstarch. Mix well and set aside.

2. Heat a wok or skillet over high heat. Swirl in the oil, then add the shallot, garlic, gingerroot, and hot pepper. Stir-fry for a few minutes, until the mixture becomes aromatic.

3. Add the chicken and stir-fry, just until it loses its pink color. Add the snap peas, corn, and bell pepper and stir-fry a few minutes more.

4. Mix the reserved sauce again, then stir it into the chicken and mix well. Cook, stirring, until the food is evenly coated with the sauce and is hot. Stir in the cashews and scallions. Serve hot with rice.

Serves 3 to 4

Chiles Stuffed with Pork and Peanuts

If, like most Thais, you have a taste for hot stuff, try these delightfully spicy little stuffed jalapeños as an appetizer at your next party or barbecue. The ultimate crossroads ingredient is the ketchup in the dipping sauce: America's favorite condiment had its origins in Asia as a sweet and tangy sauce and was refashioned in the New World with the tomato as its primary component. It returned to Asia to function once again as an ingredient in dips and cooking sauces.

8 ounces ground pork
2 cups finely chopped napa
   cabbage
⅓ cup chopped peanuts
1 shallot, minced
3 cloves garlic, crushed
1 tablespoon fish sauce
1 teaspoon sugar
¼ teaspoon freshly ground
   black pepper

¼ cup finely chopped fresh
   coriander leaves
2 teaspoons finely minced
   lemongrass, or 1 teaspoon
   dried powdered
15 to 20 medium jalapeño
   peppers (see Tip)
½ cup dipping sauce (recipe
   follows)

1. Combine the pork with the cabbage, peanuts, shallot, garlic, fish sauce, sugar, black pepper, coriander, and lemongrass. Mix thoroughly.

2. Cut the jalapeños in half lengthwise. Remove the seeds and the membranes (see Tip).

3. Stuff the pork mixture into the jalapeño halves, mounding the mixture slightly.

4. Place the stuffed jalapeños in a steamer, cover, and steam for 15 to 20 minutes. Serve warm or at room temperature with the dipping sauce.

Makes 30 to 40 stuffed peppers

DIPPING SAUCE

2 tablespoons ketchup
2 tablespoons fish sauce
2 tablespoons rice vinegar

2 teaspoons sugar
1 teaspoon grated gingerroot

Combine all the ingredients and mix thoroughly.

Makes about ½ cup

TIP: Preparing 15 to 20 jalapeños will expose you to a heavy dose of capsaicin, the hot or irritant compound that is concentrated in the inner membranes and seeds of the chiles. Remember always, when dealing with hot chile peppers, to keep your hands away from your eyes and any other sensitive parts, including cuts and scratches.

Masaman Beef Curry with Peanuts and Potatoes

Indian spices and Malaysian flavors mingle in this dark and fragrant dish, which gets its special character from the aromatics and the touch of sweetness so dear to the Thai palate. "Masaman" is a variant spelling of "Muslim"—the presence of potatoes, otherwise little used in Thai cuisine, indicates the affiliation with Indian tradition.

1 tablespoon coriander seeds
2 teaspoons cumin seeds
6 to 8 cardamom pods
2 shallots, finely minced
2 cloves garlic, crushed
1 tablespoon finely minced gingerroot
1 tablespoon finely minced lemongrass, or 1 teaspoon dried powdered
1 to 2 teaspoons crushed dried hot pepper
¼ teaspoon cinnamon
¼ teaspoon nutmeg
2 tablespoons peanut oil
¾ to 1 pound boneless beef, cut into small (⅛-inch to ½-inch) cubes

1 can (5 to 6 ounces) unsweetened coconut milk
1 tablespoon fish sauce
1 tablespoon fresh lime juice
2 kaffir lime leaves (optional but good)
1½ teaspoons sugar
2 medium potatoes, peeled and cut into small cubes
⅓ cup coarsely chopped roasted peanuts
3 to 4 tablespoons chopped fresh coriander leaves, for garnish

1. In a small skillet, toast the coriander seeds, cumin, and cardamom over moderate heat, gently shaking the pan, until the seeds are just lightly browned and aromatic. Let cool slightly, then grind the seeds in a spice mill.

2. Combine the ground spices with the shallots, garlic, gingerroot, lemongrass, hot pepper, cinnamon, and nutmeg. Mix thoroughly.

3. Heat the oil in a heavy skillet and brown the beef over moderate to high heat. While the meat is browning, add the spice mixture and turn it frequently as you turn the beef.

4. Add the coconut milk, fish sauce, lime juice, lime leaves if us-

ing, and sugar. Mix well, bring to a simmer, then cover and cook over low heat for about 1 hour, until the beef is tender.

5. Add the potatoes, cover, and cook, stirring occasionally, for about 30 to 40 minutes, until the potatoes are tender and the mixture is thick and dark.

6. Stir in the peanuts. Garnish the curry with the chopped coriander and serve with rice.

Serves 4 to 6

Sweet-and-Spicy Bean Curd with Peanuts

A fine example of the Asian talent for taking something essentially tasteless and, with but a few characteristic ingredients, making it bounce with flavor. Note that deep-fried bean curd, in cubes or slices, is frequently available in Asian groceries. If you can get it, you can dispense with the first step of frying the bean curd. Serve the dish as an appetizer or as one of several dishes in a Thai meal.

1 pound extra-firm bean curd, cut in slices about ⅜ inch thick	1 teaspoon salt
	1 large clove garlic, minced
	3 tablespoons finely chopped roasted peanuts
3 to 4 tablespoons peanut oil	
½ cup rice vinegar	3 tablespoons chopped fresh coriander leaves
3 tablespoons sugar	
1 teaspoon crushed dried hot pepper	

1. Pat the bean curd slices thoroughly dry with paper towels. Heat the oil in a skillet. Fry the bean curd over high heat, turning once, until golden brown on both sides. Place the fried bean curd slices on a rimmed serving dish and set aside.

2. In a small, nonreactive saucepan, combine the vinegar, sugar, hot pepper, salt, and garlic. Bring to a boil, then cook over moderate heat for about 5 minutes, or until slightly syrupy. Let cool slightly.

3. Pour the sauce over the bean curd; sprinkle with the chopped peanuts and coriander. Serve at room temperature.

Serves 4 to 6

the philippines

The long arms of India and China reached out to touch all the cuisines of Asia, and though their influence is ancient and pervasive, other, more distant cultures have also played a major role. The Arabs, the Spanish, the Portuguese, the Dutch, and the French have all left their culinary imprints, sometimes small and subtle, at times profound.

The Philippines is such a crossroads, an invigorating mixture of Chinese, Malay, and Spanish. The evidence of more than three hundred years of Spanish occupation is clear in the names, the preparation, and the ingredients of many of the characteristic dishes. There is a heavy use of onions and garlic slowly sautéed in oil (though not necessarily the olive oil so typical of Spanish cooking), and a decided taste for sour, provided primarily by vinegar. Such familiar Spanish ingredients as chickpeas, green peas, ham, sausage, and olives show up frequently, as well as a number of products from Mexico, Spain's major colony in the New World. Foremost among these are tomatoes, bell peppers and chiles, sweet potatoes, and achiote, the whole or ground seeds of the annatto tree, used in Filipino cooking (as in the Caribbean) to provide a rich red-orange color and delicate flavor.

All these Spanish elements entered a system thoroughly Asian in its foundation. At the core are the rice and seafood common to all of Southeast Asia, flavored with the fish sauce (patis) and coconut so dear to the Malay palate. Here, once again, are Chinese noodles, frequently tinted an attractive yellow and pan-fried with bits of meat, seafood, and vegetables. And from the Chinese comes as well a deep appreciation of pork, of soy sauce, and of gingerroot.

Spanish chorizo and Chinese sausage, fried rice and paella, empanadas and egg rolls! The Mediterranean and Asia have come together in an unusual and appealing integration, within individual dishes and side by side on the Filipino table.

RECIPES

Garlic Chicken and Corn Soup

Pan-Fried Spring Rolls with Peanuts and Shrimp

Marinated Rock Shrimp with Coconut and Chile

Filipino Paella with Shrimp and Chorizo

Adobo of Fish with Tomatoes

Braised Sweet Pork with Plantains

Beef and Vegetable Stew in Spicy Tomato
   Sauce

Beef Braised with Vegetables in Peanut Sauce

Vegetable Adobo with Noodles

Caramel Coconut Flan

Garlic Chicken and Corn Soup

Like many other Asian people, Filipinos took kindly to the corn introduced by the Spanish from Mexico, but only in the form of a fresh vegetable, never as a ground meal or flour for bread or stuffing. Indeed, Filipino "tamales" retain only the name and the form of the Mexican favorite; the steamed corn husks filled with limed cornmeal are replaced by banana leaves filled with ground rice. This simple chicken-and-corn soup is easy to prepare and full of good flavor.

1 tablespoon vegetable oil
3 to 4 scallions, separated into
    green and white parts,
    thinly sliced
4 large cloves garlic, minced
4 cups chicken stock
1 tablespoon cider vinegar
Plenty of freshly ground black
    pepper

1 cup thinly sliced bok choy,
    with leaves
1 cup coarsely torn spinach
    leaves
1 cup fresh or frozen corn
    kernels
½ cup coarsely shredded
    cooked chicken
Fish sauce, to taste, if needed

1. Heat the oil in a medium saucepan and sauté the white parts of scallion and the garlic over moderate heat, stirring, until the scallions wilt.

2. Add the stock, vinegar, and black pepper. Bring to a simmer and cook for about 5 minutes.

3. Add the bok choy, spinach, and corn and simmer for 5 to 10 minutes.

4. Stir in the chicken and the reserved green tops of scallion. Taste for salt and add some fish sauce, if necessary. Serve hot.

Serves 4 to 6

Pan-Fried Spring Rolls with Peanuts and Shrimp (Lumpia)

Delicate, crispy fried rice-paper wrappers enclose a crunchy, flavorful filling of vegetables, peanuts, and shrimp. Dry rice papers are a useful ingredient to keep around; they store indefinitely on the pantry shelf and require only a couple of minutes of soaking in water to make them pliable. Once softened, they can be filled and eaten as they are, or they can be steamed or fried.

8 ounces raw shrimp, peeled and deveined
2 teaspoons fish sauce
2 teaspoons soy sauce
2 or 3 cloves garlic
3 to 4 scallions, finely chopped
2 cups finely chopped napa cabbage
1 cup fresh bean sprouts
¼ cup coarsely chopped salted roasted peanuts
12 to 15 (6-inch) rice-paper spring-roll wrappers
3 to 4 tablespoons peanut oil or vegetable oil
Duck sauce, for dipping

1. In a food processor, combine half the shrimp and the fish sauce, soy sauce, and garlic. Process into a paste.

2. Chop the remaining shrimp into small (pea-sized) pieces. Combine the chopped shrimp with the shrimp paste, scallions, cabbage, and bean sprouts. Mix well, then stir in the peanuts.

3. Place a rice paper in tepid water to cover for a few minutes, until it is pliable. Place the wrapper on a clean kitchen towel in a diamond position. (The towel absorbs the moisture from the soaked wrapper.)

4. Place a heaping tablespoon of the filling in a horizontal line on the center of the wrapper, coming to within 1 inch of the side points. Fold the bottom point up over the filling, then fold in the sides. Roll upward to make a closed roll. Place the filled roll on a plate; continue filling and rolling until all the filling is used.

5. Heat the oil in a heavy skillet over moderately high heat. When the oil is hot, add the spring rolls and fry until nicely browned on both sides, turning once. Drain on paper towels.

6. With a sharp knife, cut the rolls on the sharp diagonal into two or three pieces. Serve the spring rolls hot, with duck sauce or any sweet-and-spicy dipping sauce.

Makes about 12 rolls

TIP: The cooked rolls can be reheated in a 400°F oven for 15 minutes.

Marinated Rock Shrimp with Coconut and Chile

It is tempting to speculate that this zesty seafood appetizer found its way to the Philippines from Mexico, via the Spanish, for it is strikingly similar to the Mexican ceviche. The Pacific has its own traditions, however, of fish and seafood "cooked" in acidic marinades (the Hawaiian lomi-lomi salmon is a good example); wherever the origins of the practice, this dish has flavor affiliations with both Asia and the Americas. It is best served chilled in small portions as an appetizer or first course.

1 pound rock shrimp (you can also use thin strips of boneless white fish or ordinary small-to-medium shrimp)
1 to 2 lemons
1 to 2 limes
¼ cup unsweetened coconut milk
1 large tomato, coarsely chopped
4 to 6 scallions, finely chopped, or 1 medium onion, finely chopped

1 tablespoon fish sauce
2 teaspoons grated or very finely minced gingerroot
2 to 3 small fresh hot chiles, seeded and minced
1 medium green bell pepper, seeded and finely chopped
Lettuce cups or 3 to 4 avocados, halved and pitted

1. Place the shrimp in a glass, ceramic, or other nonreactive container and squeeze on enough lemon and lime juice to cover. Mix well and let stand, covered, in the refrigerator, for about 4 hours, until the shrimp turns opaque and pink (or the fish turns opaque).

2. Drain the shrimp thoroughly, then combine with the coconut milk, tomato, scallions, fish sauce, gingerroot, chiles, and bell pepper. Mix well, then refrigerate for an hour or two.

3. Serve the mixture in lettuce cups or in the pitted halves of avocados.

Serves 4 to 6

Filipino Paella with Shrimp and Chorizo

Seasoned rice dishes, embellished with all kinds of tidbits, are popular in rice cultures everywhere. Most Asian varieties are prepared from leftover cold cooked rice that is fried, then seasoned and mixed with other ingredients. The Spanish-style paella probably derives both its name and its preparation from the pilaus and pilafs of India, Persia, and the Middle East. In these, raw rice is sautéed with aromatics, then cooked in seasoned liquids to which other ingredients may be added. This paella is on the Spanish model, although some Asian ingredients make an appearance.

2 tablespoons vegetable oil
1 onion, finely chopped
4 or 5 large cloves garlic, minced
1 tablespoon finely minced gingerroot
1 teaspoon ground annatto (achiote)
1 cup long-grain rice
3 ounces cured chorizo, diced
2 medium tomatoes, coarsely chopped

2 cups chicken or fish stock
1 tablespoon fish sauce
Several good grinds of black pepper
½ to ¾ pound fresh shrimp, peeled and deveined
½ cup fresh or frozen peas
Pimiento-stuffed olives and sliced hard-boiled egg, for garnish (optional)

1. Heat the oil in a medium, heavy saucepan and sauté the onion, garlic, and gingerroot over moderate heat, stirring, until the onion wilts and the mixture becomes aromatic.

2. Stir in the annatto and mix well, then add the rice and the diced chorizo and cook, stirring, for a few minutes.

3. Add the tomatoes, stock, fish sauce, and black pepper. Mix well, bring to a simmer, then cover and cook over low heat for 10 to 15 minutes.

4. Stir in the shrimp and the peas, then cover and continue to cook over low heat until all the liquid has been absorbed and the shrimp have turned pink, about 5 to 10 minutes.

5. Remove from the heat and let stand, covered, for 5 to 10 minutes before serving. Spoon the paella into a serving dish or platter and garnish with the olives and hard-boiled egg, if desired.

Serves 4

Adobo of Fish with Tomatoes

Many varieties of fish—red snapper, bluefish, pompano, cod—can be used in this simple but delicious dish, reminiscent in technique and flavor of the Spanish-inspired escabeche (page 228) but with some typical Asian flavor elements added. This adobo can be served with rice, but it's also very good with pan-fried potatoes.

1 to 1½ pounds fish fillets
Flour for dredging
2 to 3 tablespoons vegetable oil
Salt
Freshly ground black pepper
1 medium onion, finely
    chopped
6 cloves garlic, minced

2 teaspoons finely minced
    gingerroot
2 tablespoons cider vinegar
1 tablespoon soy sauce
2 medium tomatoes, coarsely
    chopped
2 to 3 scallions, coarsely
    chopped, for garnish

1. Dredge the fish fillets lightly in flour. In a skillet, heat the oil over moderate to high heat. Sauté the fish, turning once, until lightly browned on each side. As the fillets brown, remove them from the pan, salt and pepper lightly, and set aside.

2. Add the onion, garlic, and gingerroot to the pan (add a bit more oil if necessary) and cook, stirring, over moderate heat until the onion is wilted. Add the vinegar, soy sauce, and tomatoes and several good grinds of pepper. Simmer, stirring, over low heat for about 10 to 15 minutes, until the mixture is thick.

3. Return the fish to the pan and cook until it is thoroughly heated through. Garnish with the chopped scallions.

Serves 4 to 6

Braised Sweet Pork with Plantains

A delicious dish especially popular with folks who like their savory foods on the sweet side. The rich sweetness of the sauce, particularly good with pork, comes from brown sugar, ripe plantain, and coconut milk—offset with a touch of soy sauce and vinegar, the characteristic Filipino flavor base. The dish can be made with either raw or cooked pork; it should be served with plenty of rice and another dish that is not sweet.

2 tablespoons vegetable oil
1 medium onion, coarsely chopped
1 large carrot, sliced
4 large cloves garlic, crushed
1 teaspoon ground annatto (achiote), or 1 teaspoon paprika
1 to 1¼ pounds lean boneless pork, cut into slices ½ inch thick, or 1 pound cold roast pork, trimmed of fat, cut into slices ½ inch thick

2 tablespoons firmly packed brown sugar
1 tablespoon soy sauce
1 tablespoon cider vinegar
Several good grinds of black pepper
¼ teaspoon crushed dried hot pepper
1 can (5 to 6 ounces) unsweetened coconut milk
1 large ripe plantain, peeled and cut on the diagonal into ¼-inch slices

1. Heat the oil in a large skillet and sauté the onion and carrot over moderate heat, stirring, until the onion beings to turn golden.

2. Add the garlic and annatto and cook, stirring, for a few more minutes.

3. Add the pork: If raw, brown lightly on both sides. If cooked, just turn the slices briefly in the onion mixture.

4. Add the brown sugar, soy sauce, vinegar, black pepper, hot pepper, and coconut milk. Bring to a simmer, then cover and cook over low heat for about 1 hour for the raw pork, 20 to 30 minutes for the cooked. Stir the meat in the sauce from time to time.

5. When the meat is tender, uncover the pan, add the sliced plantain, and cook for another 5 to 10 minutes. The sauce should be fairly thick; if it is too liquid, cook it down quickly.

Serves 4 to 6

Beef and Vegetable Stew in Spicy Tomato Sauce (Caldereta)

Soy sauce and olive oil, tomatoes and gingerroot! Caldereta—the name in Spanish means "little pot (of stew)"—is a classic example of a dish that started out Spanish and got Asianized along the way. Note that many of the flavor and color ingredients come, via Spain, from Mexico (sweet and hot red peppers, achiote, tomatoes).

2 tablespoons olive oil
1 medium onion, finely chopped
6 cloves garlic, minced
1 tablespoon minced gingerroot
2 to 3 small fresh hot red chiles, seeded and minced, or ½ to 1 teaspoon crushed dried hot pepper
1 teaspoon ground achiote (you can substitute paprika, if necessary)
½ to ¾ pound boneless beef stew meat, cut into ½-inch cubes

2 large carrots, sliced
2 cups tomato sauce
1 tablespoon soy sauce
1 teaspoon sugar
1 large red bell pepper, seeded and cut into ½-inch pieces
2 medium potatoes, cut into small cubes
1 tablespoon sherry vinegar
½ cup fresh or frozen peas
Pimiento-stuffed green olives, for garnish (optional)

1. Heat the oil in a heavy pot or deep, heavy skillet and sauté the onion, garlic, gingerroot, and chiles over moderate heat, stirring, until the onion wilts and the mixture becomes aromatic.

2. Stir in the achiote, then add the beef and brown on all sides.

3. Add the carrots, tomato sauce, soy sauce, and sugar. Bring to a simmer, then cover and cook over low heat for about 1 hour, or until the beef becomes tender.

4. Add the bell pepper, the potatoes, and the vinegar. Mix well, then cover and continue to cook until the potatoes are tender. Add the peas for the last 10 minutes or so of cooking.

5. Garnish the stew with the olives, if desired, and serve with plenty of rice.

Serves 4 to 6

Beef Braised with Vegetables in Peanut Sauce (Kari Kari)

A Spanish-style beef and vegetable stew, traditionally made with oxtails, is refashioned with a number of Asian seasonings, including the surprising addition of ground peanuts. It is a flavorful but mild dish, typically served with a spicy relish or sambal made from dried shrimp.

2 tablespoons vegetable oil
1 large onion, coarsely chopped
4 or 5 large cloves garlic, minced
1 pound lean beef, cut into ½-inch cubes
2 cups beef broth
1 tablespoon fish sauce
1 teaspoon tamarind concentrate
2 carrots, thickly sliced

1 large sweet potato or white potato, peeled and cut into 1-inch cubes
1 to 2 Asian eggplants, thickly sliced
8 ounces green beans, cut into 1-inch pieces
¼ to ⅓ cup peanut butter
Plenty of freshly ground black pepper

1. Heat the oil in a large, heavy pot or Dutch oven and sauté the onion and garlic over moderate heat, stirring, until just soft and aromatic.

2. Add the beef cubes and brown quickly on all sides.

3. Stir in the broth, fish sauce, and tamarind. Bring to a simmer, then cover and cook over low heat, stirring occasionally, for about 1 hour.

4. Add the carrots, sweet potato, eggplant, and green beans and mix well. Cover and cook again for about 1 hour, or until the meat is very tender. Stir in enough peanut butter to make a thick sauce, then stir in plenty of freshly ground black pepper. Taste for saltiness; add a bit of salt or more fish sauce, if necessary. Serve hot with rice and a spicy relish.

Serves 4 to 6

Vegetable Adobo with Noodles

A hearty and richly flavored mixture of vegetables and noodles, seasoned with the characteristic Filipino combination of soy sauce, garlic, and vinegar, this time with coconut added. It makes a very satisfying meatless dish, especially good with a garnish of chopped fresh chiles.

2 tablespoons vegetable oil
1 large onion, finely chopped
6 cloves garlic, minced
1 teaspoon ground annatto (achiote)
2 carrots, sliced about ½ inch thick
2 to 3 long, slender Asian eggplants (about ½ pound total), sliced ½ inch thick
1 large sweet potato, peeled and sliced about ½ inch thick

2 tablespoons soy sauce
2 tablespoons cider vinegar
1 can (5 to 6 ounces) unsweetened coconut milk
¼ teaspoon freshly ground black pepper
6 ounces fresh spinach, trimmed, washed, and coarsely chopped
4 ounces dry Chinese wheat noodles
Chopped fresh hot chiles, for garnish (optional)

1. Heat the oil in a large, deep skillet or large, heavy pot and sauté the onion and garlic over moderate heat, stirring, until the vegetables soften and become aromatic. Stir in the annatto and mix for a few minutes.

2. Add the carrots, eggplants, and sweet potato and mix well.

3. Add the soy sauce, vinegar, coconut milk, and black pepper. Mix well, then bring to a simmer. Cover and cook over low heat, stirring occasionally, for 30 to 40 minutes, until the vegetables are tender. Stir in the spinach and cook until it is just wilted.

4. Cook the noodles in boiling water for 3 to 4 minutes, until just tender but still firm. Drain thoroughly, then gently mix the noodles into the vegetable mixture. Bring to a simmer, then serve hot, garnished with fresh chopped chiles, if desired.

Serves 4 to 6

Caramel Coconut Flan

Sweet egg custards and creams are popular all over the world, and the traditional Spanish flan has been enthusiastically accepted into cultures where it was unknown before the Spanish arrived. In Mexico, it is frequently flavored with cinnamon or almonds, while Filipino cooks have individualized it with the flavor of their beloved coconut.

1 cup sugar	3 eggs
1 cup unsweetened coconut milk	3 egg yolks
	½ teaspoon vanilla
2 cups milk	

1. In a small, heavy saucepan or skillet, cook ½ cup of the sugar over moderate heat, shaking or tilting the pan until the sugar melts and turns richly brown and syrupy. Pour the syrup into a shallow 1½-quart casserole or baking dish (or six to eight small individual ramekins), tilting the dish so that the caramel covers the entire bottom.

2. In a medium saucepan, combine the coconut milk, the milk, and the remaining ½ cup sugar. Mix well, then heat just to the scalding point (small bubbles form around the edge). Remove from the heat.

3. Beat the eggs and the egg yolks thoroughly in a medium bowl. Slowly add some of the hot milk, whisking as you add it, until you have added about half the milk. Return the egg mixture to the remaining milk in the pot. Stir in the vanilla. Preheat the oven to 350°F.

4. Carefully pour the custard over the caramelized baking dish(es). Set the baking dish in a larger pan, then pour boiling water into the larger pan until it comes about halfway up the sides of the smaller dish.

5. Bake for 55 to 60 minutes for a larger dish, 35 to 40 for small ones. Remove from the water bath and let cool, then chill thoroughly. To unmold, if desired, dip the bottom of the baking dish in hot water, then invert onto a rimmed serving plate.

Serves 6 to 8

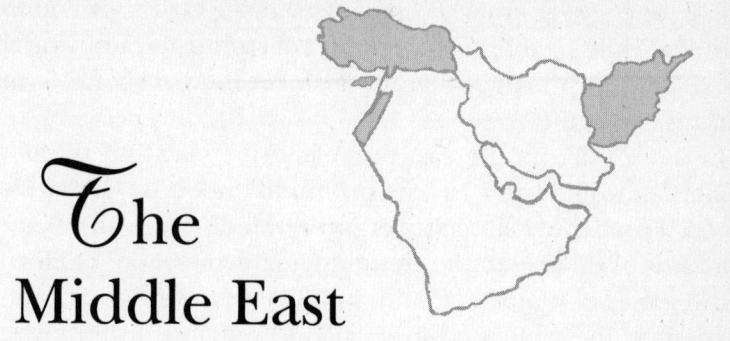

The
Middle East

For untold centuries, until well into modern times, anything beyond Europe's eastern borders was regarded as
"Oriental," a part of the unknown and mysterious East.
The most exotic—and the most coveted—was the far-
thest away, the fabled realms of the Spice Islands, China,
and Japan, brimming with fragrant spices, shimmering
silks, and glittering jewels. To get to this treasure, Europeans had to traverse the lands in between, a largely un-
explored passageway from the West to the East.

To regard this huge landmass as a mere throughway
from spice-starved Europe to the riches of Cathay was
at best uninformed, for in fact it was this piece of earth
that was the birthplace of Western culture and civilization, home of the three great religions of the Western
world—Judaism, Christianity, and Islam—and the source
of much of Europe's culinary traditions.

The Middle East is an area vast and diverse, from the Black Sea to the Arabian Sea, from the Caucasus of central Asia to the shores of the eastern Mediterranean. It encompasses arid mountain steppes, temperate highlands, fertile river valleys, deserts, and flat coastal plains. This geographic diversity spawned a variety of cultures and cuisines, while establishing a number of strong and unifying themes, products, and practices that would form the backbone of many of the cuisines of the West.

In the south and the east originated the vine and the olive, two plants that would come to have profound importance in Western tradition. From the wine cultures of the Mediterranean, to the great vineyards of France, to the contemporary wineries of California and South America, Australia, and South Africa, wine is central to the kitchen, to the table, and to social and religious experience. Ironically, it has had far less importance in its ancient homeland, because alcoholic beverages are prohibited by the Koran to the faithful of Islam. The olive has retained its prominence in the Middle East, of course, while extending its crucial influence to all the cuisines of the Mediterranean and North Africa.

If wine and olives were not treasure enough, the Middle East had other gifts as well. It was here that wheat and barley were first cultivated, some ten thousand years ago, and with that came the development of the world's most elaborate tradition of breads, one given new vitality and complexity by the discovery of yeast-leavened dough in Egypt about four or five thousand years ago. It was in this area, too, that sheep, goats, and cattle were first domesticated; along with the herding and breeding of these domestic animals for their meat, there arose an intense corollary tradition of dairying. Those of us for whom yogurt, cheese, butter, and milk are ordinary foods of everyday life owe this rich legacy to the lands between the Occident and the Orient.

And there is yet more. The Middle East was home to a number of valuable legumes—lentils, chickpeas, and fava beans. In the highlands there flourished from ancient times the cultivation of some of the world's most popular nuts and fruits—walnuts, hazelnuts, almonds, pistachios, apricots, plums, rhubarb, pomegranates, and quince.

The Middle East was a great agricultural hearth that gave rise to many of our most familiar and widely used foods, sending them both east and west to reach every corner of the world. But while much was given, much also was received; by virtue of its strategic location between the East and the West, this land assimilated the goods and influences of many who ventured through it.

From the East, from Asia, came rice, a staple that has become as fundamental to the region as wheat—cooked as a simple grain, in delicately flavored and garnished pilafs, as savory stuffings for vegetables, and in rich creamy sweets. India contributed eggplant and cucumbers, two vegetables that are central to the Middle Eastern kitchen. The Eastern connection also provided many of the spices that flavor the food to this day—cinnamon, cardamom, nutmeg, and cloves—and that blended so gracefully with the native herbs and spices: cumin, coriander, parsley, and dill.

From the West came many of the foods indigenous to the Americas, especially tomatoes, sweet and hot peppers, potatoes, and a variety of beans and squashes. These joined an established vegetable tradition of salads, stews, and stuffed dishes, unctuous with olive oil and perfumed with onions, garlic, and a variety of fresh herbs.

Rightly called the cradle of Western civilization, the Middle East nurtured many different cultures and many different people—Persians, Turks, Copts, Kurds, Arabs, Hittites, Huns, and Jews. All contributed their unique beliefs and traditions to the pot; all shared in the rich heritage of native foods enriched and elaborated with a wealth of foreign imports. From skewered chunks of savory grilled lamb, eaten with freshly baked pita and dollops of tart yogurt, to tender slices of eggplant simmered in thick aromatic tomato sauces, from hearty pots of grains and beans to delicate seafood and chunky colorful salads, the food of the Middle East is neither East nor West but a distinctive mixture of both. And we will see how three of its cultures—very different by reasons of history, geography, and religious belief—translated that rich tumult into their own special traditions, in some ways very different from one another, in other ways very much alike.

afghanistan

The Silk Road! The ancient passage between the East and the West still resonates with the romance and high adventure of travel to distant foreign lands. And lying right on the Silk Road is Afghanistan, a landlocked country high in central Asia. Throughout the centuries it has been visited by travelers and merchants, overrun by armies, used as a stopover by pilgrims and adventurers. Alexander the Great went through it on his way from Greece to conquer India; Marco Polo stopped by on his historic voyage to China. And from the opposite direction, the Mongols thundered through on their pillaging push to the West.

Afghanistan's cuisine is firmly rooted in the highland tradition of the Middle East. Lamb, rice, wheat bread, and yogurt are staple foods, along with eggplant and lentils. The traditional cooking fats are sheep fat and butter; the olive oil cultures lie well to the south and east. While some familiar Mediterranean vegetables, like tomatoes and peppers, have had a major impact, there is a heavier dependence on hearty root vegetables, and an intense use of onions to enrich and flavor sauces.

Afghan cookery reflects both ancient Persian and Indian elements. The spices are predominantly Indian, with cumin, coriander, cinnamon, cardamom, black onion seed, and hot red pepper most widely used, though with far greater restraint than in the Indian kitchen. Also Indian are the kormas, savory braised dishes of meat and vegetables, and the keema, a spiced ground meat sauce. A heavy use of fresh green herbs—parsley, dill, coriander, mint—is closer to Persian tradition, as is the technique of thickening sauces with split peas. And from both cuisines comes an elaborate and complex tradition of rice cookery. There is as well a repertoire of stuffed dumplings, thought to have been introduced from western China, and samosas, the spiced fried pastries from India.

The vibrant spices of India, the delicacy and refinement of Persian cooking, a soupçon of Chinese, a smidgen of the Mediterranean—all have left their mark on the Afghan table. But it has not been a one-way exchange: Much of what is now understood as the traditional cooking of northern India—the tandoor oven, grilled spitted meat, elaborate breads, and yogurt—was introduced into India and Pakistan from this part of the world.

RECIPES

Spiced Lentil Soup with Yogurt

Meat Dumplings in Broth

Roast Chicken with Spiced Tomato Glaze

Savory Braised Lamb Shanks

Spiced Lamb with Plums

Golden Rice Pilau with Carrots, Raisins, and
 Saffron

Savory Eggplant with Yogurt

Korma of Root Vegetables

Fresh Onion and Coriander Chutney

Sweet Rice with Fruit and Nuts

Spiced Lentil Soup with Yogurt

If, like me, you are a devotee of lentil soups, try this one for a refreshing flavor, robust and hearty but not heavy. Afghans traditionally make the soup with a meat (usually lamb) or poultry stock, but if you want to keep it completely vegetarian, it can be done with a vegetable stock or tomato juice. Just be careful to taste for salt and adjust the seasoning to your palate. Like most soups of this type, this one improves with age, so don't be afraid to make it early in the day or even the day before.

1 tablespoon butter or
    vegetable oil
1 medium onion, finely
    chopped
¼ teaspoon crushed dried hot
    pepper
1 teaspoon ground cumin
1 teaspoon ground coriander

1 cup lentils
6 cups meat or chicken broth
1 cup plain yogurt
Several good grinds of black
    pepper
Salt, if needed
½ cup finely chopped
    coriander leaves

1. Heat the butter in a medium, heavy saucepan and sauté the onion and hot pepper over moderate heat, stirring, until the onions wilt.

2. Stir in the cumin and the ground coriander and mix briefly with the onions.

3. Add the lentils and the broth, bring to a boil, then simmer over low heat, uncovered, for about 30 minutes, until the lentils are tender.

4. With the soup off the heat, whisk in the yogurt until it is smooth and well blended. Stir in the black pepper. Taste for salt.

5. Add the chopped coriander; mix well and bring just to a simmer.

Serves 6 to 8

Meat Dumplings in Broth
(Mantu)

A number of stuffed-dough traditions converge in Afghanistan—fried spiced meat or potato turnovers, delicate ravioli-like pasta stuffed with leeks and served with meat sauce and yogurt, and these hearty dumplings, a likely legacy from western Asia. They are called momo in Tibet, mantoo or mandoo in Korea, manti throughout central Asia. The pork and soy sauce filling of Asia is here replaced with lamb, cumin, and mint.

1 pound ground lamb
1 medium onion, finely
   chopped
1 clove garlic, crushed
1 teaspoon salt
1 teaspoon ground cumin
¼ teaspoon cayenne
1 tablespoon crushed dried
   mint

1 package wonton wrappers
4 cups beef broth or chicken
   broth
Small handful of chopped fresh
   coriander leaves
1 cup plain yogurt, lightly
   beaten, for serving

1. In a medium bowl, combine the ground meat with the onion, garlic, salt, cumin, cayenne, and mint. Mix thoroughly.
2. Have a small cup of cold water at hand. Place a wonton wrapper in a diamond position. Place a heaping teaspoonful of filling in the center of the wonton wrapper. With your finger, moisten the four edges of the wrapper. Bring the bottom point of the wrapper up to meet the top point, forming a triangle. Pinch the edges to seal completely. Then bring the two side points of the triangle together, moisten, and pinch to seal.
3. In a pot or deep skillet, heat the broth to a simmer. Place the filled dumplings in the broth (you may need to do this in two batches), cover, and cook over low heat for 10 to 12 minutes.
4. To serve, place the dumplings in a rimmed serving dish or bowl with some of the broth. Sprinkle the chopped coriander over the top. Pass the yogurt separately.

Makes 30 to 36 dumplings,
serving 4 to 6 as a main course,
6 to 8 as an appetizer

Roast Chicken with Spiced Tomato Glaze

Lamb, in a variety of cuts and preparations, is the most widely used meat of the Afghan kitchen, but chicken is a festive alternative. This chicken recalls some of the spicy chicken dishes of northern India, except that the seasoning is more delicate and tomato replaces the yogurt in the sauce. If you prefer, the chicken, split into halves, can be grilled over hot coals. The chicken is typically served with fresh naan or lavash.

3½- to 4½-pound roasting chicken

About 3 tablespoons ghee or butter, melted, or vegetable oil

Salt

Freshly ground black pepper

1 medium onion, finely chopped

2 cloves garlic, crushed

2 teaspoons finely minced gingerroot

½ teaspoon ground cumin

½ teaspoon ground coriander

½ teaspoon cinnamon

¼ teaspoon ground cardamom

1 cup tomato sauce

Fresh coriander leaves, slivers of sweet onion, and lemon wedges, for garnish

1. Preheat the oven to 350°F. Wash and dry the chicken and place, breast side up, on a rack in a roasting pan. Brush the chicken lightly all over the skin with about two thirds of the ghee, then salt and pepper lightly. Place in the oven to roast.

2. Heat the remaining ghee in a small, heavy saucepan and sauté the onion, garlic, and gingerroot over low heat, until the onion wilts and begins to turn golden.

3. Stir in the cumin, coriander, cinnamon, and cardamom. Add ¼ teaspoon of salt and several good grinds of pepper, then add the tomato sauce. Simmer, stirring, for about 5 minutes.

4. After the chicken has roasted for about 1 hour and the skin is beginning to turn golden and crisp, start basting with some of the tomato sauce. Baste two or three times and roast for about 30 to 40 minutes more.

5. When the chicken is done, let it rest for 5 to 10 minutes, then carve into serving pieces. Place the chicken on a serving plate, spoon the remaining sauce over it, and garnish with the coriander leaves, onion slivers, and lemon wedges.

Serves 4 to 6

Savory Braised Lamb Shanks

Lamb shanks are a treat in any tradition, but the Afghan kitchen has a special affinity for this rich, succulent cut of meat braised in a gently spiced sauce. The cooking must be slow and easy so that the lamb achieves its full flavor and melting tenderness.

2 tablespoons vegetable oil
2 large onions, finely chopped
4 lamb shanks (3 to 4 pounds), trimmed of excess fat
1 teaspoon salt
¼ teaspoon cayenne
¼ teaspoon freshly ground black pepper
2 teaspoons ground cumin
2 teaspoons ground coriander
½ teaspoon ground cardamom

½ teaspoon cinnamon
2 cloves garlic, crushed
2 to 3 carrots, thickly sliced
2 large tomatoes, coarsely chopped
2 medium potatoes, peeled and cut into small cubes
1 cup fresh or frozen peas
Chopped fresh mint leaves, for garnish

1. Heat the oil in a heavy pot or Dutch oven and sauté the onions over moderate heat, stirring, until the onions just begin to turn golden.

2. Push the onions to the side of the pot, then add the lamb shanks and sprinkle them with the salt, cayenne, and black pepper. Brown the shanks, turning to brown on all sides.

3. While the lamb is browning, stir in the cumin, coriander, cardamom, cinnamon, and garlic.

4. When the shanks are browned, add the carrots and tomatoes. Bring just to a simmer, then cover and cook over low heat for a total of about 2½ to 3 hours. Turn the shanks in the sauce from time to time. Add the potatoes after about 1 hour of cooking.

5. The shanks are done when the meat is very tender and falling off the bone. If the sauce is very liquid, cook it down quickly until it is quite thick. Add the peas for the last 10 minutes of cooking.

6. Garnish the lamb with the chopped mint and serve with rice or naan.

Serves 4

Spiced Lamb with Plums

The cooking of meat with fruit in delicately seasoned sauces is an ancient Persian tradition that has extended throughout the Middle East. In this dish, the flavor of tart plums combines with a number of spices from Indian practice in an unusual and distinctive sauce that goes well with the full flavor of lamb. Choose plums that are firm and just slightly underripe, for the appropriate fruity and acidic effect. The dish is always served with rice.

2 tablespoons butter or vegetable oil
2 medium onions, finely chopped
1 pound boneless lamb, cut into ½-inch cubes or into strips
1 teaspoon salt
Plenty of freshly ground black pepper
2 teaspoons ground coriander

1 teaspoon ground ginger
1 teaspoon cinnamon
½ teaspoon ground cardamom
2 tablespoons tomato paste
1 pound (about 5 or 6) firm black or red plums, pitted and coarsely chopped
1½ tablespoons fresh lemon juice
Chopped fresh coriander leaves, for garnish

1. Heat the butter in a heavy skillet or pot and sauté the onions over moderate heat until the onions wilt and begin to turn golden.

2. Add the lamb and brown lightly, turning to brown on all sides.

3. Sprinkle the lamb with the salt, pepper, ground coriander, ginger, cinnamon, and cardamom. Mix thoroughly, then stir in the tomato paste.

4. Add the chopped plums, mix well, then cover and cook over low heat for 1 to 1½ hours, or until the lamb is very tender. Stir the mixture from time to time; if too much liquid evaporates during the cooking, add a small amount of water.

5. When the lamb is tender and the sauce thick, stir in the lemon juice and taste for salt. Garnish the lamb with some chopped coriander and serve with rice.

Serves 4

Golden Rice Pilau with Carrots, Raisins, and Saffron

Throughout India, the Middle East, and the Mediterranean, saffron, the costliest and most coveted of spices, is used to add delicate flavor and unparalleled golden color to special dishes for special occasions. This festive rice pilau gets additional flavor and color from grated carrots, orange zest, and raisins; it is an excellent accompaniment to almost any grilled or roasted meat, and can also be used as a stuffing for chicken or turkey.

2 tablespoons butter
1 large onion, finely chopped
2 carrots, grated
2 teaspoons ground cumin
1 cup basmati rice
2 cups chicken broth

½ teaspoon saffron threads
2 teaspoons grated orange zest
Good dash of white pepper
½ cup golden raisins
Salt, if needed

1. Heat the butter in a medium saucepan and sauté the onion over medium heat, stirring occasionally, until the onion is soft and just beginning to turn golden.

2. Add the carrots and cumin and cook, stirring, for another few minutes.

3. Add the rice and mix thoroughly.

4. Add the broth, saffron, orange zest, white pepper, and raisins. Mix well and bring to a simmer. Cover and cook over low heat for about 20 minutes, until all the liquid has been absorbed. Taste for salt. Let stand, covered, for 5 minutes, then fluff up and turn into a serving dish.

Serves 4 to 6

Savory Eggplant with Yogurt

The two sauces in this dish represent two distinct traditions in the Middle East, the yogurt a product of the meat and dairy cultures of the temperate highlands, the zesty tomato sauce more closely allied with the vegetable cookery of the Mediterranean. Typically, they are not combined, but in Afghan cooking they frequently coalesce in an intriguing mix of flavor and tartness. Strained thick yogurt is a constant ingredient in Afghan dishes.

2 cups plain yogurt
2 medium-to-large eggplants
About ¼ cup vegetable oil
1 large onion, finely chopped
3 large cloves garlic, minced
½ teaspoon crushed dried hot pepper
2 cups canned crushed tomatoes

1 teaspoon cinnamon
1 teaspoon ground cumin
1 teaspoon salt
Several good grinds of black pepper
1 tablespoon crumbled dried mint leaves
1 large clove garlic, crushed
Snipped fresh chives, for garnish

1. Spoon the yogurt into a strainer lined with cheesecloth and let stand over a bowl for 1 to 2 hours.
2. Peel the eggplants, cut into ½-inch slices, then cut the slices into quarters.
3. Heat 2 tablespoons of the oil in a large skillet and sauté the onion, minced garlic, and hot pepper over moderate heat, stirring, just until the onion begins to turn golden.
4. Turn the heat up to moderately high, add the remaining oil and the eggplants, and fry the eggplant slices, turning them to brown lightly on both sides.

5. Add the tomatoes, cinnamon, cumin, salt, and black pepper. Mix well, then cook over moderate heat, stirring occasionally, for 20 to 30 minutes, until the eggplant is soft and the sauce is thick.

6. In a small saucepan combine the strained yogurt with the mint and the crushed garlic. Heat, stirring, just until very warm.

7. To serve, spoon half the yogurt over the bottom of a shallow bowl or rimmed serving platter. Spoon the eggplant mixture over the yogurt, then top the eggplant with the remaining yogurt. Sprinkle with the snipped chives.

Serves 4 to 6

Korma of Root Vegetables

The korma is a classic preparation in the northern Indian repertoire—a dish, usually of meat, braised with spices and aromatics in a small amount of liquid. In the Afghan tradition, with its close ties to the Indian, the korma is a familiar and valued dish, generally prepared with lamb but in lean times with vegetables alone. This satisfying, earthy mixture is a korma of winter root vegetables slowly cooked in a lightly spiced sauce.

2 tablespoons butter or vegetable oil
1 large onion, coarsely chopped
2 cloves garlic, minced
2 medium potatoes, peeled and cut into ½-inch cubes
2 carrots, thickly sliced
2 medium white turnips, or 1 small waxed yellow turnip (about 8 ounces), peeled and cut into ½-inch cubes
1 small knob celery root (about 8 ounces), peeled and cut into ½-inch cubes

1 teaspoon salt
2 teaspoons ground cumin
1 teaspoon ground coriander
½ teaspoon cinnamon
¼ teaspoon cayenne
Several good grinds of black pepper
1½ cups tomato juice, or more if needed for thinning the korma
Chopped fresh coriander leaves, for garnish (optional)

1. Heat the butter in a heavy pot and sauté the onion and garlic over moderate heat, stirring, just until the onion wilts and begins to turn golden.

2. Add the potatoes, carrots, turnips, celery root, salt, cumin, coriander, cinnamon, cayenne, and black pepper and mix well. Add the tomato juice, bring to a simmer, then cover and cook over low heat, stirring from time to time, for about 40 to 50 minutes, or until the vegetables are tender. If too much liquid evaporates during the cooking, add a bit more tomato juice. At the end of the cooking, the mixture should be quite thick. Taste for salt.

3. Serve the korma hot, with rice or naan. Garnish with the chopped coriander leaves, if desired.

Serves 4 to 6

Fresh Onion and Coriander Chutney

This pungent, refreshing mixture has clear affiliations with India's vast repertoire of fresh and preserved relishes and chutneys, but with the distinctly Persian addition of chopped walnuts. Its piquant flavor enhances all sorts of dishes, from grilled meat and kebabs to rice dishes and stews.

1 large onion, very finely chopped
1 large handful fresh coriander leaves, finely chopped (about ½ cup)
2 to 3 tablespoons fresh lemon juice
1 teaspoon sugar
¼ teaspoon (or more) cayenne
½ teaspoon salt
¼ cup finely chopped, freshly toasted walnuts

Combine the onion, coriander, lemon juice, sugar, cayenne, and salt. Mix thoroughly, then stir in the walnuts. Taste for salt and hotness. Serve at room temperature.

Makes about 2 cups

Sweet Rice with Fruit and Nuts

A festive and extravagant dish usually served at holidays and on special occasions, this rice pudding combines a number of valued and costly ingredients—almonds, pistachios, saffron, and dried fruit. It is a fairly thick mixture best served in the Afghan fashion, spread while still warm on a shallow serving dish, sprinkled with chopped nuts, and chilled.

1 cup short-grain rice
2 cups water
3 cups milk
½ cup sugar
½ teaspoon salt
8 cardamom pods
½ teaspoon saffron threads
½ cup dried pitted sour
    cherries (you can also use
    raisins or dried
    cranberries)

3 to 4 tablespoons chopped
    blanched almonds
3 to 4 tablespoons finely
    chopped pistachios
Additional chopped pistachios,
    for garnish

1. In a medium saucepan, combine the rice and water. Bring to a simmer and cook over low heat, covered, for 15 to 20 minutes, until all the water has been absorbed.

2. Add the milk, sugar, salt, cardamom, and saffron to the cooked rice in the pot. Mix well, then cook, uncovered, over low heat, stirring occasionally, for about 20 to 25 minutes. Stir in the dried fruit. Continue to cook, stirring, for another 5 minutes or so. Remove from the heat and stir in the chopped almonds and pistachios.

3. Spread the mixture while still warm in a shallow serving dish and garnish with a sprinkle of chopped pistachios. Cover with plastic wrap and chill before serving.

Serves 6 to 8

turkey

Straddling the Bosporus, the glittering city of Istanbul stands with one foot in Europe and the other in Asia, patrolling the natural gateway between the two worlds. For centuries the Turks have acted as powerful middlemen in the unceasing flow of people, goods, and ideas between the East and the West, a role that augmented both the riches of her coffers and the bounty of her table.

Turkish cuisine is both cosmopolitan and rustic, delicate and hearty, traditional and experimental. Its character and vitality are the result of a successful fusion of elements from Persia and Afghanistan to the east, the Mediterranean to the south, and central Europe to the west. These elements sometimes merge in individual dishes but are often maintained as separate traditions that come together at the table, if not in the pot.

Shish kebab is, of course, the signature meat dish, but lamb is prepared in dozens of ways—braised, baked, and minced for meatballs, croquettes, and stuffings. Wheat serves not only as the flour for bread and the delicate sheets of phyllo pastry for the savory borek and the sweet baklava, but also in such processed forms as bulgur and semolina. Creamy, thick, tart yogurt is a focal ingredient, as are a number of cheeses—the sharp, tangy feta types of the Middle East and the milder, creamier varieties from European tradition. Rice and eggplant are indispensable staples, eaten at almost every meal, along with a rich variety of vegetables, including peppers, tomatoes, potatoes, squash, artichokes, celery root, carrots, and peas.

The seasoning profile of Turkish food is more delicate than that of Afghanistan, showing a lighter touch with spices and a more intense use of herbs such as parsley, dill, mint, thyme, and bay leaf. Indeed, Turkish bay leaves are renowned for their aromatic properties and are used effectively in marinades and braising sauces. The Turkish palate appreciates a bit of sweetness to balance the acid in salads and marinated dishes, and savors the characteristic flavor and texture of raisins, pine nuts, and currants.

From earthy lamb and root vegetables to delicate seafood perfumed with herbs, from sun-drenched peppers lavish with olive oil to eggplant baked with rich cheese sauces, Turkish cuisine is a complex amalgam of East, West, North, and South, a compelling magnet for many traditions at one of the world's great centers of commerce and culture.

RECIPES

Mussels Pilaki

Turkey Braised with Garden Vegetables

Cabbage Rolls with Bulgur, Lamb, and Herbs

Tiny Spiced Meatballs with Pine Nuts

Braised Lamb with Chickpeas

Ali Pasha Rice Pilaf

Leek and Cheese Pie

Marinated Eggplant with Olive Oil and
   Tomatoes

Marinated Artichokes with Mixed Vegetables

Smoky Eggplant Cream

Apricot Yogurt with Hazelnuts

Pistachio Revani with Saffron Syrup

Mussels Pilaki

A popular part of the meze, the traditional assortment of cold appetizers, is this dish of mussels cooked with vegetables in a light, aromatic tomato sauce. Note the slight touch of sweetness in the sauce, typical of Turkish salads and marinated dishes.

2 to 3 pounds fresh mussels
3 to 4 tablespoons olive oil
1 medium onion, finely
    chopped
2 carrots, sliced
2 cloves garlic, crushed
2 medium tomatoes, coarsely
    chopped
1 tablespoon tomato paste
2 bay leaves

½ teaspoon salt
¼ teaspoon sugar
1 large potato, peeled and
    diced
Plenty of freshly ground black
    pepper
Good handful of flat-leaf parsley
    leaves, finely chopped
Juice of 1 lemon
Lemon wedges, for garnish

1. Scrub and debeard the mussels, discarding any that are cracked or open. Steam the mussels in a cup or two of water until they open. Shell the mussels; reserve the cooking liquid.

2. Heat the oil in a skillet and sauté the onion and carrots until the onion turns translucent. Stir in the garlic for a few minutes.

3. Add the tomatoes, tomato paste, bay leaves, salt, and sugar and about ½ cup of the reserved mussel liquid. Add the potato, mix well, then bring to a simmer. Cook over low to moderate heat for 20 to 30 minutes, until the potatoes are just tender. Add more mussel liquid if necessary.

4. When the potatoes are tender and the sauce is thick, add the shelled mussels and mix well. Remove from the heat and stir in the black pepper, parsley, and lemon juice. Serve at room temperature, with lemon wedges, as an appetizer.

Serves 4 to 6 as an appetizer

Turkey Braised with Garden Vegetables

Because the Turks were frequent middlemen in the exchange of goods between the East and the West, their name was often attached to unfamiliar, exotic new foods. Native American corn was sometimes called Turkish wheat, and the domesticated bird of Mexico was dubbed the "Turkey cock" by some Europeans, a name that shortened in time to just plain "turkey." For those of us more accustomed to the roasted fowl of Thanksgiving fame, this dish is an interesting change of pace: braised breast of turkey in a fresh herb-and-vegetable sauce.

2 tablespoons olive oil
1 large onion, thinly sliced
2 cloves garlic, minced
2 to 2½ pounds boneless breast of turkey, in one piece (sometimes called London broil cut)
½ teaspoon salt
¼ teaspoon freshly ground black pepper
1 medium green bell pepper, seeded and cut into ½-inch pieces
2 carrots, sliced

1 small knob celery root, peeled and cut into small chunks
2 large tomatoes, coarsely chopped, or 1 cup canned crushed
2 large bay leaves
½ teaspoon dried thyme
2 zucchini, sliced or cut into ½-inch chunks
½ cup fresh or frozen peas
Small handful of flat-leaf parsley leaves, finely chopped

1. Heat the oil in a heavy pot or Dutch oven and sauté the onion until it wilts and just starts to turn golden. Add the garlic and cook, stirring, a few minutes more.

2. Sprinkle the turkey breast with the salt and black pepper, then brown lightly on both sides.

3. Add the bell pepper, carrots, celery root, tomatoes, bay leaves, and thyme. Bring to a simmer, then cover and cook over low heat for about 50 minutes, turning the meat once or twice in the sauce.

4. Remove the turkey to a carving board and let rest for 10 minutes. Add the zucchini and peas to the sauce in the pot and cook, uncovered, until the sauce is thickened and all the vegetables are

tender. Stir in the parsley. Taste for salt; you may need more at this point.

5. Slice the turkey and spoon the sauce and vegetables over and around the slices.

Serves 6 to 8

VARIATIONS: Other vegetables—such as string beans, artichoke hearts, and potato cubes—can be added or substituted.

Cabbage Rolls with Bulgur, Lamb, and Herbs

There arose in the central Middle Eastern hearth a rich tradition of stuffed vegetables cooked in savory sauces that spawned a multitude of variations throughout the Mediterranean, the Balkans, and central Europe. The meatless versions, typically stuffed with rice and cooked in olive oil, are frequently eaten cold, while the vegetables stuffed with meat mixtures are often cooked with butter and are always eaten warm. These cabbage rolls use bulgur (cracked wheat), a Turkish staple, combined with lamb and a number of fresh herbs that show a clear Persian influence.

½ cup bulgur (medium- or coarse-grain)
⅓ cup very hot water
8 to 10 large outer leaves from a head of cabbage
1 pound lean ground lamb (you can substitute beef if you wish)
1¼ teaspoons salt, more if needed
¼ teaspoon freshly ground black pepper
1 teaspoon ground cumin
3 tablespoons finely chopped fresh mint leaves, or 1 tablespoon crumbled dried
3 to 4 tablespoons finely chopped parsley leaves
3 to 4 tablespoons finely snipped fresh dill
2 tablespoons butter or olive oil
1 large onion, thinly sliced

1 cup meat stock or chicken
   stock
2 tablespoons tomato paste
1 tablespoon fresh lemon juice,
   more if needed

1 to 2 tablespoons each
         additional chopped fresh
         mint, parsley, and dill, for
         garnish

1. In a large bowl, combine the bulgur and the hot water; mix well and let stand for 20 to 30 minutes.

2. Trim the cabbage leaves of tough stem ends, then cook in boiling water for 3 to 4 minutes. Drain in a colander and set aside.

3. Add the ground meat, salt, black pepper, cumin, mint, parsley, and dill to the soaked bulgur. Mix thoroughly (best to knead with the hands).

4. Place a heaping tablespoon of the filling on each cabbage leaf. Fold the bottom of the leaf up over the filling, fold down the top, then fold the sides in. Fasten the packet with a wooden toothpick.

5. Heat the butter in a large heavy pot or Dutch oven and sauté the onion until it is soft and translucent. Add the stock, tomato paste, and lemon juice. Mix well and bring to a simmer.

6. Place the stuffed cabbage rolls in the sauce. Cover and cook over low heat for about 1 hour, turning the rolls in the sauce once or twice during the cooking. Taste the sauce for salt and lemon.

7. Serve the cabbage rolls with the sauce on a large rimmed platter or dish; sprinkle with the additional chopped herbs.

Serves 4

Tiny Spiced Meatballs with Pine Nuts

The Turkish kitchen is a treasure house of ground or minced meatballs and croquettes. Called kofte, from the Persian word for "pounded," they come in every size and shape, some stuffed, others sauced. These savory little meatballs are typically served with a rice pilaf, but they also make an excellent cocktail tidbit, served hot with toothpicks. They are quick and easy to prepare, but be careful not to overcook them.

1 pound finely ground lean lamb or beef	¼ teaspoon freshly ground black pepper
1 medium onion, very finely chopped	2 teaspoons ground cumin
2 tablespoons pine nuts	½ teaspoon ground allspice
1 teaspoon salt	Flour for dredging
	2 to 3 tablespoons vegetable oil

1. In a medium bowl combine the meat, onion, pine nuts, salt, pepper, cumin, and allspice. Mix thoroughly, preferably with your hands, kneading the mixture with your fingers.

2. Form into small balls, about the size of a cherry tomato. Try to keep the pine nuts inside the meatballs. Dredge the meatballs lightly with flour.

3. In a large skillet, heat the oil over moderate heat. Add the meatballs and fry, turning frequently, until they are just nicely browned on all sides. Remove from the pan and serve hot.

Makes about 35 to 40 small meatballs

Braised Lamb with Chickpeas

Typical of the richly flavored meat and vegetable stews of the Middle East, this savory dish shows the remnants of a complex spice tradition that originates in northern India and Pakistan and that becomes more and more subtle as it moves from east to west. As the spicing declines, the tomato becomes more dominant, as influences from the Mediterranean come into play. Serve this with rice or bread and a crisp salad.

2 tablespoons olive oil
1 large onion, finely chopped
1¼ pounds lean boneless lamb, cut into ½-inch cubes (beef can also be used, but lamb is more typical)
1 carrot, sliced
1 teaspoon salt
1 teaspoon ground cumin
1 teaspoon cinnamon

¼ teaspoon freshly ground black pepper
2 cups canned crushed tomatoes
3 cups cooked or canned chickpeas, drained
3 to 4 tablespoons finely snipped fresh dill
Additional chopped dill for garnish (optional)

1. Heat the oil in a heavy pot or deep skillet and brown the lamb cubes over moderate heat. While the meat is browning, add the onion and sauté in the oil as you turn the lamb to brown it.

2. Add the carrot, then sprinkle the salt, cumin, cinnamon, and pepper over the lamb. Mix well, then stir in the tomatoes. Bring to a simmer, then cover and cook over low heat for about 1 hour, until the lamb is quite tender. Stir the stew occasionally as it cooks.

3. Add the chickpeas and dill and cook, stirring occasionally, for another 45 minutes or so, or until the lamb is very tender.

4. Serve hot, garnished with some additional chopped dill, if desired.

Serves 4 to 6

Ali Pasha Rice Pilaf

Although rice is central to most Turkish meals, pasta also plays a part, having converged in Turkey from three separate traditions—the meat-filled dumpling from western Asia via Afghanistan, macaroni in a variety of shapes and sizes from Greece and Italy, and noodles from Persia. It is the Persian *rishte* (threads) that embellish this delicate, buttery pilaf, along with currants and pine nuts. For a festive presentation, press the hot cooked pilaf into an oiled ring mold, then unmold onto a serving plate and surround with tiny meatballs (see page 124).

3 tablespoons butter	2 cups chicken stock
1 cup thin egg noodles	3 tablespoons dried currants
3 tablespoons pine nuts	Salt, if needed
1 medium onion, finely	A bit of finely chopped parsley
chopped	leaves, for garnish
1 cup long-grain rice	

1. Heat 1 tablespoon of the butter in a medium skillet and sauté the noodles and the pine nuts over moderate heat, shaking the pan frequently, until the noodles and pine nuts are golden brown. Do not allow them to overbrown. Remove from the heat and set aside.

2. In a medium, heavy saucepan, sauté the onion in the remaining 2 tablespoons of butter until it is just beginning to turn golden. Add the rice and stir into the butter for a minute or two.

3. Add the stock and the currants, bring to a simmer, then cover and cook over low heat for about 15 minutes. Gently stir in the reserved noodles and pine nuts, cover, and continue to cook for about 5 minutes, until the rice is cooked and all the liquid has been absorbed. Taste for salt.

4. Serve as is, garnished with a bit of chopped parsley, or mold in a ring mold as described above.

Serves 4 to 6

Leek and Cheese Pie

This savory "pie" can be prepared in a number of ways: The leek-and-cheese filling can be layered between sheets of phyllo pastry, or baked within a bottom and top of short pastry crust, or, as in this version, between layers of spicy bread crumbs. It is a wonderfully rich and intense dish, best served in small portions; it makes an excellent addition to the buffet table.

5 tablespoons olive oil
5 to 6 large leeks, mostly white part, washed thoroughly and finely chopped (about 4½ to 5 cups chopped)
6 eggs
1 pound farmer cheese
6 to 8 ounces feta cheese, finely crumbled

½ teaspoon salt
¼ teaspoon freshly ground black pepper
½ cup finely chopped flat-leaf parsley leaves
¾ cup soft bread crumbs
¼ teaspoon cayenne pepper

1. Heat 2 tablespoons of the oil in a large skillet and sauté the leeks over moderate heat, stirring occasionally, until they are soft and just beginning to turn golden. Remove from the heat and let cool slightly.

2. In a large bowl, whisk or beat the eggs thoroughly, then blend in the farmer cheese and feta cheese and mix well. Stir in the leeks, salt, black pepper, and parsley and mix thoroughly. Preheat the oven to 350°F.

3. Combine the bread crumbs, the cayenne, and the 3 remaining tablespoons of oil; mix well.

4. Butter a 12- x 8-inch baking dish or shallow casserole. Sprinkle about two thirds of the crumb mixture evenly over the bottom of the casserole. Spoon the cheese mixture evenly over the crumbs. Sprinkle the remaining crumbs evenly over the top of the cheese.

5. Bake the pie for about 30 to 35 minutes, until it is firm and nicely browned. Let it stand for at least 10 minutes before cutting into small squares to serve. It can be served warm or at room temperature.

Makes 15 to 20 small squares

Marinated Eggplant
with Olive Oil and Tomatoes
(Imam Bayeldi)

This recipe is from an earlier book, but I include it here because it is a wonderful dish, a classic of the Turkish kitchen, and an exultant expression of the Mediterranean aspect of Turkish cuisine, in its lavish use of olive oil, garlic, and tomatoes. The sweet-and-sour element is a characteristic Turkish touch, one that had an important influence on the cooking of Sicily and the Balkans. For best flavor, prepare the dish a day in advance.

4 to 5 baby Italian eggplants
     (3 to 5 inches long)
Salt
1 to 2 cups olive oil
3 large onions, sliced
4 cloves garlic, crushed
1 can (35 ounces) Italian-style
    tomatoes, drained and
    coarsely chopped

½ cup finely chopped flat-leaf
    parsley leaves
Juice of 2 lemons
¼ teaspoon freshly ground
    black pepper
2 teaspoons sugar

1. Cut the stem ends off the eggplants and cut in half lengthwise. On the peel side of each half, make two or three small slits with a sharp knife, being careful not to cut all the way through the eggplant.

2. Place the eggplant halves on a large tray and salt both sides generously. Let stand for 30 minutes. At the end of this time, wipe off all excess salt and moisture from the eggplant.

3. Pour in enough olive oil to cover the bottom of a large skillet. (The glory of this dish is to use as much olive oil as possible.) Over moderate heat, sauté the eggplant halves on both sides until lightly browned. Add more oil as needed. As the halves brown, transfer them cut side up to a large shallow baking dish or casserole.

4. When all the eggplant is browned, add a couple more tablespoons of oil to the pan. Add the onions and cook slowly, stirring occasionally, until they are soft and richly browned, about 30 minutes.

5. Stir in the garlic, then add the tomatoes, parsley, lemon juice,

1 teaspoon salt, the black pepper, and the sugar. Mix well. Simmer over moderate heat for about 10 minutes. Preheat the oven to 400°F.

6. Pour the sauce mixture over the eggplant, then generously drizzle some more olive oil over the top. Cover and bake for 30 to 40 minutes. Remove the cover for the last 10 minutes of baking.

7. Let cool, then cover and refrigerate for at least 4 to 6 hours, or preferably overnight. Bring to room temperature before serving.

Serves 6 to 8

Marinated Artichokes with Mixed Vegetables

It is difficult to imagine a Turkish meal without at least one dish of vegetables dressed with olive oil and lemon juice or vinegar. Each dish takes its name from the major component—green beans, artichokes—but almost all are composed of mixtures of vegetables that frequently include potatoes, carrots, and peas. You can certainly use canned or jarred artichoke bottoms, but they will not have the same firm texture and delicate flavor of the fresh-cooked vegetables.

2 small potatoes, peeled and cut into ½-inch cubes
2 carrots, sliced
6 to 8 small boiler onions, peeled and cut in half
6 to 8 cooked artichoke bottoms, cut into quarters or thickly sliced
½ cup cooked fresh or frozen peas

3 tablespoons fresh lemon juice
3 tablespoons olive oil
½ teaspoon salt
½ teaspoon sugar
Plenty of freshly ground black pepper
2 to 3 tablespoons finely chopped flat-leaf parsley leaves or finely snipped dill

1. Cook the potatoes, carrots, and onions in boiling water just until the potatoes are tender but still firm. Drain and combine with the artichokes and peas in a bowl.

2. In a small bowl, combine the lemon juice, oil, salt, sugar, and pepper and whisk until well blended and creamy.

3. Pour the dressing over the vegetables and mix well. Let stand at room temperature for an hour or two. Taste for salt and lemon; garnish with the parsley or dill.

Serves 4 to 6

Smoky Eggplant Cream

Sometimes called "sultan's delight" in Turkey, this rich creamy purée is a perfect marriage between East and West, combining a traditional Middle Eastern favorite, grilled eggplant, with a European-style cheese sauce. The eggplant can also be roasted in a hot oven until soft, but it won't have the wonderful smoky flavor of the grill. The cream is typically served with shish kebabs but is good with almost any grilled or roasted meat or poultry.

2 medium eggplants, about 1 pound each
2 tablespoons fresh lemon juice
2 tablespoons butter
2 tablespoons flour
½ cup milk
1 teaspoon salt
Plenty of freshly ground black pepper
½ cup grated Gruyère or Emmentaler cheese
2 tablespoons grated Parmesan or other sharp grating cheese

1. Grill the eggplants over charcoal, turning from time to time, until they are very soft when pierced with a sharp knife, about 15 minutes. Let cool until easy to handle, then peel.

2. Purée the peeled eggplant and the lemon juice in a food processor.

3. In a medium saucepan, melt the butter over moderate heat. Add the flour and stir in to make a roux. Cook, stirring, for 2 to 3 minutes.

4. Add the milk and whisk until smooth. Cook, stirring, until the mixture becomes smooth and thick. Stir in the salt and pepper.

5. Add the eggplant purée and cook, stirring, for about 5 minutes, until the mixture is smooth and thick. Remove from the heat and stir in the Gruyère and Parmesan. Mix until well blended and smooth. Taste for salt and pepper.

6. Serve the cream as is from the pot, or spoon into a buttered shallow casserole or gratin dish and heat in a 350°F oven for about 15 minutes.

Serves 4 to 6

Apricot Yogurt with Hazelnuts

I know that your local supermarket has at least a half dozen brands of apricot yogurt, as well as blueberry crunch and praline cinnamon swirl. So why bother to make your own? Because, my friends, this one is better, from that part of the world that has long relished the combination of real yogurt, tart and creamy, with a variety of fresh and dried fruits and nuts. A sheep's-milk yogurt would be good, if you can get it, but in any case choose a high-quality yogurt with no gums, emulsifiers, or added flavors.

1 cup dried apricots (Turkish, of course!), cut into quarters
2 teaspoons julienne strips lemon zest
1½ cups water

1 tablespoon sugar
2 cups plain yogurt
⅓ to ½ cup finely chopped freshly toasted hazelnuts
4 to 6 fresh mint leaves, for garnish (optional)

1. In a saucepan, combine the apricots, lemon zest, and water. Bring to a simmer, then cook, uncovered, over low to moderate heat for about 15 minutes. Stir in the sugar and cook about 5 minutes more, until the apricots are tender.

2. Let the mixture cool, then stir it into the yogurt. Chill thoroughly.

3. Serve the yogurt in small dishes; sprinkle with the chopped nuts. Garnish with a mint leaf, if desired.

Serves 4 to 6

Pistachio Revani with Saffron Syrup

Semolina is a product milled from hard wheat, which has a drier, coarser texture than the soft wheat flours typically used in European cakes and pastries. It makes an ideal sponge for the sweet syrups that are so fundamental a part of Middle Eastern cuisine, and it can be seen as a kind of confectionary cross between the tender sweet baked goods of the West and the syrup-soaked pastries of the East.

¼ pound (1 stick) unsalted butter, at room temperature, plus additional butter for pan
2½ cups sugar
6 eggs
1 cup fine semolina (farina)

1 cup finely chopped unsalted pistachios
1 teaspoon vanilla
1 cup water
Juice of 1 lemon
½ teaspoon saffron threads

1. In a large bowl, cream the butter and 1 cup of the sugar until pale and smooth.

2. Beat in the eggs, one at a time, beating well after each addition, until the mixture is fluffy.

3. Stir in the semolina, pistachios, and vanilla and mix until thoroughly blended. Preheat the oven to 350°F.

4. Generously butter a 13x9x2-inch baking pan or a 12-inch round pan. Spread the batter evenly in the pan. Bake the cake for 30 to 35 minutes.

5. While the cake is baking, combine the remaining 1½ cups sugar with the water and lemon juice in a small, nonreactive saucepan. Mix well, bring to a boil, and cook over moderate heat for about

10 minutes. Stir in the saffron threads for the last few minutes of cooking.

6. When the cake is lightly browned and firm to the touch, remove it from the oven and turn off the heat. If the syrup has cooled, bring it just to a simmer. Pour the hot syrup slowly and evenly all over the cake, tilting the pan to make sure the entire cake is covered. Return the cake to the oven for 5 minutes.

7. Let the cake cool completely, then cut into small diamonds or squares to serve.

Makes about 40 pieces

israel

The birthplace of the Bible is a typical part of the Middle Eastern landscape, differing from its neighbors only in the nature of the people who made it their home. The religion and culture of the Jews, which had their origin here so many centuries ago, have shaped the cuisine from those earliest times to the present day.

Expelled from their ancient homeland by the Romans, the Jewish people wandered all over the world, in a mass migration known as the Diaspora. And wherever they settled, throughout Europe, the Mediterranean, and North Africa, they adapted their culinary practice to the foodways and resources of their new homes, but always within the constraints of the dietary laws set down in the Old Testament. Those laws, lengthy and detailed, specify the prohibitions against certain animal foods, focusing in modern times primarily on pork and shellfish. Another powerful injunction prohibits the mixing of meat and dairy products, stemming from the command "Thou shalt not seethe a kid in its mother's milk." Finally, the consumption of blood is forbidden, as a substance sacred to the Lord; this law resulted in the ritual slaughter and koshering of meat, as well as the practice of long, slow cooking to remove any trace of blood from the finished dish.

The observance of the dietary laws was a powerful force in preserving tradition among Jews scattered throughout the world. But while some features of their adopted cuisines were necessarily rejected, others less controversial were assimilated, in a stunning display of both faith and flexibility. Alsatian Jews developed a taste for sweet-and-sour and rich pâtés; Polish Jews for rye bread and sour cream; Moroccan Jews for dishes fragrant with spices, nuts, and fruits; Italian Jews for pasta and pine nuts.

Jews from all over the world have returned in this century to the land from which they first emerged. Each brings back to the ancestral homeland a different set of ethnic foodways, all still mediated by the ancient dietary laws. Israel is a culinary hodgepodge, but a Jewish hodgepodge, and its cuisine, like its exuberant young nationhood, is very much a cuisine-in-process. Pita sits next to bagels, pickled herring is served along with hummus, lemon-and-chile-laced salads walk hand-in-hand with sauerkraut and sour pickles. Is peaceful coexistence the end of the story, or some distant unknowable fusion?

RECIPES

Sweet-and-Sour Salmon with Raisins and Mint

Roasted Sea Bass with Spiced Yogurt Crust

Sweet-and-Sour Stuffed Peppers

Lentils, Rice, and Chickpeas

Mixed Peppers with Eggplant and Tahini

Meatless Chopped Liver

Lemony Leeks with Olives and Tomatoes

Chunky Mixed Salad

Spiced Hot Pepper Relish

Double Orange Salad with Honey and Mint

Sephardic Fruit and Nut Paste

Rich Chocolate Macaroon Cake

Jewish Apple Cake

Sweet-and-Sour Salmon with Raisins and Mint

The Jewish taste for sweet-and-sour is thought to have originated in Alsace, but this dish comes from the tradition of Jews who settled in Italy. The raisins, pine nuts, and mint, so typical of Sicilian cooking, suggest a prior Turkish influence. The fish should be marinated and chilled for 24 hours; it is intensely flavored and is best served in small portions as an appetizer, or as a first course on some mixed greens or lettuce leaves.

¼ cup fresh lemon juice
¼ cup white vinegar
½ cup water
2 tablespoons sugar
1 medium onion, thinly sliced
⅓ cup dark raisins
½ teaspoon salt
8 to 10 black peppercorns
2 bay leaves

1½ pounds salmon or salmon trout fillet, ¾ to 1 inch thick
½ cup fresh mint leaves, finely chopped
2 tablespoons lightly toasted pine nuts
Additional coarsely chopped mint leaves, for garnish

1. In a deep nonreactive skillet or top-of-range casserole, combine the lemon juice, vinegar, water, sugar, onion, raisins, salt, peppercorns, and bay leaves. Mix well, then simmer the mixture for 5 to 7 minutes.

2. Place the fish in the pan; if it does not fit in one piece, you can cut it into pieces to fit. Bring to a simmer, then cover and cook over low heat, turning once, for 15 to 20 minutes, or until the salmon is just cooked through. Remove from the heat and stir in the ½ cup chopped mint. Let cool for an hour or two, then cover and refrigerate overnight.

3. Before serving, remove the bay leaves and peppercorns and stir in the pine nuts. Serve the fish in small portions as an appetizer, or as a first course on some mixed greens or lettuce leaves. Garnish with the additional chopped mint and spoon some of the broth over each portion.

Serves 6 to 8

Roasted Sea Bass with Spiced Yogurt Crust

Fish is an animal food that is exempt from the ritual dietary law forbidding the mixture of meat and dairy products, and the combination of fish and dairy results in such well-loved traditional Jewish dishes as herring in sour cream and cream cheese and lox. This contemporary roasted sea bass is flavored with some typical Middle Eastern seasonings incorporated in an egg-and-yogurt crust that is very characteristic of Balkan cuisine, where it is frequently used as a topping for baked casseroles.

2 tablespoons olive oil, plus
    additional for baking dish
1 medium onion, finely
    chopped
¼ cup plain yogurt
¼ teaspoon crushed dried hot
    pepper
1 teaspoon ground cumin
1 tablespoon fresh lemon juice
1 egg, lightly beaten

2 to 3 tablespoons finely
    chopped flat-leaf parsley
    leaves
2 to 3 tablespoons finely
    chopped coriander leaves
1¼ to 1½ pounds sea bass
    fillets, about ½ to ¾ inch
    thick
Salt
Freshly ground black pepper

1. Heat the oil in a small skillet and sauté the onion over moderate heat until it just begins to turn golden.

2. In a small bowl, combine the sautéed onion with the yogurt, hot pepper, cumin, lemon juice, egg, parsley, and coriander. Mix thoroughly. Preheat the oven to 450°F.

3. Place the fish fillets in a lightly oiled baking dish or casserole. Salt and pepper lightly. Spoon the yogurt mixture evenly over the fish. Bake for about 20 minutes, until the fish just flakes easily when tested with a fork and the crust is lightly browned.

Serves 4

Sweet-and-Sour Stuffed Peppers

The Middle East has long been a center of stuffed vegetables—grape leaves, cabbage, eggplant, peppers—and the tradition migrated into Eastern Europe and the Balkans. This recipe may well have begun its long trek in its original homeland, been refashioned by the sweet-and-sour practice of European Jews, and returned home once again to join its savory brethren.

1 pound lean ground beef
1 cup cold cooked rice
1 medium onion, grated or very finely chopped
1 teaspoon ground ginger
1¼ teaspoons salt
¼ teaspoon freshly ground black pepper
4 to 6 small-to-medium green bell peppers, cut in half lengthwise and seeded
2 tablespoons vegetable oil, plus extra for baking dish

1 large onion, thinly sliced
2 cloves garlic, finely chopped
1 large carrot, thinly sliced
2 cups canned crushed tomatoes
2 tablespoons fresh lemon juice
2 teaspoons sugar
1 teaspoon ground ginger
½ teaspoon salt
¼ teaspoon freshly ground black pepper
½ cup dark raisins

1. In a large bowl, combine the ground beef, rice, grated or finely chopped onion, ginger, salt, and black pepper. Mix thoroughly, then pack the mixture into the prepared pepper shells, mounding it slightly. Any extra stuffing can be formed into meatballs to cook in the sauce. Place the stuffed pepper halves in a single layer in a lightly greased baking dish or casserole. Preheat the oven to 350°F.

2. Heat the 2 tablespoons oil in a skillet and sauté the sliced onion, garlic, and carrot over moderate heat until the vegetables are limp. Add the tomatoes, lemon juice, sugar, ginger, salt, black pepper, and raisins. Mix well and simmer for about 5 minutes. Pour the sauce over and around the stuffed peppers.

3. Cover the baking dish with foil and bake for 45 to 55 minutes, basting the peppers with the sauce from time to time. Uncover the casserole for the last 10 to 15 minutes of cooking.

Serves 4 to 6

Lentils, Rice, and Chickpeas

Two of the Middle East's most ancient foods—lentils and chickpeas—combine with rice in this traditional dish that offers hearty flavor and a complete balance of vegetable proteins. The seasoning combination of garlic, cumin, and mint indicates a probable Egyptian origin. Served with yogurt, a salad, and fresh pita, this dish makes a tasty and satisfying meatless meal.

¾ cup lentils
½ cup rice
2 cups water
3 tablespoons olive oil
1 large onion, thinly sliced
1 medium onion, finely
    chopped
4 large cloves garlic
2 teaspoons ground cumin
2 cups tomato sauce
1 teaspoon salt

Several good grinds of black
    pepper
1 small bunch fresh mint leaves,
    finely chopped, or
    2 tablespoons crushed dry
    mint
2 cups cooked or canned
    chickpeas, drained
Good handful of flat-leaf parsley
    leaves, finely chopped
Plain yogurt, for garnish

1. In a pot, combine the lentils, rice, and water. Bring to a simmer, then cover and cook over low heat for about 20 minutes, until all the liquid has been absorbed. Remove from the heat and let stand, covered.

2. Heat the oil in a medium saucepan and sauté the sliced onion over moderate heat, stirring occasionally, until the onion is a rich golden brown. Remove the onion from the pot, leaving behind as much of the oil as possible. Set the onions aside.

3. In the same saucepan, sauté the chopped onion and the garlic in the remaining oil, stirring, until the onion wilts and just begins to turn golden. Stir in the cumin.

4. Add the tomato sauce, salt, pepper, mint, and chickpeas, then add the reserved lentils and rice. Mix well, then cook, stirring occasionally, over low heat for 15 to 20 minutes. Just before serving, stir in the parsley.

5. Serve hot, garnished with the reserved caramelized onions, and pass the yogurt.

Serves 4 to 6

TIP: Like most bean and lentil dishes, this will thicken considerably on standing. If you need to thin the mixture, add some water and adjust the seasoning as necessary.

Mixed Peppers with Eggplant and Tahini

Some typical Lebanese seasoning ingredients—lemon, parsley, sesame tahini—flavor this hearty mixture of vegetables well loved throughout the Middle East. Unlike its more familiar cousins, hummus bi tahini and baba ghanouj, it has a chunky texture. It can serve as a salad or a vegetable side dish, or as a dip or spread with fresh pita or crisp crackers.

¼ cup olive oil
4 large bell peppers, mixed colors (red, green, yellow), seeded and diced
2 medium eggplants, peeled and diced
1 large onion, finely chopped
4 or 5 cloves garlic, crushed
2 to 3 small fresh hot chiles, seeded and minced, or 1 teaspoon crushed dried hot pepper (optional)

2 to 3 tablespoons fresh lemon juice
1 teaspoon salt, or more to taste
Plenty of freshly ground black pepper
Large handful of flat-leaf parsley leaves, finely chopped
2 to 3 tablespoons sesame tahini
Black olives and tomato wedges, for garnish

1. Heat the oil in a large skillet and add the peppers, eggplants, onion, garlic, and chiles. Cook over low to moderate heat, stirring from time to time, for about 30 to 40 minutes, until the mixture is soft and thick.

2. Stir in the lemon juice, salt, pepper, and parsley and mix well. Then stir in the tahini and blend thoroughly. Taste for salt and lemon.

3. Serve at room temperature as a salad or spread. Garnish with black olives and tomato wedges.

Makes about 3 cups

Meatless Chopped Liver

The traditional dish of chopped chicken livers, eggs, and onions, lubricated with savory chicken fat, is thought to have originated in the rich pâté culture of Alsace, but it was popular with Jews throughout Eastern Europe, served as an appetizer at festive meals and special occasions. A number of "mock" or meatless versions were created, made from vegetables such as green beans and mushrooms. When the dish traveled to Israel, it was reinvented once again, this time with the ubiquitous eggplant as the primary component, made unctuous with plenty of olive oil. It makes an excellent party spread.

About ¼ cup olive oil
2 large onions, coarsely
   chopped
1 large eggplant, peeled and
   diced
2 or 3 large cloves garlic,
   crushed

1 teaspoon salt
¼ teaspoon freshly ground
   black pepper
2 hard-boiled eggs

1. Heat the oil in a heavy skillet and sauté the onions over low to moderate heat, stirring occasionally, for about 20 minutes, or until the onions are a rich golden color.

2. Add the eggplant and garlic, mix well, then cook, stirring from time to time, until the mixture is soft and richly browned. Add a tablespoon or two more of oil if necessary.

3. Stir in the salt and pepper. Let the mixture cool slightly.

4. Turn the mixture out into a food processor, making sure to scrape up all the brown bits from the bottom of the pan. Process into a coarse purée.

5. In a bowl, chop the eggs finely. Add the eggplant purée and mix thoroughly. Taste for salt. Spoon the mixture into a serving bowl or mound on a plate. Serve at room temperature with bread or crackers.

Makes about 1½ cups

Lemony Leeks with Olives and Tomatoes

Both leeks and olives are ancient biblical foods that continue to this day to nourish the children of Israel. Combined with tomatoes, lemon juice, and a touch of hot pepper, they can be served warm, as a vegetable, or at room temperature as a salad or spread for fresh pita.

6 large leeks
3 to 4 tablespoons olive oil
2 medium tomatoes, coarsely chopped
¼ teaspoon crushed dried hot pepper

10 to 12 small oil-cured black olives
2 to 3 tablespoons fresh lemon juice
Salt to taste

1. Trim the leeks, discarding most of the green tops. Wash thoroughly, then slice crosswise in thin slices.

2. Heat the oil in a large skillet and sauté the leeks over low heat, stirring occasionally, until they are quite soft, 10 to 15 minutes.

3. Stir in the tomatoes and hot pepper and cook over moderate heat, stirring, until the tomatoes are soft and the mixture is thick.

4. Stir in the olives and lemon juice and mix well. Add salt to taste. Serve warm or at room temperature.

Makes about 2 cups

Chunky Mixed Salad

Cucumbers, peppers, and tomatoes are the basis for salads through-out the Middle East, and there are endless variations on the theme. Israelis frequently add a handful of fresh hot chiles or a spoonful of zhoug (see page 144) to spice up the mixture, and other vegetables—such as chickpeas, kidney beans, and green beans—can be added. The salad is good with almost anything, or served by itself with some fresh pita.

2 tomatoes, cut into ½-inch chunks

2 cucumbers, peeled (or not) and cut into ½-inch chunks

2 green and/or red bell peppers, seeded and cut into ½-inch chunks

1 bunch (5 to 6) scallions, coarsely chopped

Good handful of flat-leaf parsley leaves, coarsely chopped

Good handful of coriander leaves, coarsely chopped

3 tablespoons olive oil

3 tablespoons fresh lemon juice

1 large clove garlic, crushed

Plenty of freshly ground black pepper

Salt to taste (about 1 teaspoon)

1. In a large bowl, combine the tomatoes, cucumbers, bell pep-pers, scallions, parsley, and coriander.

2. In a small bowl or measuring cup, combine the olive oil, lemon juice, garlic, and pepper and whisk to blend thoroughly. Pour the dressing over the vegetables and mix well. Just before serving, mix again, then add salt to taste.

Serves 4 to 6

Spiced Hot Pepper Relish
(Zhoug)

This pungent relish came to the Israeli table with Yemenite Jews, whose cuisine incorporates much of the complex spicing and hot peppers of the Gulf states and parts of North Africa. Israelis use a different variety of fresh hot peppers; I have substituted jalapeños, which are widely available here. The relish is typically eaten as a dip with fresh pita, or as an enhancing additive to salads and soups.

8 cardamom pods
1 teaspoon cumin seeds
1 teaspoon coriander seeds
8 to 10 medium-to-large
    jalapeño peppers, seeded
1 large clove garlic
1 cup flat-leaf parsley leaves

1 cup coriander leaves
¼ teaspoon salt

1. In a small skillet, toast the cardamom, cumin, and coriander seeds over moderate heat, shaking the pan frequently, until the seeds are hot and aromatic. Do not brown. Let cool slightly, then grind in a spice mill.

2. In a food processor, combine the ground spices, jalapeños, and garlic. Process into a paste.

3. Add the parsley, coriander leaves, and salt and process into a coarse purée. Let stand at room temperature for a couple of hours before serving.

Makes about ½ cup

Double Orange Salad with Honey and Mint

Modern Israel has made the growing of oranges a major industry, and the well-loved fruit is used imaginatively in a variety of sweet and savory dishes. The flavor and visual appeal of this refreshing salad depend on the contrast between two types of orange—a sweet eating orange, like the navel, and the blood orange, with its vivid red color and intense flavor, long a favorite of Sicily and North Africa. The tart creaminess of yogurt makes a wonderful optional garnish, and if you like the tangy flavor, a sheep's-milk or goat's-milk yogurt would be an excellent choice.

3 to 4 navel oranges (or other sweet eating oranges)
3 to 4 blood oranges
3 tablespoons honey
1 tablespoon fresh lemon juice

2 to 3 tablespoons chopped fresh mint leaves
Plain yogurt, for serving (optional)

1. Peel the navel and blood oranges, carefully removing all the white pith.
2. With a sharp serrated knife, cut each orange crosswise into four or five slices. Arrange the slices, overlapping, in an attractive pattern on a serving plate.
3. Combine the honey and the lemon juice and mix well. Drizzle the mixture over the orange slices. Sprinkle the chopped mint over the plate.
4. Serve chilled or at room temperature, with yogurt to pass, if desired.

Serves 4 to 6

Sephardic Fruit and Nut Paste
(Haroseth)

The haroseth is one of the ritual foods of the Passover table, a sweet paste that symbolizes the mortar used by Jewish slaves to build the temples of the Egyptian pharaoh. Jewish communities all over the world developed their own versions of haroseth, based on locally available ingredients; the familiar European variety is made from apples, walnuts, and wine, while North African and Middle Eastern mixtures feature a different variety of fruits and nuts and tend to be more heavily spiced. Although the haroseth is prepared only for Passover, it makes a delicious confection, rolled into small balls or served as a garnish for ice cream or cake.

10 ounces pitted dates, coarsely chopped
6 blood oranges, peeled and coarsely chopped
½ cup freshly toasted almonds, finely chopped
1 cup dark raisins, coarsely chopped
½ teaspoon cinnamon
2 to 3 tablespoons cream sherry (the older and sweeter, the better)

Combine all the ingredients and mix thoroughly. Let stand, covered, in the refrigerator, several hours or overnight.

Makes about 5 cups

Rich Chocolate Macaroon Cake

Sweet and chewy macaroons, of Italian origin, were enthusiastically adopted by Jews as a valuable addition to the Passover table, because they contain none of the wheat flour that is ritually avoided in the commemoration of the exodus from Egypt. They contribute a dense texture and a delicious flavor to this flourless chocolate cake, further enhanced by the orange zest and candied orange peel so dear to the contemporary Israeli palate.

¼ pound (1 stick) unsalted
    butter
12 ounces bittersweet or
    semisweet chocolate
5 eggs, separated
½ cup sugar
10 ounces almond macaroons,
    processed into crumbs
    (about 2 cups crumbs)

1 teaspoon vanilla
2 teaspoons grated orange zest
½ teaspoon salt
½ cup heavy cream
2 to 3 tablespoons finely
    chopped almonds
Slivers of candied orange peel,
    for garnish (optional)

1. Place the butter and 8 ounces of the chocolate in a small, heavy saucepan and stir constantly over low heat until the mixture is melted and smooth. Remove from the heat and set aside.

2. In a mixing bowl, beat the egg yolks until frothy. Add the sugar and continue to beat until the mixture is thick and pale. Preheat the oven to 350°F.

3. With the mixer at low speed, add the chocolate mixture to the egg yolks and mix until well blended. Stir in the macaroon crumbs, vanilla, and orange zest and mix gently but thoroughly.

4. Beat the egg whites with the salt until they are stiff but not dry. Fold the beaten egg whites into the chocolate mixture.

5. Butter a 9-inch springform pan. Spoon the batter evenly into the pan. Bake for 35 to 40 minutes, until the cake is just firm to the touch and just beginning to crack on the top. Remove from the oven and let cool thoroughly.

6. When the cake is completely cooled, run a sharp knife around the edge and release the springform. Place the cake on a serving plate.

7. In a small saucepan, heat the cream just to the scalding point (small bubbles around the edge). Remove from the heat and stir in

the remaining 4 ounces of chocolate until melted and smooth. Let cool until the mixture is of spreading consistency.

8. Spread the chocolate over the top of the cake. Sprinkle the chopped almonds in a ring around the outer edge. Chill.

9. Serve the cake in small wedges, garnished with candied orange peel, if desired. Very good with vanilla ice cream.

Serves 10 to 12

Jewish Apple Cake

Dense and moist, crammed with sweet cinnamony fruit, this popular cake is thought to come from the rich tradition of baked goods of German or Alsatian Jews. The cake is a great favorite of family and friends, and the recipe has evolved over the years in my kitchen; I now make it with equal amounts of apples and pears, which give it an even richer flavor and moister texture.

3 Granny Smith apples, peeled, cored, and cut into small slices
3 Bartlett pears, ripe but firm, peeled, cored, and cut into small slices
1 tablespoon cinnamon
2¼ cups sugar
3 cups flour

1 teaspoon salt
1 tablespoon baking powder
1 cup vegetable oil
4 eggs
2 teaspoons vanilla
1 teaspoon almond extract
¼ cup apple cider or apple juice

1. In a large bowl, combine the apples, pears, and cinnamon and ¼ cup of the sugar. Mix well and set aside.

2. In a large mixing bowl, combine the flour, the remaining 2 cups sugar, the salt, and the baking powder. Mix thoroughly, then make a well in the middle of the mixture.

3. Pour the oil, eggs, vanilla extract, almond extract, and cider into the well, then mix the batter until it is well blended and smooth. The batter will be very stiff.

4. Preheat the oven to 375°F. Generously butter a deep 10-inch Bundt pan or angel food cake pan.

5. Spoon one third of the batter into the pan. Spoon half the fruit mixture over the batter; take care that the fruit does not touch the sides or inner ring of the pan. Spoon another third of the batter over the fruit. Spoon the remaining fruit over the batter, then spread the remaining batter over the fruit.

6. Bake for 65 to 75 minutes, until the cake is firm and nicely browned. Allow the cake to cool in the pan, then unmold onto a serving plate.

Serves 10 to 12

$\mathcal{E}$urope

We are inclined to conceptualize Europe as a single entity, because it has been for so long the center of political, economic, and cultural influence in the Western world. Yet for all that presumed uniformity, much of it quite real and profound, Europe is from a number of perspectives a place of extraordinary diversity, encompassing geographic areas, cultures, and traditions that are unique and distinctive.

The landscape of southern France is as remote and different from that of Scandinavia as the thickly wooded forests of central Europe are from the gentle downs of England or the rough, isolating hills of Portugal and Spain. And as the landscape and the climate vary, so do the people and the food. Many different kinds of people in many different places have formed the traditions of Europe, and when they came together at various times throughout the centuries, they produced fascinating new sets of culinary configurations. Perhaps because Europe's history is better known to many of us and the geographic features are so clearly defined in our minds, it is somewhat easier to delineate the differences and to see more readily when they merge.

In the south, along the Mediterranean, lie the warm, sunny lands that are the ancient domain of wine and olives, of wheat refined into flour for bread and pasta, of such robust seasonings as garlic, capers, and anchovies and a variety of pungent fresh herbs. This is the area that embraced most enthusiastically the New World tomato, turning it into a variety of vividly colored and richly flavored sauces that dress the food of southern Europe from Spain and Portugal in the west to Greece and Turkey in the east, and that reached a pinnacle of expression in the kitchens of southern Italy.

As we move north from the Mediterranean, the climate, the terrain, and the ingredients begin to shift, and the farther north we go, the more dramatic the change. Olive oil fades out, to be replaced by butter in the fertile central valleys and by lard and bacon fat, beef drippings and goose fat to the north and east. Wine gives way to beer, a liquid reflection of the shift in emphasis from wheat to such hardier grains as barley, oats, and rye and the production of dark whole-grain breads. The vegetable focus of the balmy south reverses to a preference for meat and dairy products, with beef, veal, and pork, and hundreds of fresh and cured cheeses taking a central place in the culinary repertoire. Hardy root and winter vegetables—potatoes, beets, cabbage, turnips—replace the tender greens and the eggplant, peppers, and squash of the nurturing southern climate.

In this movement from the south to the north, with its gradually shifting focus from plant foods to animal foods, there is a corresponding change in the seasoning practices: Strong, salient flavoring additives diminish in proportion to the dependence on meat, animal fats, and dairy products. The exuberant, mouth-filling flavors of the south—the garlic, the herbs, the seafood and salted fish, the savory tomato sauces—give way to subtler flavors, fewer spices, less-pungent herbs. The gustatory experiences we call flavor come more surely from the animal products themselves, the rich chewy meats, the fatty sausages and smoked hams, the savory meat stocks, the unctuous sweet butter, tart smooth sour cream, and rich cheeses, which themselves offer an extraordinary range of flavors, from subtle to strong, buttery to belligerent.

In addition to these clear demarcations of ingredients, shaped initially and profoundly by geographic and climatic factors, there is the ancient and ongoing human migration, the movements of people from one area to another. To the ancient inhabitants of Europe, those names that echo from our history books—Greeks and Romans, Angles and Saxons, Gauls and Franks, Germans and Celts—must be added influences from other, more faraway places: in the Iberian peninsula a heavy infusion from the Arab cultures of North Africa; in Eastern Europe an intense overlay of people and traditions from Turkey and the Middle East. And we can trace the route of those fierce nomadic marauders from central Asia, the Huns (who gave their name to Hungary), by following the "sauerkraut trail," an unlikely legacy from Asia to the West: a piece of human history made palpable in fermented cabbage!

In more recent times the reverse effects of European colonialism have become amply evident: curries in Great Britain, Indonesian rijsttafels in the Netherlands, Algerian couscous in France, and through all of Europe the many foods from the Americas that have become as entrenched and familiar as any that came before. Imagine Ireland without potatoes, Italy without tomatoes and polenta, Hungary without paprika, Spain without sweet peppers, Switzerland without chocolate, and you will have some idea of how dramatically European tables have been refashioned in the last five hundred years.

In some very real way, all of Europe is a crossroads, a continually unfolding saga of people, places, and food. But despite the seeming clutter of the centuries, there are distinct traditions and unique practices to observe, for people inevitably define themselves through their foodways, absorbing new influences and creating innovations in characteristic ways. And so we shall look at three different areas that have given rise to three very coherent cuisines—one in the Mediterranean, one in Eastern Europe, one in Western Europe—each with a distinctive profile that reflects its own particular history and the people who made it.

sicily

Anchored smack in the middle of the Mediterranean, just under the toe of Italy, the island of Sicily has been from the earliest times the focus of traditions from every direction, assimilating and refashioning the ingredients and the tastes of many different cultures. From Spain to the west came the anchovy, the tiny fish so perishable it is salted almost immediately after its catch and used as a pervasive and characteristic seasoning ingredient. The cuisines of North Africa contributed couscous, in Sicily prepared exclusively with fish and seafood, and a penchant for fragrant cinnamon in both sweet and savory dishes. Arab cultures provided a rich heritage of sweet concoctions, aromatic with lemon and orange, given flavor and substance with almonds. From Turkey and the eastern Mediterranean came a taste for raisins and currants, pine nuts, and mint, and a near-obsessive fascination with the eggplant, prepared in a variety of forms unparalleled anywhere else in Europe. And in the sixteenth century, from the brave New World across the Atlantic, the ruddy tomato made its triumphant conquest of the Italian palate, a fresh young upstart bringing new life and vigor to age-old traditions.

Central to these many different influences were the foods that had formed the backbone of this Mediterranean cuisine for unnumbered centuries—olives, green and ripe, spiced and cured, pressed for the oil that melds everything in its liquid gold embrace; robust garlic, pungent capers, sweet basil, and spicy oregano; a wealth of seafood, from tiny sardines, to succulent little clams, to the giant meaty tuna and swordfish; chewy rustic breads; and pasta in every size and shape, with a variety of textures to tease a thousand tongues.

The cuisine of Sicily has been evolving and transforming from ancient times to the present, yet it preserves its fundamental patterns. Arriving on these shores with nineteenth-century immigrants, and then again at the end of World War II with American GIs whose tastes were newly wakened to the pleasure of pizza and pasta, it underwent yet another metamorphosis, inevitable in a new land and a new era. Still, it continues to enchant not only those who claim it as their heritage, but also those many more of us who have adopted it as our own. Through all its modulations, its graceful acceptance of new ingredients and ideas, it has stubbornly retained its own character—robust, earthy, full of life, the satisfying food of family and of love.

RECIPES

Hearty Vegetable and Sausage Soup

Sardine and Olive Spread

Ragù of Swordfish with Tomatoes and Mint

Chicken with Eggplant in Tomato-Fennel Sauce

Braised Lamb with Rosemary, Olives, and
    Tomatoes

Eggplant and Anchovy Sauce for Pasta

Pasta with Olives, Garlic, and Hot Peppers

Layered Casserole of Eggplant and Pasta

Zucchini with Raisins and Pine Nuts

Baked "Stuffed" Tomatoes

Mixed Olive Salad

Ricotta Cheesecake with Macaroon Crust

Hearty Vegetable and Sausage Soup

Colorful, chunky, and filled with zesty flavor, this soup exemplifies the rustic, forthright goodness of southern Italian cooking. It is brimming with vegetables, bits of sausage, and pasta, so it can easily serve as a whole meal, along with some good crusty bread for dunking. Make the soup early in the day or even the day before, so that its deep, vibrant flavor can develop properly.

8 ounces Italian sausage, removed from casings
2 tablespoons olive oil
1 medium onion, finely chopped
1 red or green bell pepper, seeded and diced
2 carrots, sliced
2 stalks celery, thinly sliced
3 or 4 cloves garlic, minced
¼ teaspoon crushed dried hot pepper
½ teaspoon fennel seeds

2 cups canned Italian-style tomatoes, with juice, coarsely chopped
6 cups chicken stock
Several good grinds of black pepper
½ teaspoon crumbled dried oregano
⅓ cup orzo or semi di melone (seed-shaped pasta)
½ cup fresh or frozen peas
Freshly grated Romano or Parmesan cheese, for serving

1. Brown the sausage over moderate heat, crumbling the meat as it cooks. When the sausage is completely browned, remove from the pan with a slotted spoon and set aside.

2. Heat the oil in a large pot and sauté the onion, bell pepper, carrots, celery, garlic, hot pepper, and fennel seeds over moderate heat, stirring, until the onion wilts and just begins to turn golden.

3. Add the tomatoes, stock, black pepper, and oregano. Bring to a simmer, then cook, uncovered, over low heat for about 20 to 30 minutes.

4. Add the reserved sausage and the pasta, mix well, and cook for another 15 to 20 minutes, stirring frequently at the beginning to make sure the pasta doesn't stick to the bottom of the pot.

5. Stir in the peas for the last few minutes of cooking.

6. Serve the soup hot, and pass the grated cheese.

Serves 6 to 8

Sardine and Olive Spread

This intensely flavored mixture, compounded from a number of familiar Sicilian staples, is extremely versatile. It can be served at room temperature as a savory spread for good crusty bread, as a broiled topping for thick slices of fresh tomato, or as a sauce to toss with hot cooked pasta.

4 to 4½ ounces canned
    sardines, packed in
    olive oil
12 to 15 Sicilian green olives,
    pitted (about ½ cup)
4 to 5 cloves garlic
1 tablespoon fresh lemon juice

½ teaspoon crushed dried hot
    pepper
Small handful of fresh basil
    leaves
Small handful of flat-leaf
    parsley leaves
2 tablespoons olive oil

1. In a food processor, combine the sardines, with their oil, and the olives, garlic, lemon juice, and hot pepper. Purée into a coarse paste.

2. Add the basil and parsley and purée until fairly smooth.

3. Dribble in the olive oil slowly and blend thoroughly.

Makes about 1 cup

Ragù of Swordfish with Tomatoes and Mint

A simple rustic stew with exemplary flavor, this is equally good prepared with fresh tuna. The fundamental Sicilian base of olive oil, garlic, and tomatoes is here enhanced with pungent capers, the slight astringency of white wine, and the unexpected fresh flavor of mint. The mixture can be tossed with hot cooked pasta or served as a simple stew in shallow bowls with grilled slices of crusty bread.

3 to 4 tablespoons olive oil
1 large onion, thinly sliced
4 or 5 cloves garlic, finely
    chopped
8 to 10 plum tomatoes (about
    2 pounds), coarsely
    chopped
1 teaspoon salt
Plenty of freshly ground black
    pepper

Generous pinch of crushed
    dried hot pepper
½ cup dry white wine
1 tablespoon capers, drained
1 pound swordfish or tuna, cut
    into 1-inch chunks
¼ cup chopped fresh mint
    leaves

1. Heat the oil in a large skillet and sauté the onion and garlic over moderate heat until the onion wilts and the garlic just begins to turn golden.

2. Add the tomatoes, salt, black pepper, and hot pepper. Bring to a simmer, then cook over moderate heat, uncovered, stirring occasionally, until the mixture is soft and thick.

3. Stir in the wine and capers and simmer for about 5 minutes.

4. Add the fish and cook, stirring, just until the chunks are cooked through, about 5 minutes.

5. Stir in the mint and serve hot.

Serves 4

Chicken with Eggplant in Tomato-Fennel Sauce

Italians have long appreciated fennel, both as a flavoring ingredient and as a vegetable. It works well in this robust dish of chicken and eggplant in a zesty tomato sauce. Slow cooking makes the dark meat of chicken a better choice than white meat, and if you want a leaner dish, remove the skin of the chicken before browning.

4 to 5 tablespoons olive oil
1 medium-to-large eggplant, peeled and cut into ½-inch slices
Salt
Freshly ground black pepper
2 to 2½ pounds chicken thighs (skinless, if desired)
1 medium onion, coarsely chopped

3 or 4 cloves garlic, minced
½ teaspoon crushed dried hot pepper
1 medium red bell pepper, seeded and diced
2 cups canned crushed tomatoes
½ medium bulb fresh fennel, thinly sliced (about 1½ to 2 cups sliced)

1. Heat about 3 tablespoons of the oil in a large skillet and fry the eggplant slices over moderate to high heat, turning once to brown lightly on both sides. As the slices brown, remove them to a casserole or Pyrex baking dish. Salt and pepper lightly and set aside.

2. In the same skillet, heat 1 to 2 more tablespoons of the oil over moderate heat, then add the chicken and brown on both sides. As the chicken is browning, add the onion, garlic, hot pepper, and bell pepper and fry them in the oil. Sprinkle the chicken with about 1 teaspoon salt and some black pepper.

3. Add the tomatoes and fennel to the pan, mix well, then cover and cook over low heat for about 30 to 40 minutes. Preheat the oven to 350°F.

4. Lay the chicken pieces over the eggplant in the baking dish. Spoon all the sauce and vegetables from the pan over the chicken and eggplant. Bake for about 30 minutes, until the chicken is very tender and the sauce is thick. Serve with good bread and a green salad.

Serves 4 to 6

Braised Lamb with Rosemary, Olives, and Tomatoes

The warm, resiny tang of rosemary and the pungent saltiness of Sicilian green olives are a wonderful complement to succulent lamb, slow-cooked on the bone. This fragrant, earthy stew gets better as it ages, so make it early in the day or the day before. It is best served with a good crusty bread or a simple polenta.

2 tablespoons olive oil
2 to 2½ pounds meaty lamb
    stew on the bone, trimmed
    of excess fat
1 medium onion, coarsely
    chopped
4 cloves garlic, minced
½ teaspoon crushed dried hot
    pepper
½ teaspoon salt, or more to
    taste
Several good grinds of black
    pepper

1 tablespoon chopped fresh
    rosemary leaves, or
    1½ teaspoons dried
½ cup pitted green Sicilian
    olives, cut in half
2 cups canned crushed
    tomatoes
2 medium potatoes, cut into
    small cubes
Small handful of flat-leaf parsley
    leaves, finely chopped

1. Heat the oil in a large, heavy pot or deep skillet and brown the lamb slowly over moderate heat, turning the pieces to brown on all sides.

2. While the lamb is browning, add the onion, garlic, and hot pepper and sauté them in the oil. Sprinkle the lamb with the salt and pepper.

3. Add the rosemary, olives, and tomatoes and mix well. Cover and cook over low heat for 1½ to 2 hours, until the lamb is tender.

4. Add the potatoes, cover, and cook until the potatoes are tender. If the sauce becomes too thick while cooking, add a bit of water or dry white wine.

5. When the lamb and the potatoes are fully cooked, stir in the parsley. Taste for salt.

Serves 4

Eggplant and Anchovy Sauce for Pasta

A hallmark dish, this rich, full-bodied sauce pushes all the preferred flavor buttons of the Sicilian palate, with its robust mix of olive oil, garlic, anchovies, eggplant, and tomatoes. It needs no garnish of any kind, although it is sometimes served with a sprinkle of bread crumbs lightly browned in olive oil.

3 tablespoons olive oil
4 or 5 large cloves garlic, finely chopped
1 can (2 ounces) anchovies, packed in olive oil
½ teaspoon (or more to taste) crushed dried hot pepper
1 large eggplant, peeled and diced

1 can (28 ounces) crushed tomatoes
Several good grinds of black pepper
Good handful of flat-leaf parsley leaves, finely chopped
1 pound freshly cooked hot spaghetti or other pasta

1. Heat the oil in a large skillet and sauté the garlic over low to moderate heat, stirring, just until the garlic becomes very lightly browned and aromatic. Stir in the anchovies with their oil, mashing the anchovies with a fork or the back of the spoon. Stir in the hot pepper and cook, stirring, for a minute or two.

2. Add the diced eggplant and sauté, stirring, over moderate to high heat, just until the eggplant is becoming soft and lightly browned.

3. Add the tomatoes and black pepper, mix well, and cook over low heat, stirring occasionally, for about 15 minutes. Stir in the parsley.

4. Toss the hot drained pasta with the sauce and serve hot.

Serves 4

Pasta with Olives, Garlic, and Hot Pepper

Variations on the theme of garlic, olives, and tomatoes are seemingly endless—and endlessly delicious. The depth of flavor in this robust sauce comes not just from olive oil but from the olives themselves, as well as from the crushed dried hot peppers for which Sicilians have a special fondness. My choice for the pasta would be spaghetti or linguine, but almost any variety will serve.

2 to 3 tablespoons olive oil
4 or 5 large cloves garlic, finely chopped
½ to 1 teaspoon crushed dried hot pepper
1 can (28 ounces) crushed tomatoes
20 to 24 oil-cured black olives, pitted and coarsely chopped
Several good grinds of black pepper
⅓ cup finely chopped flat-leaf parsley leaves
Salt to taste (start with about ½ teaspoon)
1 pound freshly cooked hot pasta
Freshly grated Parmesan or Romano cheese, to pass

1. Heat the oil in a deep skillet or medium saucepan and sauté the garlic and hot pepper over low to moderate heat, stirring, just until the garlic softens and becomes aromatic.

2. Add the tomatoes, olives, and black pepper. Simmer over low heat, uncovered, for 15 to 20 minutes, stirring occasionally.

3. Stir in the parsley and add salt to taste.

4. Toss the hot drained pasta with the sauce. Pass grated cheese to add as desired.

Serves 4 to 6

Layered Casserole of Eggplant and Pasta

The baked casseroles of southern Italy—with their savory layers of pasta, vegetables, sauce, and cheese—have long been embraced as a beloved addition to the American scene. This recipe is but one further variation on the theme. As with all such preparations, there is a fair amount of work in cooking and assembling the components, but this can be done early in the day. Note that although the sausage adds rich flavor and texture, it can be omitted for a wholly meatless dish.

4 to 5 tablespoons olive oil
8 ounces fennel-flavored fresh Italian sausage, removed from casings
1 medium onion, coarsely chopped
3 or 4 cloves garlic, minced
1 medium green or sweet red pepper, seeded and diced
½ teaspoon crushed dried hot pepper
1 can (28 ounces) crushed tomatoes
1 teaspoon dried oregano

1 teaspoon dried basil
½ to 1 teaspoon salt
¼ teaspoon freshly ground black pepper
3 tablespoons grated pecorino Romano or Parmesan cheese
2 medium-to-large eggplants, peeled and cut into ½-inch slices
8 ounces small, short-cut pasta (cut fusilli, catanisella, gemelli, etc.)
8 ounces thinly sliced or shredded mozzarella

1. Heat about 2 tablespoons of the oil in a saucepan or deep skillet and brown the sausage over moderate heat, crumbling the sausage coarsely as it browns. While the sausage is browning, add the onion, garlic, and sweet and hot pepper and sauté.

2. When the sausage is browned and the onion soft, add the tomatoes, oregano, and basil, about ½ teaspoon of the salt, and the black pepper. Bring to the simmer, then cook, uncovered, over low heat, stirring occasionally, for 15 to 20 minutes. Remove from the heat, stir in the grated cheese, and taste for salt.

3. Brown the eggplant slices in the remaining 2 to 3 tablespoons olive oil over moderate to high heat, turning to brown on both sides.

As the slices brown, remove them from the pan, salt and pepper them lightly, and set aside.

4. Cook the pasta in boiling salted water for 8 to 10 minutes, until just tender but still firm. Drain. Preheat the oven to 350°F.

5. Mix the hot pasta with half the tomato sauce. Lightly oil a 2½- to 3-quart casserole or baking dish.

6. Spoon half the sauced pasta into the casserole. Top the pasta with half the eggplant slices. Spoon half the remaining sauce over the eggplant, then layer half the mozzarella over the sauce. Repeat with layers of the remaining pasta, eggplant, sauce, and cheese.

7. Bake the casserole for about 30 minutes, until bubbly.

Serves 4 to 6

Zucchini with Raisins and Pine Nuts

The use of raisins and pine nuts in lightly sweet-and-sour sauces probably came to Sicily from Turkey; these ingredients also turn up in the cooking of Venice, long a commercial gateway to Turkey and the East, but less commonly in the anchovy-and-tomato sauces that are so fundamental to the Sicilian kitchen. Note that the zucchini in this dish is cooked rather soft, in the traditional Italian manner; if you want a more contemporary crisp product, add the zucchini toward the end for a quick cooking in the thickened sauce.

2 to 3 tablespoons olive oil
3 large cloves garlic, very thinly sliced
4 small-to-medium zucchini, trimmed and cut into slices about ⅜ inch thick
2 medium tomatoes, coarsely chopped

1 teaspoon anchovy paste
2 tablespoons golden raisins
1 tablespoon red wine vinegar
Several good grinds of black pepper
1 tablespoon pine nuts, lightly toasted

1. Heat the oil in a medium skillet and sauté the garlic over moderate heat, stirring, just until the garlic begins to turn golden and becomes aromatic. Do not allow the garlic to overbrown.

2. Add the sliced zucchini and sauté for a few minutes, stirring.

3. Add the tomatoes, anchovy paste, raisins, and vinegar. Mix well, then cook over moderate heat, stirring occasionally, for about 10 to 12 minutes, until the sauce has thickened and most of the liquid has cooked away.

4. Stir in the black pepper and pine nuts. Serve warm or at room temperature.

Serves 4 to 6

Baked "Stuffed" Tomatoes

Highly seasoned bread crumbs are a common feature of Sicilian cooking, used as toppings for cooked vegetables and pasta. This is an extremely simple dish, but it is filled with all the rich flavor of the Mediterranean, and it's a wonderful way to enjoy the best tomatoes of the summer harvest.

4 to 5 medium tomatoes, fully ripe but firm (choose only high-quality tomatoes with good flavor)
¼ cup soft bread crumbs
2 tablespoons olive oil
2 teaspoons anchovy paste

1 tablespoon capers, drained
4 or 5 cloves garlic, crushed
Several good grinds of black pepper
3 to 4 tablespoons finely chopped flat-leaf parsley leaves

1. Cut the tomatoes into very thick slices (about 3 slices per tomato). Place the slices in a single layer in a lightly oiled shallow casserole or baking dish. Preheat the oven to 450°F.

2. In a small bowl, combine the bread crumbs with the oil, anchovy paste, capers, garlic, pepper, and parsley and mix thoroughly.

3. Sprinkle the bread crumb mixture evenly over the tomatoes.

Bake in a hot oven for 8 to 10 minutes, just until the crumb topping is lightly browned. Serve warm or at room temperature.

Serves 4

Mixed Olive Salad

This aromatic mixture is traditionally called a salad, but it is really more of a condiment or appetizer, best served as a savory tidbit with drinks or as part of an antipasto platter. Its special character comes from the tang of lemon, a flavor cherished by Sicilians in sweets, savories, and beverages. Let the flavors mellow for two or three days before serving, then store, covered, in the refrigerator.

8 ounces pitted Sicilian green olives
8 ounces brine-cured black olives
2 stalks celery, thinly sliced
1 red bell pepper, seeded and cut into small, thin slices
3 to 4 cloves garlic, thinly sliced
1 tablespoon capers, drained

1 tablespoon julienne strips lemon zest
½ teaspoon crushed dried hot pepper
½ teaspoon crumbled dried oregano
2 tablespoons red wine vinegar
¼ cup olive oil

Combine all the ingredients and mix thoroughly. Let stand, covered, at room temperature for two to three days, mixing occasionally. Cover and refrigerate to store, but let come to room temperature before serving.

Makes about 4 cups

Ricotta Cheesecake with Macaroon Crust

The word "macaroon," meaning a little cake, is related to "maca-roni," little pieces of dough, and both may derive from an ancient Greek term for pasta. Crumbled, the sweet, chewy, almond-flavored cakes make an unusual crust for this rich cheesecake, with a touch of orange and cinnamon that probably comes from the Arab cuisines of North Africa.

3 extra-large eggs
15 to 16 ounces ricotta
8 ounces cream cheese, at room temperature
1 cup sugar
1 teaspoon vanilla
2 teaspoons grated orange zest
½ teaspoon cinnamon
½ cup finely chopped bittersweet or semisweet chocolate, or mini-morsels

Butter for the pan
10 ounces almond-flavored macaroons, processed into crumbs (about 2 cups)
2 tablespoons pine nuts
Confectioners' sugar
Shaved chocolate curls and orange slices or segments, for garnish (optional)

1. In a food processor, combine the eggs, ricotta, cream cheese, and sugar (do this in several batches, if necessary). Purée until smooth.

2. Transfer the mixture into a bowl; stir in the vanilla, orange zest, cinnamon, and the ½ cup chocolate and mix thoroughly. Preheat the oven to 350°F.

3. Lightly butter the bottom and sides of a 9-inch springform pan. Press the macaroon crumbs evenly into the bottom of the pan. Sprinkle the pine nuts on top of the crumbs and press them lightly into the crumbs.

4. Pour the cheese filling over the crust. Bake for about 55 to 60 minutes, or until the cake is just firm in the center and very lightly browned. Let the cake cool thoroughly, then chill.

5. Run a sharp knife around the edge of the pan and release the springform. Place the cake on a serving plate. Sift a little confection-

ers' sugar over the top. Cut into small wedges and garnish each serving with a couple of chocolate curls and an orange slice or two on the side.

Serves 8 to 10

the balkans

It is no accident that many of the cuisines described in this book come from areas with a history of turmoil and strife, for crossroads are a natural focus for conflict. The Balkans are perhaps the most unfortunate example, a region split and ravaged by enmities as ancient as the hills from which the name derives: "balkan" is the Turkish word for mountain.

Many different people and worldviews have come into uneasy alliance in this triangular part of Eastern Europe. Muslims, Christians, Jews, Croats, Serbs, and Slavs have all left their mark, but the food has been most powerfully affected by three distinctive traditions—from the east, Turkey and the Middle East; from the south, the Mediterranean cuisines of Greece and Italy; from the west and north, the cuisines of central Europe. Like the people and the politics, the elements sometimes blend harmoniously, at others merely coexist, and occasionally jar.

This is the region where sour cream comes head-to-head with yogurt, where lard and butter vie for dominance with olive oil, where the eggplant and tomatoes of the south face off against the mushrooms, cabbage, and potatoes of the north, where the lamb and grilled kebabs of the Middle East butt up against the pig and the cured pork products so dear to middle Europe.

Of special interest in this multiethnic confluence is a variety of acidic flavors, nicely manipulated to produce a number of characteristic dishes. The Balkan palate resonates to the age-old tang of sauerkraut, used as both food and flavoring. From the ancient wine cultures of the Mediterranean comes the graceful flavor of wine and its sour offspring, vinegar. From Greece and Turkey, the tart citrusy flavor of lemon provides a distinctive note to both sweet and savory dishes. Add to these the mild, round acidic taste of tomatoes and the lactic acid tang of sour cream and yogurt. Ferment in the politics, fermentation in the food. Does the kitchen reflect the culture, or the culture the kitchen?

Also typical of the Balkans is a rich tradition of vegetable cookery, with a particularly intense focus on peppers, both sweet and hot. They are enjoyed roasted, fried, pickled, and dried, in salads, sauces, relishes, and savory spreads. Esteemed as well is a wide variety of fruits, dried, cooked in sweet syrups, and preserved in a number of excellent jams and conserves.

The food of the Balkans is as diverse as the people who produce it and the many traditions they comprise. It is both rustic and earthy, sophisticated and complex. The legacy of conflict is everywhere, yet it seems at times that coexistence and even collaboration can be achieved.

RECIPES

Hearty Vegetable Soup with Yogurt and Herbs

Mushroom Ciorba

Savory Herring Spread

Dalmatian Marinated Tuna

Walnut-Crusted Salmon with Vegetables

Chicken with Olives and Fennel

Pork Cutlets with Peppers, Wine, and Sour
    Cream

Mushroom-Spinach Roll with Caraway and Dill

Cornmeal-Stuffed Cabbage Braised with
    Sauerkraut

Red Pepper, Tomato, and Garlic Purée

Red Pepper Caviar with Cheese

Roasted Beet Salad with Yogurt and Dill
Summer Fruits in White-Wine Syrup
Chocolate Hazelnut Cake

Hearty Vegetable Soup with Yogurt and Herbs

An earthy peasant soup, chunky with vegetables and rice, and filled with the refreshing flavor of mixed green herbs and the tang of lemon juice and yogurt. The yogurt-egg mixture, commonly used throughout the Balkans as a baked golden topping for casseroles, serves in the liquid medium of a soup as an enriching, smoothing, and thickening agent.

2 tablespoons olive oil
1 medium onion, coarsely chopped
1 small red or green bell pepper, seeded and diced
1 large carrot, coarsely diced
1 small potato, peeled and diced
2 cups coarsely chopped cabbage
4 cups water
4 tablespoons tomato paste
1 teaspoon salt
¼ teaspoon freshly ground black pepper

2 tablespoons uncooked rice
2 tablespoons fresh lemon juice
3 to 4 tablespoons finely snipped fresh dill
3 to 4 tablespoons finely chopped flat-leaf parsley leaves
2 tablespoons finely chopped chives
1 egg
½ cup plain yogurt

1. Heat the oil in a medium, heavy pot and sauté the onion over moderate heat until the onion wilts and begins to turn golden.

2. Add the bell pepper, carrot, potato, and cabbage. Add the water, tomato paste, salt, and black pepper. Bring to a simmer, then cook, uncovered, over low heat for about 20 minutes.

3. Add the rice, mix well, and continue to cook for another 20 minutes. Stir the bottom of the pot occasionally to make sure the rice does not stick. When the rice is tender, stir in the lemon juice and the herbs.

4. In a small bowl, whisk the egg thoroughly, then add the yogurt and mix well. Add a little of the hot soup to the egg mixture, stirring constantly, then, with the pot off the heat, add the warm mixture to the soup, stirring constantly. Taste for salt.

Serves 6 to 8

Mushroom Ciorba

The ciorba is a Romanian specialty, a category of "sour" soups, made of meat, fish, or vegetables, that derive their characteristic tangy flavor from sauerkraut juice, as well as other acidic ingredients like wine, lemon, sour cream, and yogurt. This version combines the earthy flavor of fresh and dried mushrooms so typical of middle Europe with the egg-lemon addition from Greece. If you were brought up on the little red can of cream of mushroom soup, try this one for a refreshing change of pace!

½ ounce dried mushrooms
2 tablespoons butter
1 leek, mostly white part, thoroughly washed and finely chopped
1 medium onion, finely chopped
1 pound fresh mushrooms, coarsely chopped
2 cups beef broth (see Variation)

1 cup sauerkraut juice
Several good grinds of black pepper
1 egg
½ cup sour cream
1 tablespoon fresh lemon juice
2 to 3 tablespoons finely snipped fresh chives

1. Cover the dried mushrooms with about ⅓ cup warm water; let stand 30 minutes to 1 hour.
2. Heat the butter in a medium saucepan and sauté the leek and onion over moderate heat, just until the vegetables wilt.
3. Add the chopped fresh mushrooms and cook, stirring occasionally, until the mushrooms are soft and dark and most of the liquid has cooked away.
4. Add the beef broth, sauerkraut juice, and black pepper. Bring to a simmer and cook, uncovered, over low heat for about 15 to 20 minutes.
5. Drain the soaked mushrooms, reserving the liquid. Strain the liquid through cheesecloth to remove any grit; coarsely chop the mushrooms. Add the mushrooms and the strained liquid to the soup.
6. In a small bowl, whisk the egg, then stir in the sour cream and the lemon juice. Slowly add some of the hot soup to the egg mixture, whisking as you add it, until the egg mixture is warmed.

7. With the soup off the heat, add the warmed egg mixture to the pot, whisking as you add it. Blend thoroughly, then heat just to a simmer—do not boil. Taste for salt; you may need a bit at this point.

8. Serve the soup hot, sprinkled with the chives. Leftover soup can be reheated, but do not allow it to come to a boil.

Serves 4 to 6

VARIATION: A friend made the soup substituting vegetable stock for the beef broth and reported that it worked very well.

Savory Herring Spread

In addition to the many vegetable spreads that abound in Balkan cuisines, there are an assortment of fish and fish-roe salads and spreads, built on the model of the Greek taramosalata, a rich mixture of carp or other red fish roe, moistened bread, and olive oil. This recipe features the popular Eastern European pickled herring in a similar preparation. It's a good choice for a brunch or party buffet.

1 cup soft bread crumbs
½ cup milk
8 ounces pickled herring, drained, in small chunks
1 small onion, coarsely chopped
2 tablespoons fresh lemon juice
3 to 4 tablespoons olive oil

¼ teaspoon freshly ground black pepper
1 tablespoon capers, drained
Chopped parsley or dill sprigs, tomato wedges, cucumber slices, black olives, and red onion rings, for garnish

1. In a medium bowl, combine the bread crumbs and milk and mix well.

2. In a food processor, combine the herring, onion, and lemon juice and process into a paste.

3. Mix the herring paste into the bread crumbs, then vigorously beat the olive oil into the mixture. Stir in the pepper and capers.

4. To serve, mound the herring spread onto a serving dish. Garnish with a bit of parsley or dill, and surround with the tomato wedges, cucumber slices, olives, and onion rings. Serve with crackers or thinly sliced black bread.

Makes 2 cups

Dalmatian Marinated Tuna

From the Dalmatian coast of the Adriatic comes this traditional dish of tuna, its meaty texture and flavor enhanced with a savory astringent marinade. The preparation is similar to certain Turkish dishes, except that the touch of sweetness has disappeared and the addition of wine and mustard seeds shifts the flavor to a more European mode. The tuna should be marinated overnight and served cold in small portions as an appetizer.

2 tablespoons olive oil
1 to 1¼ pounds fresh tuna
    steaks, 1 inch thick
1 large onion, cut in half and
    thinly sliced
2 carrots, thinly sliced
1 teaspoon mustard seeds
1 cup dry white wine

¼ cup white wine vinegar
1 large bay leaf
½ teaspoon salt
¼ teaspoon freshly ground
    black pepper
1 small lemon, thinly sliced
Chopped parsley, for garnish

1. Heat the oil in a heavy skillet over moderately high heat. Sear the tuna steaks, about 2 minutes on each side, so that the outsides are nicely browned and the inside is just slightly rare. Remove the steaks from the pan with a slotted spoon and place in a glass or ceramic dish.

2. Add the onion and carrots to the oil in the pan and sauté over moderate heat, stirring, until the onion wilts and becomes translucent. Stir in the mustard seeds and cook for a few minutes more.

3. Add the wine, vinegar, bay leaf, salt, and pepper and bring to a simmer. Cook, stirring, for about 5 minutes. Add the lemon slices to the sauce.

4. Pour the sauce over the tuna, then cover and refrigerate 6 to 8 hours or overnight. Turn the steaks in the marinade once or twice.

5. Cut the tuna into thin slices and layer the slices onto some torn greens. Remove the bay leaf and as many of the mustard seeds as possible from the marinade, then spoon the marinade over the tuna slices. Garnish with some chopped parsley.

Serves 4 to 6 as an appetizer

Walnut-Crusted Salmon with Vegetables

The subtle flavor of this Bulgarian dish comes from some surprising elements: The vegetable mixture, so typical of the Middle East, is cooked with wine, a distinctly European addition, while the walnut topping almost certainly originates in Turkish tradition. Other fish can be substituted, but salmon works particularly well.

4 to 5 tablespoons olive oil
1 pound salmon fillets or small
   salmon steaks, about ½
   inch thick
Salt
Freshly ground black pepper
1 medium onion, coarsely
   chopped
2 or 3 cloves garlic, crushed
1 medium eggplant, peeled and
   diced
1 large green or red bell
   pepper, seeded and diced

1 medium zucchini, diced
1 large tomato, coarsely
   chopped
½ cup dry white wine
Good squeeze of lemon juice
¼ cup finely chopped walnuts
2 tablespoons soft bread
   crumbs
½ teaspoon paprika (preferably
   Hungarian sweet)
2 tablespoons butter, melted

1. Heat 2 tablespoons of the oil in a skillet over high heat. Add the fish and brown quickly, turning once to brown on both sides.

Note that the fish should not be cooked through, just browned on both sides. Salt and pepper the fish lightly, then remove from the pan and set aside.

2. Add the remaining 2 to 3 tablespoons oil to the pan. Add the onion and garlic and sauté over moderate heat just until the onion wilts.

3. Add the eggplant and sauté for a few minutes.

4. Add the bell pepper, zucchini, tomato, wine, about 1 teaspoon of salt, and several good grinds of black pepper. Mix well, bring to a simmer, then cook, uncovered, over moderate heat, stirring occasionally, for about 20 minutes, until the vegetables are soft and most of the liquid has cooked away. Stir in the lemon juice. Preheat the oven to 400°F.

5. Spoon the vegetable mixture evenly into a shallow casserole or baking dish. Place the reserved fish in a single layer over the vegetables.

6. Combine the walnuts, bread crumbs, paprika, and butter and about ¼ teaspoon salt. Mix well, then sprinkle the mixture over the fish and vegetables.

7. Bake for 15 to 20 minutes, until the topping is browned and the fish flakes easily when forked.

Serves 4

Chicken with Olives and Fennel

Compare this recipe with the Sicilian Chicken on page 159. Although many of the ingredients are the same, the effect of this Romanian dish is very different: The intensity of the tomatoes has been diminished, while the white wine and the sour cream add richness, subtle flavor, and interesting acidic notes. In a nod to both central Europe and the Mediterranean, you can serve the chicken with noodles, rice, or polenta.

2 tablespoons olive oil
2 to 2½ pounds chicken
    parts (breast quarters,
    thighs, etc.)
Salt
Freshly ground black pepper
1 medium onion, finely
    chopped
3 or 4 cloves garlic, minced

1 small bulb fresh fennel,
    finely chopped (reserve
    feathery green fronds for
    garnish)
½ cup kalamata olives
1 cup dry white wine
2 tablespoons tomato paste
½ cup sour cream

1. Heat the oil in a heavy skillet and brown the chicken parts over moderate heat, turning once to brown on both sides. Salt and pepper the chicken lightly, remove from the pan, and set aside.

2. Add the onion to the pan and sauté until the onion begins to turn golden.

3. Stir in the garlic and fennel and cook for another 5 minutes or so, stirring occasionally. Add ½ teaspoon salt, several grinds of pepper, and the olives, wine, and tomato paste. Mix well.

4. Return the chicken (with juices) to the pan, bring to a simmer, then cover and cook over low heat for 40 to 50 minutes, or until the chicken is very tender.

5. Remove the chicken from the pan and place on a warm serving plate. Rapidly reduce the sauce until it is quite thick. Turn the heat low and stir in the sour cream until it is blended and hot. Taste for salt.

6. Pour the sauce over the chicken. Coarsely chop the reserved fennel fronds and sprinkle them over the top.

Serves 4

Pork Cutlets with Peppers, Wine, and Sour Cream

In this richly sauced pork dish from Bulgaria, influences from central Europe, and especially from Hungary, are evident in the mushrooms, paprika, and sour cream. The red wine, tomato paste, and sour cream blend to make a sauce that has depth and roundness but with ever-present acidic highlights. Almost any fresh mushroom can be used in the dish, but I have found that shiitakes, which are not traditional, are particularly good.

1 pound lean pork tenders or cutlets, cut or pounded ¼ inch thick
Flour for dredging
2 to 3 tablespoons olive oil, more if needed for vegetables
Salt
Freshly ground black pepper
1 medium onion, coarsely chopped
1 medium red bell pepper, seeded and diced

2 cloves garlic, minced
1 teaspoon Hungarian sweet (rose) paprika
½ teaspoon Hungarian hot paprika or crushed dried hot pepper
8 ounces fresh sliced mushrooms
½ cup dry red wine
2 tablespoons tomato paste
3 to 4 tablespoons sour cream

1. Dredge the pork tenders lightly in flour. Heat the oil in a heavy skillet over moderate to high heat. Fry the tenders, turning once, until just nicely browned on both sides. Salt and pepper the pork, remove from the pan, and set aside.

2. To the oil remaining in the pan (add a tablespoon or so more if necessary), add the onion, bell pepper, and garlic. Sauté over moderate heat, stirring, until the onion wilts. Stir in the sweet paprika, hot paprika, and mushrooms and sauté a few minutes more.

3. Add ¼ teaspoon salt, several grinds of the black pepper, the wine, and the tomato paste. Cook over moderate heat, stirring occasionally, until the sauce is fairly thick and most of the liquid has cooked away.

4. Lower the heat to low, stir in the sour cream, and mix until smooth. Taste for salt and hotness; the sauce should have a slight but not overwhelming pungency. Bring to a simmer, then pour over the warm cutlets—or place the cutlets in the pan to warm, and coat them in the sauce. Serve the cutlets with steamed new potatoes or buttered noodles.

Serves 4

Mushroom-Spinach Roll with Caraway and Dill

Rolls or "pies" wrapped or layered in multiple sheets of fine, fragile pastry are known throughout the Balkans as strudel, pita, or borek, and were introduced into Eastern Europe from Turkey. The filling for this savory roll—with its rich mix of mushrooms, sour cream, caraway, and dill—is typical of middle Europe. If you wish, the vegetable mixture can be used on its own as a side dish, with the addition of some extra sour cream—spoon it into a shallow buttered baking dish, top with some buttered bread crumbs, and bake at 350°F until hot.

2 to 3 tablespoons olive oil
1 medium onion, finely
    chopped
2 cloves garlic, minced
1 pound mushrooms, coarsely
    chopped
1 teaspoon salt
¼ teaspoon freshly ground
    black pepper
½ teaspoon caraway seeds

1 box (10 ounces) frozen
    chopped spinach, defrosted
¼ cup sour cream
2 to 3 tablespoons finely
    snipped fresh dill
2 to 3 tablespoons finely
    chopped parsley leaves
6 large sheets (11 x 14 inches)
    phyllo pastry sheets
About ½ stick butter, melted

1. Heat the oil in a skillet and sauté the onion and garlic just until the onion wilts.

2. Add the mushrooms and cook over moderate heat, stirring occasionally, until the mushrooms are soft and dark and all the liquid has cooked away. Stir in the salt, pepper, and caraway seeds.

3. Squeeze out as much water as possible from the defrosted spinach. Add the spinach to the mushrooms, then add the sour cream, mix thoroughly, and cook, stirring, until the mixture is hot and well blended. Stir in the dill and parsley. Remove from the heat and taste for salt. Preheat the oven to 375°F.

4. Keep the phyllo sheets lightly covered with a damp cloth while working. Remove one sheet at a time and place it, long side across, in front of you. Brush it lightly but completely with melted butter. Place another sheet on top of the first and brush it with butter. Repeat, using all six sheets of dough.

5. Spoon the filling in the center of the pastry sheets, to within 1 inch of the short sides and 2 inches of the long sides. Fold the long side closest to you up over the filling, then brush that surface completely with melted butter. Fold the short sides in, then brush them with butter. Fold the other long side over the filling and brush with butter. Make sure that all exposed surfaces of the pastry are brushed with butter.

6. Place the rolled pastry, seam side down, on a baking sheet. Brush the top surface completely with butter. Bake the roll for 35 to 45 minutes, until it is golden brown and crisp. Let stand for 5 to 10 minutes before cutting into slices to serve.

Serves 4 to 6

Cornmeal-Stuffed Cabbage Braised with Sauerkraut

I never met a stuffed cabbage I didn't like, and this eccentric Romanian version is a personal favorite. Instead of the more familiar rice or minced-meat fillings of the Middle East and Eastern Europe, this uses an inexpensive popular staple, mamaliga (cornmeal mush), flavored with caramelized onions and enriched with cheese. The sauerkraut and tomato sauce provide an unusual acidic tang that might be more typically delivered by lemon juice or vinegar. Garnished with sour cream, this stuffed cabbage makes a delicious and satisfying meatless meal.

10 to 12 whole cabbage leaves
4 to 5 tablespoons olive oil
2 medium onions, coarsely
    chopped
2½ cups water
1½ teaspoons salt
1 cup yellow stone-ground
    cornmeal
8 ounces farmer cheese
¼ teaspoon freshly ground
    black pepper

1 large onion, thinly sliced
3 or 4 large cloves garlic,
    minced
2 cups sauerkraut, drained
1 cup tomato juice
3 to 4 tablespoons finely
    snipped fresh dill
Sour cream, for serving

1. Trim the tough stem ends of the cabbage leaves, then cook the leaves in boiling water for 5 minutes. Drain the leaves and set aside.

2. Heat 2 tablespoons of the oil in a medium, heavy saucepan and sauté the chopped onion, stirring occasionally, until the onions are a rich golden brown. This will take at least 15 to 20 minutes.

3. Add the water and salt to the pot and bring to a boil. Slowly add the cornmeal to the boiling water, stirring or whisking constantly as you add it. When all the cornmeal has been added, continue to cook, stirring, for a few more minutes. The mush should be fairly thick. Remove from the heat and stir in the cheese and pepper. Set aside to cool.

4. Heat 2 more tablespoons of the oil in a heavy pot or Dutch oven and sauté the sliced onion and garlic over moderate heat, stirring, just until the onion wilts.

5. Add the sauerkraut, tomato juice, and dill and mix well. Remove from the heat while you make the cabbage rolls.

6. Place a large spoonful of the cornmeal mixture on the middle of a cabbage leaf. Fold up the edges of the leaf to form an envelope and fasten with a wooden toothpick. Continue until all the leaves and the filling have been used.

7. Place the stuffed cabbage rolls over the sauerkraut sauce. Drizzle a little olive oil over the rolls. Bring to a simmer, then cover and cook over low heat for about 1½ hours. Turn the rolls carefully in the sauce once or twice while cooking. If too much liquid evaporates during cooking, add a little more tomato juice.

8. Serve the cabbage rolls and sauce hot, with sour cream. Remind diners to remove the toothpicks before eating.

Serves 4 to 6

Red Pepper, Tomato, and Garlic Purée (Ajvar)

This brilliant red spread, as flavorful as it is colorful, is a prime example of the Balkan devotion to peppers in a wide variety of forms—sweet and hot, pickled and raw, in salads, relishes, sauces, and spreads. A similar pepper "jam" is made in Hungary from simple boiled peppers; this Bulgarian version intensifies the flavor and color with tomatoes, garlic, and olive oil. It is an extremely versatile product; use it by itself as a dip or spread for crackers, bread, or raw vegetables; as a spread for sandwiches or cold meats (it's particularly good with cold sliced beef); or as a flavor enhancement for soups or sauces.

About ⅓ cup olive oil
5 or 6 large cloves garlic, sliced
4 large fleshy red bell peppers, seeded and coarsely chopped
2 to 3 small fresh hot red chiles, seeded and chopped, or ½ to 1 teaspoon crushed dried hot pepper (optional but good)

2 large, very ripe tomatoes, coarsely chopped
1 teaspoon salt
Plenty of freshly ground black pepper

1. Heat about ¼ cup of the oil in a large skillet and sauté the garlic over moderate heat, stirring, until it just begins to turn golden and becomes aromatic. Do not allow the garlic to burn.

2. Add the bell peppers, the hot peppers, if using, and the tomatoes and cook over moderate heat, stirring occasionally, for about 30 to 40 minutes, until the vegetables are very soft and all the liquid has cooked away. Continue to cook, stirring, for another 5 to 10 minutes, until the mixture is very thick. Remove from the heat and let cool a bit.

3. Purée the mixture in a food processor with an additional 2 tablespoons or so of oil. There is no need to purée until absolutely smooth; a little texture is nice. Stir in the salt and black pepper and mix well. Taste for salt.

Makes about 2 cups

TIP: The ajvar stores well, covered, in the refrigerator. To keep it longer than a week or two, store it in a glass jar; smooth the top of the purée, then cover it with a thin layer of olive oil, cover, and refrigerate.

Red Pepper Caviar with Cheese

A characteristic feature of Balkan cookery is a wide variety of highly seasoned mixtures to spread on bread. Very popular are the vegetable "caviars" made of eggplant or mushrooms or peppers, richly flavored with garlic, spices, and herbs and at times enriched with dairy products such as cheese and sour cream. This is an excellent do-ahead party dish; for an attractive presentation, line a 1-quart mold or bowl with plastic wrap, then pack in the caviar and chill. Unmold onto a serving plate, remove the plastic wrap, and garnish the caviar with black olives, sprigs of dill, and red pepper rings.

¼ cup olive oil
1 large onion, finely chopped
4 medium red bell peppers, seeded and finely chopped
4 large cloves garlic, minced
1 teaspoon crushed dried hot pepper
1 teaspoon caraway seeds
1 tablespoon Hungarian sweet (rose) paprika
½ teaspoon salt
¼ teaspoon freshly ground black pepper

3 to 4 tablespoons finely snipped fresh dill
3 to 4 tablespoons finely chopped flat-leaf parsley leaves
8 ounces farmer cheese
6 to 8 ounces feta cheese
2 tablespoons sour cream
Black olives, cucumber slices, sprigs of dill, red pepper rings, for garnish, if desired

1. Heat the oil in a heavy skillet and cook the onion and bell pepper over low to moderate heat, stirring occasionally, for 30 to 40 minutes, until the vegetables are very soft and the onions are richly browned.

2. Add the garlic, hot pepper, caraway, paprika, salt, and black pepper and cook, stirring, for a few minutes more.

3. Add the dill and parsley, mix well, and remove from the heat.

4. In a bowl, mash the farmer cheese, then finely crumble the feta and mix it thoroughly into the farmer cheese. Add the reserved vegetable mixture and mix well. Stir in the sour cream and blend thoroughly.

5. Chill the mixture as is, or pack it firmly into a mold lined with plastic wrap. Chill, then unmold and garnish. Serve with crisp flat bread, crackers, or a variety of thinly sliced dark and light breads.

Makes about 3 cups

Roasted Beet Salad with Yogurt and Dill

The yogurt-based salad and relish tradition of India and the Middle East makes a colorful alliance here with the Eastern European beet in a tangy and attractively pink salad. In traditional practice, the beets would be boiled, but I think that roasting produces a better flavor; you can, if you wish, substitute canned beets as a convenient shortcut.

4 to 5 medium beets
½ cup plain yogurt
Good squeeze of fresh lemon
    juice
1 clove garlic, crushed
¼ teaspoon salt
¼ teaspoon sugar

Several good grinds of black
    pepper
2 to 3 tablespoons finely
    snipped fresh dill
Additional sprigs or chopped
    dill, for garnish

1. Wash the beets, then trim the stems close to the top of the beets. Place the beets in a baking pan and roast in a 400°F oven for 50 to 60 minutes, or until the flesh is easily pierced with a sharp knife.

2. Let the beets cool, then peel and dice.

3. Mix the yogurt, lemon juice, garlic, salt, sugar, and pepper into the beets, then stir in the chopped dill. Chill the mixture thoroughly. Garnish the salad with a bit of additional dill.

Serves 4

Summer Fruits in White-Wine Syrup

The sweet sugar syrups of the Middle East get an added dimension of flavor from wine in this dish, one that is commonly prepared throughout the Balkans. It is very easy to make and produces a simple but delicious dessert that captures the best of firm summer fruits. A handful of walnut halves can be added to the mixture, if desired.

1 cup dry white wine
½ cup sugar
1 cinnamon stick
1 tablespoon fresh lemon juice
6 nectarines, pitted and thickly sliced
6 red or black plums, or a mixture of both, pitted and thickly sliced

1 cup cherries, halved and pitted
Handful of walnut halves (optional)

1. In a large skillet, combine the wine, sugar, cinnamon stick, and lemon juice. Bring to a simmer, then cook over moderate heat, stirring occasionally, for 7 to 10 minutes.
2. Add the nectarines, plums, and cherries, and the nuts, if using, and turn gently in the syrup. Bring to a simmer, then cook for just a minute or two.
3. Let the mixture cool, then chill before serving.

Serves 6 to 8

Chocolate Hazelnut Cake

Chocolate, one of the most unusual foods indigenous to the Americas, had its most profound impact on Western Europe, where it joined an elaborate tradition of pastries, cakes, and confections. The Balkans are the site of chocolate's last stand in Europe, for beyond them to the east its use diminishes sharply. Balkan chocolate cookery reflects both the egg-and-dairy-rich products of Western Europe and the highly sweetened nut pastes more typical of Turkey and the Middle East. They come together in this high, handsome Yugoslavian cake.

CHOCOLATE LAYERS

Butter for greasing pans
10 eggs
1 cup sugar
8 ounces bittersweet or
     semisweet chocolate
¼ cup coffee
⅔ cup flour

HAZELNUT FILLING

½ stick (4 tablespoons) unsalted
     butter, at room temperature
½ cup sugar
1 cup freshly toasted, very finely
     chopped hazelnuts
2 tablespoons hazelnut liqueur
     (Frangelico)
1 to 2 tablespoons milk or light
     cream

FROSTING

½ stick (4 tablespoons)
     unsalted butter
3 tablespoons milk or light
     cream
6 ounces bittersweet or
     semisweet chocolate
½ teaspoon vanilla

To make the layers:

1. Butter two 9-inch round springform pans. Line the bottoms of the pans with waxed paper or aluminum foil, then butter the paper or foil.

2. Beat the eggs until light and frothy. Gradually add the sugar and continue to beat until the mixture is quite thick and pale.

3. In a small saucepan, melt the chocolate with the coffee until it is smooth and well blended. Let cool slightly. Preheat the oven to 350°F.

4. Stir the cooled chocolate mixture into the egg mixture until well blended. Sift the flour into the mixture and mix until it is completely blended in.

5. Divide the batter equally between the two pans and smooth into even layers. Bake for 40 to 45 minutes. Let cool completely in the pans.

To make the filling:

6. Cream the butter and sugar together until light and smooth. Reserve 2 tablespoons of the chopped nuts, then add the rest to the butter mixture and mix well. Stir in the hazelnut liqueur and enough milk or cream to make the mixture a good spreading consistency.

To make the frosting:

7. In a small saucepan, combine the butter and milk. Heat until the butter is melted and the mixture is just at the scald. Remove from the heat and stir in the chocolate until it is smooth and well blended. Stir in the vanilla.

To assemble the cake:

Remove the cooled cakes from the pans. Place one layer, smooth side up, on a serving plate. Carefully peel off the waxed paper or foil. Spread the hazelnut filling over the layer. Peel the paper or foil off the second layer. Place the second layer, smooth side down, over the filling. Spread the frosting over the top and sides of the cake. Sprinkle the reserved chopped nuts around the outer edge of the cake.

Serves 10 to 12

alsace

If there is any place in the world that eloquently illustrates the power of food to transcend borders and ethnicities, that place is Alsace. Lying on the fertile northeast edge of France, across the Rhine River from Germany, it has been for untold centuries the gustatory confluence of French and German cooking, a unique amalgam of two very different traditions.

Is there another cuisine that pays such dedicated and graceful homage to meat and animal fat? Both Gauls and Teutons participate in an ardent celebration of pork in a multitude of forms—fresh, cured, spiced, smoked. From Germany comes a long tradition of sausages, from France a rich repertoire of pâtés, and from both a sure hand with bacon and ham. This wealth of charcuterie is enriched by a superb dairy tradition—creamy butter, thick cream, and a host of fine cheeses. And if this were not richness enough, throw in for good measure the fine fat liver of the famed Strasbourg goose!

Although essentially French in style, the influence of German products is clear. Alsace is the westernmost end of the sauerkraut trail in Europe, and sauerkraut is of significance here and nowhere else in France. Also favored are such characteristic German foods as noodles and dumplings, a variety of whole-grain breads, and an old tradition of buttery cakes and yeast-raised sweet breads.

But Alsatian cooking is more than the simple merging of French and German; it brings its own distinctive elements to the creative mix. Excellent wines are produced, with the Riesling the most admired variety. A fine assortment of cultivated fruits are appreciated in cakes, tarts, preserves, and a number of fruit liqueurs and eaux de vie, including kirschwasser, the potent firewater distilled from cherries.

One curious element is the eccentric taste for sweet-and-sour, exhibited nowhere else in France. It may derive from the German penchant for vinegary sauces, softened and sweetened by local fruits and wines. It finds expression in tart-sweet condiments and sauces for meat and fish dishes. It is said that the Jewish taste for sweet-and-sour developed in Alsace, although, interestingly, carp with sweet-and-sour sauce is called in Alsace "carp in the Jewish style." And so the crossroads intersect, leading who knows where!

The success of Alsatian cooking is the refining and softening of hearty, substantial German fare by the exquisite palate and technical expertise of French tradition. It is a merger that defies expectation and validates the power of food to give us pleasure and value—a triumph of the pig over politics.

RECIPES

Onion Soup with Beer

Savory Lentil Soup with Knockwurst

Braised Sweet-and-Sour Beef

Calf's Liver with Apples, Onions, and Riesling

Sauerkraut with Mixed Sausages

Smoked Pork with Vegetables in Wine Sauce

Bacon, Mushroom, and Muenster Tart

Potatoes with Cream and Cheese

Warm Cabbage and Bacon Salad

Sweet-and-Sour Huckleberry Sauce

Plum Tart with Almonds

Fresh Raspberry Cream

Onion Soup with Beer

Onion soup is a classic dish beloved throughout France, based on such French fundamentals as well-made, fully flavored stock, high-quality cheese, and onions slowly browned in butter. This Alsatian version offers some interesting variations: The flavor of the beer makes an intriguing foil to the richness of the caramelized onions, and a chewy light rye bread makes a refreshing change from the more typical baguette.

2 tablespoons unsalted butter
4 large onions, thinly sliced
4 cups beef broth
1 cup beer (a crisp light variety is best)
¼ teaspoon freshly ground black pepper
2 to 3 slices chewy light Jewish-style rye bread, cut into quarters, or 6 to 8 slices (½ inch thick) baguette or other French bread

Butter, at room temperature
4 ounces shredded or thinly sliced Gruyère or Emmentaler cheese

1. Heat the 2 tablespoons butter in a heavy saucepan and sauté the onions over low heat, stirring occasionally, for 30 to 40 minutes, until the onions are very soft and richly browned.

2. Add the broth, beer, and pepper. Bring to a simmer, then cook, uncovered, over low heat for 15 to 20 minutes.

3. Spread the bread slices lightly on both sides with softened butter, then toast in a 400°F oven for 10 minutes or so, until browned and crisp.

4. Spoon the hot broth and onions into ovenproof bowls or soup ramekins. Place a slice of toasted bread (two if small) on each serving. Top the bread with a handful of shredded cheese.

5. Place the bowls under the broiler for a few seconds, until the cheese is melted and bubbly. Serve immediately.

Serves 4 to 6

Savory Lentil Soup with Knockwurst

The mainstream American palate was heavily influenced by many foods brought here by German immigrants, a taste eloquently manifested by our apparently unquenchable lust for hot dogs, hamburgers, potato salad, and such old familiar favorites as lentil soup with frankfurters. This Alsatian version of the soup is somewhat gentler than the German original, softened and enriched with chicken stock and a buttery mirepoix of onions, leeks, celery, and carrots. You can, of course, choose to omit the knockwurst, but don't serve it to an Alsatian if you do!

2 tablespoons unsalted butter
1 medium onion, finely chopped
1 large leek, mostly white part, thoroughly washed and finely chopped
2 carrots, coarsely diced
1 large stalk celery, with leaves, thinly sliced
1 cup lentils

6 cups chicken broth
¼ teaspoon freshly ground black pepper
⅛ teaspoon nutmeg
2 good-quality knockwurst (about 6 ounces), thickly sliced
Small handful finely chopped parsley leaves

1. Heat the butter in a heavy pot and sauté the onion, leek, carrots, and celery over moderate heat, stirring occasionally, until the onion and leek are soft and just beginning to turn golden.

2. Wash the lentils and drain. Add the lentils to the pot, along with the broth, pepper, and nutmeg. Bring to a simmer, then cook, uncovered, over low heat for about 45 minutes, or until the lentils are very tender.

3. Add the sliced knockwurst and cook for another 10 to 15 minutes. Stir in the chopped parsley and taste for salt. Serve hot.

Serves 6 to 8

TIP: Like most other dried pea and bean soups, this will thicken considerably on standing. It can be thinned with water or additional broth; then taste, and adjust the seasoning if necessary.

Braised Sweet-and-Sour Beef

This rich marinated beef, another example of the Alsatian taste for sweet-and-sour, is much mellower than the German sauerbraten from which it undoubtedly derives, with herbs and a soft pinot noir substituting for the spices and tangy vinegar of the original. For proper flavor, the meat should be marinated for three to seven days. Serve it in thin slices with buttered noodles or steamed new potatoes.

2 tablespoons vegetable oil
1 large onion, finely chopped
2 carrots, diced
2 cups pinot noir
2 tablespoons red wine vinegar
1 tablespoon sugar
1 teaspoon salt
¼ teaspoon freshly ground
    black pepper

2 bay leaves
1 teaspoon dried thyme
2 to 2½ pounds boneless
    bottom round roast
⅓ cup heavy cream or crème
    fraîche

1. Heat 1 tablespoon of the oil in a medium saucepan and sauté the onion and carrots just until the onion wilts. Add the wine, vinegar, sugar, salt, pepper, bay leaves, and thyme. Bring just to a simmer, stirring, then remove from the heat and let cool.

2. Cut the beef into 3 or 4 slices of about the same thickness. Place the beef in a glass, enamel, or stainless-steel container. Pour the marinade over the beef, cover, and refrigerate for three to seven days. Turn the beef occasionally while it is marinating.

3. Remove the beef slices from the marinade and pat dry with paper towels. In a heavy pot or Dutch oven, heat the remaining tablespoon of oil over moderate heat. Brown the beef in the oil, turning the slices to brown on both sides.

4. When the beef is browned, add the reserved marinade with the vegetables. Bring to a simmer, then cover and cook slowly over low heat for about 1½ hours, until the beef is fork-tender.

5. Remove the beef from the pot and allow it to rest for 10 minutes. Cut it into thin, even slices, then return it to the pot. Continue to cook for another 45 minutes to 1 hour, until the meat is very tender.

6. Remove the beef slices from the pot and place in a serving dish. Remove the bay leaves from the sauce. Add the cream to the liquid in the pot and cook quickly, stirring, until the sauce is somewhat thick. Pour the sauce over the beef and serve with noodles or potatoes.

Serves 6

Calf's Liver with Apples, Onions, and Riesling

A complex blend of flavors characterizes this simple but delicious sauce—a rich, fruity sweetness from the caramelized apples and onions, a light touch of flavorful acidity from the wine, everything highlighted and enhanced by a spoonful of pungent mustard. Serve the dish with steamed or mashed potatoes and a simple green salad.

About ½ stick (about
    4 tablespoons) unsalted
    butter
1 medium onion, cut in half
    and thinly sliced
1 tart-sweet apple (Granny
    Smith are good), peeled,
    quartered, and thinly sliced
1 pound calf's liver, thinly sliced

Flour for dredging
½ teaspoon salt
Plenty of freshly ground black
    pepper
½ cup dry Riesling
1 heaping teaspoon coarse-
    grain mustard
2 tablespoons finely chopped
    parsley leaves

1. Heat about 2 tablespoons of the butter in a skillet and sauté the onion and apple over low heat, stirring occasionally, until they are soft and richly browned. This should take about 20 to 30 minutes. Remove the apple and onion from the pan and set aside.

2. Melt the remaining 2 tablespoons butter in the skillet over moderate heat. Dredge the liver slices lightly in flour, then sauté over moderate heat for 2 to 3 minutes on each side. Salt and pepper generously, then remove from the pan and keep warm while preparing the sauce.

3. Return the apple-onion mixture to the pan. Over moderate to high heat, add the wine, then stir in the mustard. Cook, stirring, for a few minutes.

4. Pour the hot sauce over the liver, sprinkle with the chopped parsley, and serve hot.

Serves 3 to 4

Sauerkraut with Mixed Sausages (Choucroute Garni)

It is interesting that the French word for sauerkraut, *choucroute,* is an amalgam of the French word for cabbage, *chou,* and the German word for cabbage, *Kraut*—linguistic fusion reflects the culinary! Almost any cured pork product can be used to "garnish" the sauerkraut, including smoked pork chops, cured ham, and a variety of coarse- and fine-grained sausages. Serve the choucroute with boiled potatoes, coarse-grained mustard, and an assortment of dark and light breads.

4 slices thick-sliced bacon, cut in half
1 large onion, sliced
2 bay leaves
5 to 8 juniper berries
½ teaspoon cracked black pepper
1 small onion, stuck with 3 or 4 whole cloves
2 pounds good-quality sauerkraut, drained (see Tip)

12 ounces (about 4) knockwurst, or other plump, fine-grained sausages
12 to 16 ounces smoked garlic sausage (kielbasa is a good substitute), cut into large chunks
2 cups dry Riesling or other dry white wine

1. Preheat the oven to 350°F. Layer the bacon slices over the bottom of an ovenproof casserole or Dutch oven. Place the sliced onion, bay leaves, juniper berries, pepper, and whole onion over the bacon.

2. Add the sauerkraut in an even layer, then place the knockwurst and the garlic sausage over the sauerkraut. Pour in the wine.

3. Cover the casserole and bake for about 1 hour. After 30 to 40 minutes, gently stir the sauerkraut and sausages. Cover and finish baking.

Serves 4 to 6

TIP: Save the drained sauerkraut juice for other dishes, such as the Romanian ciorba on page 173. It can be stored in a covered container in the refrigerator.

Smoked Pork with Vegetables in Wine Sauce

Boiled pork and cabbage is not a dish one ordinarily associates with the French, but in Alsatian hands it becomes an earthy, subtly sauced preparation in which the flavors of smoked pork, vegetables, and wine are very smoothly integrated. The odd touch of nutmeg and ginger is probably a vestige of an earlier tradition, common throughout Western Europe in medieval times, in which a number of exotic spices were used (frequently to excess) in meat and fish cookery.

2 tablespoons butter or
    vegetable oil
1 medium onion, thinly sliced
2 carrots, sliced
1 small knob celery root (about
    8 to 12 ounces), peeled
    and sliced
1 small head cabbage, coarsely
    shredded or sliced

1 cup beef or veal stock
1 cup dry white wine
2 bay leaves
⅛ teaspoon nutmeg
¼ teaspoon ginger
Several good grinds of black
    pepper
1 to 1½ pounds smoked pork
    butt

1. Heat the butter in a large, heavy pot and sauté the onion and carrots over moderate heat, stirring, until the onion wilts and begins to turn golden.

2. Stir in the celeriac and cabbage, then add the stock, wine, bay leaves, nutmeg, ginger, and pepper. Mix well, then add the pork butt. Bring to a simmer, cover, and cook over low heat for about 1 hour, or until the meat is fork-tender.

3. Remove the meat from the pot and let rest for 5 to 10 minutes. If there is a lot of liquid in the pot, cook it down quickly until the mixture is fairly thick. Taste for salt.

4. Spoon the vegetable mixture and sauce into a rimmed serving dish. Slice the meat and layer it over the vegetables. Serve with steamed or boiled potatoes or potato salad.

Serves 4 to 6

Bacon, Mushroom, and Muenster Tart

With its load of mushrooms, this rich tart is a heartier cousin of the more familiar quiche Lorraine. Muenster is the classic cheese of Alsace, mild and creamy with a distinctive nutty flavor. Try to find a high-quality Muenster rather than the presliced, plastic-wrapped supermarket varieties.

4 to 5 slices thick-sliced bacon, coarsely chopped
2 tablespoons unsalted butter
1 large leek, mostly white part, thoroughly washed and finely chopped
1 medium onion, finely chopped
1 pound mushrooms, sliced
1 teaspoon salt
¼ teaspoon freshly ground black pepper

2 eggs
1⅓ cups light cream
¼ teaspoon nutmeg
Good dash cayenne pepper
4 ounces Muenster cheese, cut into small slices
Pastry for an 8- or 9-inch fluted quiche or tart pan
2 teaspoons Dijon mustard

1. In a large skillet, cook the bacon until crisp; remove from the pan with a slotted spoon and drain on paper towels. Pour off and discard the fat from the pan.

2. In the same skillet, melt the butter over moderate heat. Add the chopped leek and onion and sauté until the vegetables are just wilted.

3. Add the mushrooms, turn up the heat a bit, and continue to cook, stirring occasionally, until the mixture is soft and dark and all the liquid has cooked away. Stir in ½ teaspoon of the salt and ⅛ teaspoon of the black pepper and mix well.

4. In a small bowl, whisk the eggs thoroughly, then stir in the cream, nutmeg, and cayenne and the remaining ½ teaspoon salt and ⅛ teaspoon pepper. Preheat the oven to 400°F.

5. Fit the pastry into the pan and spread the bottom evenly with the mustard. Sprinkle the reserved bacon bits over the mustard.

6. Spoon the mushroom mixture evenly into the pastry shell. Layer the sliced cheese evenly over the mushrooms. Carefully pour the egg mixture into the shell.

7. Bake the tart for 35 to 45 minutes, until it is puffed and nicely browned. Let stand for 5 to 10 minutes before cutting into wedges.

Serves 4 to 6 as a main course,
6 to 8 as an appetizer or first course

Potatoes with Cream and Cheese

If the French and the Germans agree on nothing else, they are in accord about the virtues of the potato, the starchy tuber introduced into Europe in the sixteenth century from its native home in the Andes mountains of South America. Originally disdained as a food fit only for the very poor or for livestock, the potato has achieved a place of honor in the French kitchen; nowhere is that more evident than in Alsace, where the potato repertoire is unrivaled. This is a simple dish with only a few ingredients, but it is utterly delicious and well worth an extra hour or two on the Exercycle!

4 to 5 medium potatoes (all-purpose or bakers)
Butter for baking dish
Salt

Freshly ground black pepper
½ to ⅔ cup heavy cream
1 cup shredded Emmentaler or Gruyère cheese

1. Cook the whole, unpeeled potatoes in boiling water until they are just tender when pierced with a sharp knife. Drain, let cool, then peel and slice about ¼ inch thick. Preheat the oven to 375°F.
2. Layer the potatoes in a well-buttered gratin dish or shallow casserole. Salt and pepper generously.
3. Pour in enough cream to barely cover the potatoes. Spread the cheese evenly over the top.
4. Bake for 20 to 30 minutes, until bubbly and very lightly browned.

Serves 4

Warm Cabbage and Bacon Salad

The German practice of flavoring cooked vegetables with bacon fat joins hands with the French love of lardons, crisp chewy little cubes of fried bacon used to garnish cooked vegetables and salads. This is a robust and full-flavored dish, best served in cold weather.

3 to 4 slices thick-sliced bacon,
        coarsely diced
1 medium onion, cut in half
   and thinly sliced
½ teaspoon caraway seeds
1 small head savoy cabbage,
   thinly sliced or shredded
   (about 6 cups)

¼ cup white wine vinegar
Salt
Freshly ground black pepper to
   taste

1. In a large skillet, fry the diced bacon until it is browned and crisp. Remove the bacon from the pan with a slotted spoon and reserve. Pour off and discard all but about 1 to 2 tablespoons of the fat in the pan.

2. Add the onion to the pan and sauté, stirring, until the onion is just beginning to turn golden. Add the caraway seeds and cook, stirring, for a few minutes.

3. Add the cabbage to the pan, then pour in the vinegar, mix well, and bring to a simmer. Cover and cook over low heat for about 10 minutes, until the cabbage is tender but still just barely crisp.

4. Add salt and freshly ground pepper to taste. Add the reserved bacon, mix well, then serve warm.

Serves 4 to 6

Sweet-and-Sour Huckleberry Sauce

A delicious example of the Alsatian flair for fruity, sweet, and sour, this vibrant sauce is traditionally served as a complement to smoked meats, game, or sausages. It is a fine addition to the Thanksgiving table, and my sweet-toothed son has discovered that it makes a spectacular sauce for ice cream or cheesecake. Blueberries can be substituted for the huckleberries, if desired.

1 quart fresh huckleberries or blueberries

1 cup sugar

½ cup cider vinegar

1 cinnamon stick

1. Wash and pick over the berries and drain thoroughly.
2. In a medium saucepan, combine the sugar, vinegar, and cinnamon stick. Bring to a simmer, then cook at a moderate boil, stirring occasionally, for 5 to 7 minutes.
3. Add the berries to the syrup and mix gently but thoroughly. Bring quickly to a simmer, then cook for just a minute or so. Spoon the mixture into a clean glass jar. Cover and let cool, then refrigerate.

Makes 1 quart

TIP: The berries will keep for a year or more, covered, in the refrigerator. When all the berries have been used, the syrup can be recycled for another batch; simply bring the syrup to a boil, add the new berries, and cook as above. Spoon into a fresh clean jar. The flavor of the new batch will be even richer than the first.

Plum Tart with Almonds

The berries and fruits of Alsace are legendary and have long been appreciated in a lavish assortment of pastries and cakes. This luscious plum tart has as its base, rather than the more familiar short crust or pastry shell, a thin, buttery cake layer. It really needs no garnish of any kind, but if you must gild the lily, serve it with a dollop of whipped cream or a spoonful or two of crème anglaise (custard sauce).

¼ pound (1 stick) unsalted butter, at room temperature, plus additional for pan
½ cup plus 2 tablespoons sugar
3 eggs
½ teaspoon almond extract

1 cup flour
10 to 12 black or red plums, or a mixture of both
½ teaspoon cinnamon
¼ cup plum jelly
2 to 3 tablespoons thinly sliced almonds

1. Cream the stick of butter with the ½ cup sugar until it is smooth. Add the eggs one at a time, beating well after each addition. Stir in the almond extract.

2. Add the flour and mix just until it is thoroughly blended in.

3. Butter the bottom and sides of an 11-inch tart pan that has a removable bottom. Spread the batter evenly in the bottom the pan. Preheat the oven to 375°F.

4. Cut the plums in half, remove the pits, then cut each plum half into 3 slices. Starting at the outer edge of the pan, place the plum slices, just touching, in a ring around the batter. Then make an inner circle of the plum slices, continuing until all the batter is covered.

5. Combine the 2 tablespoons of sugar with the cinnamon, mix well, then sprinkle evenly over the plums.

6. Bake the tart for about 30 minutes, until the cake layer is just firm to the touch.

7. Let the tart cool, then remove from the pan and place on a serving plate. Heat the jelly until it is just liquid enough to spread, then brush it evenly over the entire surface of the tart. Sprinkle the almonds over the jelly glaze.

Serves 6 to 8

Fresh Raspberry Cream

A classic example of the Alsatian genius for rich sweet cream and fruit concoctions, this dessert features a luscious, velvety baked cream, topped, when chilled, with an intensely flavored fresh raspberry purée. Serve it in small portions and savor it slowly!

1 pint fresh raspberries
1 cup sugar
4 tablespoons framboise (or other raspberry liqueur)
3 cups heavy cream
6 egg yolks
1 teaspoon vanilla

Finely shaved bittersweet chocolate curls, for garnish (optional)
Additional fresh whole raspberries, for garnish (optional)

1. Combine the raspberries, ½ cup of the sugar, and 2 tablespoons of the liqueur in a food processor and purée. Strain the purée to remove the seeds and set aside.

2. In a saucepan, combine the cream and the remaining ½ cup sugar. Mix well, then bring just to the scalding point.

3. In a bowl, beat the egg yolks until they are smooth. Slowly pour the hot cream into the eggs, stirring constantly, until the mixture is very well blended. Stir in the vanilla and the 2 remaining tablespoons liqueur. Preheat the oven to 350°F.

4. Pour the custard mixture through a strainer into a 9-inch baking dish or shallow casserole. Place the casserole in a larger baking pan, then carefully pour boiling water into the larger container so that it comes about halfway up the sides of the smaller dish.

5. Bake the cream for 40 to 45 minutes, until it is just lightly set. Remove it from the water bath, let cool, then chill thoroughly.

6. Serve the chilled cream in small portions, with the raspberry purée spooned over and around it. Garnish with shaved chocolate curls and fresh raspberries, if desired.

Serves 6

The Americas

Crossroads cooking has occurred for as long as humans have wandered the earth, shifting the patterns of people's food in numberless and unrecorded ways. But there is one date in history that marked a virtual explosion of changing foodways, a time that precipitated a profound change in what the whole world ate. The year was 1492, and it brought two worlds together, the New World of the Americas and the Old World of Europe, Asia, and Africa. The subsequent traffic between the two saw an exchange of foods and ideas unprecedented in human history.

There issued from the Americas an array of foods that would have a formidable impact on the kitchens of the Old World. From the tropics of Central and South America came manioc (cassava), sweet potatoes, pineapple, cashews and Brazil nuts, chocolate and vanilla.

From the high Andes came the potato, in a multitude of forms, and the peanut, the nutty little legume that would have such a heavy impact on the food of Africa and Southeast Asia. And from Mexico, the central hearth of the Americas, came tomatoes, corn, sweet peppers and hot chiles, turkey, an extraordinary variety of beans, and a number of squashes and pumpkins. All these foods found new homes and new uses all over the world, transforming established diets and dishes and, in the process, becoming changed themselves.

But the so-called Columbian Exchange was a two-way process; as the foods of the Americas made their way around the globe, the foods of the Old World made their impact on the New, enlarging the aboriginal repertoire with a host of exciting and valuable ingredients. Primary among these were rice and wheat, two grains of widespread appeal, which supplemented the beloved native staple, corn. Very important was the introduction of the most common domesticated meats, including beef, pork, chicken, lamb, and goat, hitherto unknown in the Americas, along with a corollary tradition of dairy products. And of special value was the introduction of such products as lard and olive oil into the cuisines of the New World, which had previously had no significant source of cooking fats and oils.

Many other ingredients from Europe, Asia, and Africa had a major impact: bananas and coconut; oranges, lemons, and limes; a large assortment of vegetables, fruits, spices, and herbs. But in addition to the goods and ingredients was the export to the Americas of new ideas and novel practices, brand new ways of processing, preparing, and presenting food. When the pig arrived, for example, it came with a whole complex of related practices—rendering out the fat to make lard; using the lard for frying or for shortening dough; preservative techniques such as pickling, salting, and smoking; the use of different cuts for such products as bacon, sausage, cracklings, and ham. The pig was eagerly accepted by Native Americans not only for its rich, succulent flesh, but also for an exciting new range of culinary possibilities.

Consider, then, that 1492 opened the floodgates to an unceasing flow of goods and ideas between the Old World and the New, and of people and cultures as well. Yet the flow of people was in one direction only—into the Americas. While their indigenous foods traveled the earth, Native Americans stayed put as the world and its people arrived on their doorstep to make new homes and new meals in a strange new land, converging in the greatest ethnic mix ever known. On these shores, fusion was inevitable and inescapable.

Initially, the immigrant cultures established themselves in small separate communities and defined territories of the Americas—the Spanish in Mexico and California, the Portuguese in Brazil, the English in Virginia, the Dutch in New York. But as more and more people arrived, the ethnic mixture swelled and became more complex, with different traditions rubbing shoulders with one another. The Scandinavians in the upper Midwest might remain relatively isolated, but in growing cities and centers of commerce, along rivers, railways, and ports, with travelers, frontiersmen, and adventurers, a legion of cultures and cuisines met and mingled, each determined to maintain as fully as possible its familiar foodways, all constrained by the resources and realities of a new land and a new way of life.

In the five hundred or so years since Columbus bumped into a small island in the Caribbean, the story of cuisine in the Americas has been an eloquent testament to the basic human need for stability and tradition, along with the necessity for flexibility and accommodation and the persistent lure of novelty and excitement. What is remarkable is how much was retained by individual ethnic traditions so far from their place of origin, as they encountered and assimilated a legion of new elements. Even the most compromised and powerless people in this ethnic mix—black slaves from Africa and most of the native peoples of the Americas—preserved much of the integrity of their food traditions as they contributed to the rich variety of the American table.

America is less a melting pot than a mega-crossroads, a place where almost every cuisine in the world has played a part and made an impact. And while there are dozens of areas that show the mingling of these many traditions, we will focus on three that express in a particularly vivid fashion the ways in which the creative merger occurred. They are not very distant from one another geographically, but their history and evolution have made each a unique and distinctive cuisine, all of them very much a part of the creative fusion movement of the contemporary scene.

old mex, new mex, tex-mex

Central to the food experience of the first foreign settlers in the New World were the regional cuisines of Mexico, which had developed over many thousands of years into complex and sophisticated systems, from the semitropical lowland enclaves of the Maya to the Aztec kingdom of the high central plateau. Fundamental to them all were two foods—corn and chile peppers—that were the distinctive hallmarks of the new dishes created in the encounter between the victorious Spanish and the vanquished Mexicans.

Corn was the basic staple grain of all native Americans, hybridized and elaborated into a myriad of forms and functions. The most pervasive and characteristic of these was the lime-treated corn, which in whole form was called posole (or hominy in North America); when wet-ground into a dough called nixtamal it was used to make tortillas and the stuffing for tamales. The unique flavor of limed corn never traveled beyond its native shores, a good example of how exported foods lose complexity when they are not accompanied by the people who actually prepare and eat them.

Similarly, the chile peppers had evolved in pre-Columbian times into an extraordinary range of products, dozens of varieties, colors, and sizes that were used fresh, smoked, roasted, pickled, and dried, and that celebrated every exquisite nuance of pungency and flavor. And although the chiles were enthusiastically accepted in many parts of the Old World, it was primarily for their hotness that they were embraced, not for their individual seasoning properties. It is only here, in traditions that radiate from the Mexican center, that anchos and chipotles, jalapeños and habañeros are individually distinguished and appreciated.

Along with corn and chile peppers, tomatoes, beans, pumpkins, and squashes were to have a significant impact on the foods introduced by the Spanish. Rice was mixed with tomatoes and native beans; cilantro and limes imported from the Mediterranean flavored Mexican avocados and seafood; olive oil and lard were used to fry tortillas and mashed beans. And as the Spanish, as well as native Mexicans, migrated north into the territories that would become the American Southwest, they encountered new tastes and new ingredients from English merchants, French trappers, and American cowboys, creating a fusion of yet new traditions. Through all these metamorphoses, however, the central Mexican theme remains clear, a tribute to its tenacity and its appeal.

RECIPES

Creamy Double Corn Chowder

Veracruz Shrimp Salad

Chile-Marinated Chicken Strips

Turkey Tamale Pie

Buffalo and Black Bean Chili

Mixed Chili with Pork and Pinto Beans

Hot and Smoky Barbecue Beef

Posole with Lamb and Green Chile

Texas Caviar

Cheese and Chile Corn Cakes

Green Chile Spoonbread

Almond, Garlic, and Chile Sauce

Mango Cream with Pineapple

Creamy Double Corn Chowder

The ancient and familiar flavors of limed corn and chile are featured in a European-style soup based on stock and enriched with cream and cheese. For an attractive alternative to the garnish of diced red pepper, try a swirl of roasted red pepper purée.

2 tablespoons butter or vegetable oil

1 medium onion, coarsely chopped

2 teaspoons ground ancho chile

2 cups cooked or canned white hominy (posole), drained

3 cups chicken or turkey stock

Kernels from 2 ears fresh sweet corn

½ cup heavy cream

Salt, if needed

4 to 6 ounces shredded Monterey Jack cheese

¼ to ⅓ cup finely diced red bell pepper, for garnish

1. Heat the butter in a medium saucepan and sauté the onion until it wilts and just begins to turn golden. Stir in the ground chile and cook, stirring, for a minute or two.

2. Transfer the onion to a food processor; add the hominy and about 1 cup of the stock. Purée until smooth.

3. Return the purée to the pot and add the remaining stock. Bring to a simmer, then cook, uncovered, over low heat for 10 to 15 minutes.

4. Add the corn kernels and cook for a few minutes more. Stir in the cream and heat to a simmer. Taste for salt.

5. To serve, place a small handful of the cheese at the bottom of each bowl. Ladle the hot soup over the cheese, then garnish with the diced pepper.

Serves 4 to 6

Veracruz Shrimp Salad

The flavor of this refreshing appetizer-salad was brand new four hundred years ago but has become familiar and characteristic of Mexican cuisine today. It is the successful fusion of native tomatoes, peppers, and oregano with the olive oil, lime, cilantro, and capers introduced by the Spanish. On the coast of Mexico, it is sometimes made with poached oysters rather than shrimp. Serve the salad in small portions as an appetizer or light lunch, with warm corn tortillas or crunchy tortilla chips.

1 pound cooked and peeled small-to-medium shrimp
1 small red onion, finely chopped
1 medium green or red bell pepper, seeded and diced
1 small-to-medium potato, cooked and diced
1 large tomato, coarsely chopped
2 to 3 serrano chiles, seeded and minced (or other fresh green chiles of choice and availability)

1 tablespoon capers, drained
3 tablespoons olive oil
2 tablespoons fresh lime juice
½ teaspoon salt, or more to taste
½ teaspoon crumbled dried oregano
Good handful (about ½ cup) of chopped cilantro
1 avocado, pitted, peeled, and sliced

1. In a bowl, combine the shrimp, onion, bell pepper, potato, tomato, chiles, and capers.

2. In a small bowl, combine the oil, lime juice, salt, and oregano. Whisk to blend thoroughly. Pour the dressing over the salad, add the chopped cilantro, and mix gently but thoroughly. Taste for salt and lime. Serve the salad garnished with the avocado slices.

Serves 4 to 6

Chile-Marinated Chicken Strips
(Pollo Adovado)

Adobo is a Spanish word used almost exclusively for spicy Mexican seasoning pastes compounded of ground chiles, garlic, and some sour element, usually vinegar (although in the Yucatán the acidic note is provided by the juice of sour oranges). The adobo traveled with the Spanish to the Philippines, where it came to designate the characteristic seasoning mixture of soy sauce, garlic, and vinegar, and to New Mexico, where it is still a popular way of preparing pork and chicken. Once the meat is marinated, it is quick and easy to cook; serve it simply with warm corn tortillas and garnish it with shredded lettuce and raw or sweet-and-sour onions.

1 medium onion, coarsely chopped
3 to 4 cloves garlic
2 tablespoons New Mexico mild red chili powder
1 tablespoon ground ancho chile
½ teaspoon crumbled dried oregano
1 tablespoon red wine vinegar

1 pound boneless, skinless chicken breasts, cut into ½-inch-thick strips
2 tablespoons vegetable oil
Salt to taste
Warm corn tortillas
Shredded lettuce
Thinly sliced raw onions or sweet-and-sour onions (see Note)

   1. In a food processor, combine the onion, garlic, red chili powder, ground chile, oregano, and vinegar. Process into a paste.

   2. In a nonreactive bowl, combine the chicken strips with the paste and mix well. Let stand, covered, in the refrigerator for 6 to 8 hours.

   3. Heat the oil in a large skillet over moderately high heat. Add the chicken, with all the marinade, and cook, turning frequently, until the chicken strips are just cooked through. Sprinkle the chicken with salt to taste.

   4. To eat, place some of the chicken strips in a warm tortilla, add some lettuce and raw or sweet-and-sour onions, and roll up.

Serves 4

NOTE: To make sweet-and-sour onions: In a nonreactive bowl, combine 1 large onion, thinly sliced, with ⅓ cup cider vinegar and 2 tablespoons sugar. Mix well and let stand for 3 to 4 hours, stirring occasionally.

Turkey Tamale Pie

Tamales are an ancient traditional Mexican dish—steamed corn husks filled with limed cornmeal and bits of meat or beans in highly seasoned chili sauces, labor-intensive and typically prepared for festive occasions. The North Americanization of this dish took the form of a pie or layered casserole, which combined all the elements in a structure more familiar and acceptable to people of Western European origin.

2 tablespoons vegetable oil
1 medium onion, coarsely chopped
1 medium green bell pepper, seeded and diced
1 medium red bell pepper, seeded and diced
4 cloves garlic, crushed
½ teaspoon crushed dried hot pepper
1 to 1½ cups diced cooked turkey
2 cups tomato sauce
2 teaspoons ground cumin
1 teaspoon crumbled dried oregano

1 tablespoon blended chili powder
1¼ teaspoons salt
2 cups cooked or canned pinto or kidney beans, drained
2 tablespoons lard or vegetable shortening
½ cup very hot water
1 cup masa harina (tortilla flour)
1 cup shredded Monterey Jack or cheddar cheese
Chopped onion, shredded lettuce, and sour cream, for serving

1. Heat the oil in a large skillet and sauté the onion, bell peppers, garlic, and hot pepper over moderate heat, stirring, until the onion just begins to turn golden.

2. Add the turkey, tomato sauce, cumin, oregano, and chili powder. Add 1 teaspoon of the salt and the beans. Mix well, bring to a simmer, then cook, uncovered, over low heat, for 30 to 40 minutes, stirring occasionally, or until the mixture is thick. Taste for salt and hotness. Preheat the oven to 350°F.

3. In a bowl, melt the lard or shortening and the remaining ¼ teaspoon salt in the hot water. Stir in the masa harina and mix until smooth.

4. Grease a 2- to 3-quart casserole or a deep 9-inch baking dish. Spread the cornmeal dough evenly over the bottom of the casserole. Spoon the chili mixture over the dough. Sprinkle the grated cheese evenly over the top.

5. Cover the casserole and bake for 30 to 35 minutes. Serve the tamale pie with the chopped onion, shredded lettuce, and sour cream.

Serves 4 to 6

Buffalo and Black Bean Chili

Chili, in an endless variety, is the tradition created from the merger of Mexico and North America in the fermentative frontier territories of the American Southwest. It was popularized by the chili "queens," Mexican women who sold their spicy concoctions from carts in the central plazas of Texas towns, and was carried throughout the West by trappers, cattle drivers, frontiersmen, and adventurers. The first commercial chili powder, a premixed blend of hot pepper and other seasonings, was developed by a German immigrant named Gebhardt living in Texas, and like curry powder, chili powder became the standardized mainstream flavor associated with the dish that bears its name. This chili is made from buffalo, a meat that is making a comeback because it is richly flavored but much leaner than beef. The chili contains some surprising flavor elements— bacon, beer, and unsweetened chocolate, long a valued seasoning for savory food in the Mexican tradition.

5 to 6 slices bacon, chopped
1 large onion, finely chopped
1 pound ground buffalo (or lean ground beef, if desired)
4 cloves garlic, crushed
1 teaspoon salt
2 to 3 teaspoons ground New Mexico red chile (or other ground red chile to taste)
2 teaspoons ground cumin
½ teaspoon crumbled dried oregano
½ cup beer
1 cup tomato sauce
2 to 3 cups cooked or canned black beans
1 tablespoon unsweetened cocoa powder
Finely chopped onions, for garnish

1. Fry the chopped bacon over moderate heat until it is just crisp. Discard all but about 2 tablespoons of the fat in the pan. Add the large onion and sauté until it just begins to turn golden.

2. Add the ground meat and fry, crumbling the meat as it browns. When the meat is all browned, add the garlic, salt, ground chile, cumin, and oregano and cook, stirring, for a few minutes.

3. Stir in the beer, tomato sauce, and beans, mix well, then cover and cook for about 30 minutes over low heat.

4. Uncover the chili and stir in the cocoa. Continue to cook over low heat, uncovered, stirring occasionally, until the mixture is thick. Taste for salt and hotness; add a bit of cayenne, if necessary.

5. Serve the chili with warm tortillas, corn chips, or corn bread, and garnish with the chopped onions.

Serves 4 to 6

Mixed Chili with Pork and Pinto Beans

In some areas, like New Mexico, that have retained closer ties with the traditional practices of the Mexican kitchen, chili is more frequently individualized with the flavor of specific chile peppers rather than the generic premixed seasoning blends. The meat is more likely to be pork than beef, cut into small pieces rather than ground. The New Mexico bean of choice is the plump and succulent pinto. Note that this chili contains anise seed, a clear Spanish touch, but no tomatoes.

2 ancho chiles
2 large dried New Mexico red chiles
2 tablespoons vegetable oil
1 medium onion, coarsely chopped
1 red bell pepper, seeded and diced
1 pound lean boneless pork, cut into pea-size pieces

5 or 6 cloves garlic, finely chopped
1½ teaspoons ground cumin
1 teaspoon crumbled dried oregano
½ teaspoon anise seeds
1 teaspoon salt
2 cups cooked or canned pinto beans, with some of the liquid

1. With a sharp knife, make a slit in the anchos and the New Mexico chiles and shake or scrape out the seeds. Cover the chiles with 1 cup warm water and let stand for 30 to 40 minutes. Remove the chiles from the water, reserving the chile water. Dice the chiles and set aside.

2. Heat the oil in a skillet and sauté the onion and the bell pepper over moderate heat, stirring, until the vegetables wilt. Add the pork and brown quickly over moderately high heat, stirring it to brown evenly.

3. When the pork is browned, add the garlic, diced soaked chiles, cumin, oregano, anise seeds, and salt. Continue to cook over moderate heat, stirring, until the mixture is aromatic and dark.

4. Stir in the reserved chile water, bring to a simmer, then cover and cook over low heat for about 1 hour.

5. Stir in the beans and a little of the bean liquid, if necessary, and cook, uncovered, for another 15 minutes, stirring occasionally. Taste for salt.

Serves 4 to 6

Hot and Smoky Barbecue Beef

The Anglo taste for beef and the Mexican tradition of spicy chile pastes and sauces were expressed in a number of popular North American dishes. Chili was one and barbecue another, but with barbecue an unexpected element entered the mix. This was a sweet and tangy component that probably originated in the sweet and spicy barbecue sauces of Asia, one that found its most widespread acceptance in the form of ketchup. This pot- or oven-cooked barbecue beef is full of robust sweet and spicy flavor. It's good served on buns, as in Sloppy Joes.

2 tablespoons vegetable oil
2 to 2½ pounds meaty beef shank, on the bone (also known as beef shin meat or hind shank)
1 large onion, coarsely chopped
1 green bell pepper, seeded and diced
4 or 5 cloves garlic, crushed
1 teaspoon salt
Plenty of freshly ground black pepper

¼ cup cider vinegar
2 tablespoons firmly packed brown sugar
1 cup canned crushed tomatoes
1 cup beer
2 ancho chiles, seeded and coarsely torn or chopped
2 chipotle chiles (smoked jalapeños)

1. Heat the oil in a heavy pot, Dutch oven, or range-to-oven casserole and brown the beef over moderately high heat, turning the beef to brown evenly. While the beef is browning, add the onion, bell pepper, and garlic and sauté, stirring.

2. When the beef is browned, sprinkle it with the salt and pepper, then add all the remaining ingredients. Mix well, bring to a simmer, then cover and cook over low heat for about 2 hours, or bake in a 300°F oven for about 2 hours. Turn the meat occasionally in the sauce while it is cooking.

3. When the meat is very tender, remove it from the pot; shred it coarsely with a knife and fork and discard the bone.

4. Mash the whole chipotles into the sauce, then return the shredded beef to the sauce. Continue to cook (or bake) until the mixture is soft and thick.

5. Serve the beef as is or on buns or rolls or with stewed pinto beans, crisp coleslaw, or corn on the cob.

Serves 4 to 6

Posole with Lamb and Green Chile

Pozole in Spanish designates a dish of boiled beans and barley, but the word, meaning "boiled," came originally from Nahuatl, the language of the Aztecs; it presumably referred to the appropriate method for cooking the dried lime-treated whole corn, which in Mexico is the defining ingredient of the dish. The Spanish enriched the tradition with the introduction of pork and lamb, but the distinctive flavor and texture of limed corn make this soupy stew an ancient and enduring favorite.

2 tablespoons vegetable oil
1 medium onion, coarsely
    chopped
2 long fresh green chiles
    (Anaheim, New Mexico,
    etc.), seeded and finely
    chopped

4 cloves garlic, crushed
8 to 12 ounces boneless lamb,
    cut into small pieces
1 teaspoon salt
2 carrots, thickly sliced
2 tomatoes, coarsely chopped

½ teaspoon crumbled dried
   oregano
2 medium potatoes, cut into
   small cubes
2 cups cooked, canned, or
   frozen white hominy
   (posole), drained

Small handful of fresh cilantro
   leaves, finely chopped

1. Heat the oil in a deep skillet or heavy pot and sauté the onion, chiles, and garlic over moderate heat, stirring, until the onion wilts.

2. Turn the heat up moderately high, add the lamb, and brown quickly, turning the pieces to brown on all sides. Sprinkle the lamb with the salt.

3. Add the carrots, tomatoes, and oregano and mix well. Bring to a simmer, then cover and cook over low heat for about 1 hour.

4. Stir in the potatoes and the posole, cover, and continue to cook for another hour or so, until the meat is very tender. If the mixture becomes too dry during the cooking, add a little water. When finished, the sauce should be slightly thickened but not too dry. Stir in the cilantro and serve hot.

Serves 4

Texas Caviar

It must be said of Texans that they were among the first "norte-americanos" to develop a sure appreciation of pungent chile peppers, a taste the rest of the country has only in recent decades begun to share. And as Texas can lay claim to the first commercial chili powder, she can also take credit for any number of salsas, spreads, and condiments fashioned from this ancient Mexican ingredient, which has become the most widely used seasoning in the world, other than salt.

3 to 4 tablespoons olive oil
1 medium onion, finely
    chopped
1 to 2 fresh serrano chiles, or
    2 to 3 jalapeños, seeded
    and minced
3 or 4 large cloves garlic,
    minced
1 medium green bell pepper,
    seeded and diced

1 large eggplant, peeled and
    diced
2 medium tomatoes, coarsely
    chopped
2 tablespoons fresh lemon juice
Good handful of chopped fresh
    cilantro leaves (about
    ½ cup)
½ teaspoon salt, or more to
    taste

1. Heat the oil in a large skillet and sauté the onion, chiles, and garlic over moderate heat, stirring, just until the onion wilts.

2. Add the bell pepper, eggplant, and tomatoes and cook, stirring occasionally, until the mixture is soft and most of the liquid has cooked away, about 20 minutes.

3. Stir in the lemon juice, cilantro, and salt and mix well. Let cool, then taste for salt, lemon, and chile.

4. Serve at room temperature as a spread or dip with crackers, corn chips, or raw vegetables.

Makes about 2½ to 3 cups

Cheese and Chile Corn Cakes

Crisp on the outside, moist on the inside, these savory little cakes are filled with many of the flavors typical of Mexican cooking. They make a nice accompaniment to a hearty soup or chili, or they can be served, with salsa or guacamole, as a cocktail snack.

1 medium onion, coarsely chopped	½ teaspoon crumbled dried oregano
2 cloves garlic	1 egg, lightly beaten
Good handful of fresh cilantro	1 jar or can (4½ ounces) chopped green chiles
1 cup masa harina (tortilla flour)	1 cup shredded Monterey Jack or mild cheddar cheese
1 teaspoon salt	3 to 4 tablespoons vegetable oil
1 teaspoon baking powder	

1. In a food processor, combine the onion, garlic, and cilantro and process into a coarse paste.

2. In a bowl, combine the masa harina, salt, baking powder, and oregano.

3. Add the onion paste, egg, and the chopped chiles to the dry ingredients. Mix thoroughly, then stir in the shredded cheese. Cover and refrigerate for 1 to 2 hours.

4. In a heavy skillet, heat enough oil to generously film the bottom of the pan over moderately high heat. Pinch off pieces of the dough, about the size of a Ping-Pong ball. Roll into a ball, then flatten into a small round cake.

5. Fry the cakes in batches, turning once, until nicely browned on both sides. Add more oil to the skillet as needed. Drain on paper towels.

Makes 10 to 12 small cakes

NOTE: The cakes can be reheated in a 400°F oven for about 10 to 12 minutes.

Green Chile Spoonbread

One of America's first comfort foods, the spoonbread, was born from the marriage of the indigenous corn-and-chile tradition with the rich dairy culture of Western Europe. Most Europeans preferred the bland unlimed cornmeal to the stronger, more distinctively fla-vored Mexican tortilla flour, and used the untreated variety as the basis of the many breads, cakes, and puddings that formed the back-bone of the colonial diet. This is more a light pudding or a soufflé than a bread (hence, eaten with a spoon), and like a soufflé, it will fall as it cools. No matter—it still tastes wonderful.

2 poblano chiles (or other large mild green chiles), or 1 can (4½ ounces) diced peeled green chiles
2 cups milk
2 tablespoons butter
1 teaspoon salt
1 teaspoon sugar
⅛ teaspoon cayenne pepper
1 cup stone-ground white or yellow cornmeal
1 can (15 to 16 ounces) cream-style corn
3 extra-large eggs

1. If using fresh chiles, grill or roast the poblanos until the skins are blackened. Place them in a paper or plastic bag until cool enough to handle. Skin the peppers and remove the seeds, then dice and set aside. (If using canned chiles, omit this step.)

2. In a medium saucepan, combine the milk, butter, salt, sugar, and cayenne. Heat over moderate heat just to the scalding point.

3. Slowly stir the cornmeal into the hot milk, whisking constantly as you add it to smooth out any lumps. Continue to cook, stirring constantly, until the mixture is smooth and thick. Remove from the heat and stir in the canned corn. Let cool slightly. Preheat the oven to 350°F.

4. Whisk the eggs thoroughly, then mix them into the cornmeal mixture, along with the reserved diced chiles. Pour the mixture into a buttered deep 2-quart casserole or soufflé dish.

5. Bake for 35 to 45 minutes, until the spoonbread is puffed and very lightly browned.

Serves 4 to 6

Almond, Garlic, and Chile Sauce

This intensely flavored pestolike sauce is a collaboration between the traditional nut-thickened sauces of Spain and the spicy pumpkinseed and peanut sauces of ancient Mexico. The pickled jalapeños add a bright pungency to a rich mixture of almonds and olive oil. The sauce is frequently served in Mexico to coat hot cooked green beans or cauliflower, but it is also very good as a dip for cold cooked shrimp or as a seasoning paste for baked or broiled fish. The sauce stores well tightly covered in the refrigerator.

⅓ cup chopped or slivered
    almonds, freshly toasted
4 cloves garlic
2 tablespoons pickled jalapeños
    (see Note)

Good handful of fresh cilantro
    (about ½ cup tightly
    packed)
¼ teaspoon salt
½ cup olive oil

1. In a food processor, combine the almonds, garlic, jalapeños, cilantro, and salt. Process the mixture into a coarse paste.

2. With the processor running, slowly add the oil in a steady stream until it is fully incorporated and the sauce is smooth and thick. Taste for salt and pungency.

Makes about ¾ cup

NOTE: Sliced, chopped, or whole jalapeños in vinegar are sold in small jars, mostly as a garnish for nachos. They can be stored almost indefinitely in the refrigerator.

Mango Cream with Pineapple

Mexican cuisine took enthusiastically to European dairy products, particularly in a sweet tradition that made the most of thick cooked creams and milk-based confections. This luscious dessert combines whipped cream with puréed mango, another popular import, in a rich, velvety mousse highlighted by tangy fresh pineapple in a cinnamon-scented brown sugar syrup.

½ cup white sugar
½ cup firmly packed brown
    sugar
¼ teaspoon cinnamon
½ cup water
1 cup diced fresh pineapple
¼ cup coarsely chopped pecans

3 to 4 medium mangoes
1 tablespoon fresh lemon juice
1½ cups heavy cream
½ teaspoon vanilla

1. In a medium saucepan, combine the white sugar, brown sugar, cinnamon, and water. Mix well, then bring to a boil and cook, uncovered, over moderate heat for about 10 minutes, stirring occasionally. Remove from the heat and stir in the pineapple and pecans. Set aside to cool.

2. Peel the mangoes and cut the flesh from the pits. Purée the mangoes with the lemon juice. You should have about 1½ to 2 cups of purée.

3. Whip the cream with the vanilla until stiff. Fold the mango purée into the whipped cream. To serve, spoon the mango purée into dessert cups, parfait glasses, or wine goblets. Top each serving generously with the pineapple sauce. If you are making this early in the day, chill the mango cream but do not spoon the sauce on top until serving time. For best flavor, the sauce should be at room temperature.

Serves 6 to 8

the caribbean

Before the Spanish conquest, a number of peoples—including the Taino, the Arawak, and the Carib—inhabited the islands of the Caribbean, their diet based on the ancient triad of corn, beans, and squashes, flavored with hot chiles, native allspice, and achiote, the tiny red seeds of the annatto tree. These foods were supplemented by sweet potatoes and cassava (manioc, or yuca), pineapple and guava, and a variety of fish, seafood, and wild game.

First to arrive were the Spanish, with their pork, ham, and sausage, their olives and capers and citrus fruits, their taste for mixed rice dishes and seafood. Much of Europe followed on their heels, with the English, the French, and the Dutch contributing a wealth of dairy products and a rich tradition of sweets and baked goods. Then black slaves hijacked from Africa to work the newly established sugar plantations brought their flair for highly seasoned stews and sauces and such familiar foods as okra and pigeon peas, plantains and yams. And finally, Chinese and Indians entered the melee, adding such characteristic ingredients as soy sauce and gingerroot, curry powder and coconut, mangoes and tamarind.

Such a multitude! Such a mixture! Such potential culinary mayhem! And yet this small string of islands has evolved an identifiable and appealing tradition, composed of a world of diverse elements that have found a way to support and enhance one another. There are, of course, variations from island to island, preferred foods and special dishes that reflect a heavier influence from one culture or another—curry dishes and stuffed roti in Trinidad and Jamaica, black beans and shredded meat in Cuba, spicy sofrito in Puerto Rico, pickled pig's feet in Barbados.

But constant to all are rice and seafood, beans and root vegetables, a riot of tropical fruits, and a shared delight in highly seasoned sauces, fried fish and savory crisp fritters, and peppery soups and stews filled with rich flavor. Shared as well by all is the smooth sweet island rum, a happy by-product of the sugar industry—in dozens of varieties, from the dark golden brews with their deep molasses tang to the silky, smooth, sophisticated whites.

Island food, like island music, resonates with the insistent pulse of the people—many people from many places, whose voices inexplicably manage to blend in a joyous celebration of spice, sun, and sea.

RECIPES

Creamy Spiced Bean and Pumpkin Soup

Seafood Escabeche

Spiced Shrimp and Pineapple with Cashews

Curried Chicken Pilau with Pigeon Peas

Shredded Pork with Onions and Peppers

Spicy Beef and Plantain Hash

Curry Goat

Spiced Fresh Corn with Tomato, Peppers, and
  Coconut

Garlic Plantain Fritters

Gratin of Rice and Hearts of Palm

Hearts of Palm, Avocado, and Orange Salad

Guava Barbecue Sauce

Plantain Coconut Bread

Candied Pumpkin

Creamy Spiced Bean and Pumpkin Soup

The lively color and rich creamy texture of this appealing soup come from a velvety purée of pumpkin, while the complex flavor is delivered by a typically Caribbean mixture of ingredients—Indian curry, English Worcestershire, Spanish sherry, Mexican peppers, and Jamaican allspice. For a shortcut version, substitute canned pumpkin purée for the homemade variety.

1 small-to-medium pie pumpkin or dumpling squash, about 2 pounds (or 2 cups canned pumpkin purée)

2 tablespoons vegetable oil, plus extra for oiling the pumpkin or squash

1 medium onion, finely chopped

1 red bell pepper, seeded and diced

2 cloves garlic, minced

2 to 3 small fresh green chiles, seeded and minced, or ½ teaspoon crushed dried hot pepper

2 teaspoons curry powder (preferably Jamaican or West Indian)

½ teaspoon ground ginger

⅛ teaspoon ground allspice

2 cups chicken stock

Several good grinds of black pepper

½ teaspoon salt

1 teaspoon Worcestershire sauce

2 to 3 cups cooked or canned kidney or pinto beans, drained

2 tablespoons cream sherry

2 to 3 tablespoons toasted pumpkin seeds (pepitas), for garnish (optional)

1. Preheat the oven to 400°F. Cut the pumpkin or squash in half horizontally and scoop out the seeds. Lightly oil the cut sides and place, cut side down, on a baking sheet. Bake for 30 to 40 minutes, until soft. Remove and let cool, then scoop out the pulp and purée it.

2. Heat the remaining 2 tablespoons oil in a medium saucepan and sauté the onion, bell pepper, garlic, and chiles over moderate heat until the onion wilts. Stir in the curry powder, ginger, and allspice and mix for a minute or two.

3. Add the chicken stock, black pepper, salt, and Worcestershire and the reserved pumpkin purée. Mix well, then simmer over low heat for about 10 to 15 minutes.

4. Stir in the beans and the sherry and simmer for a few minutes. Serve the soup hot, garnished with a sprinkle of toasted pumpkin seeds, if desired.

Serves 4 to 6

Seafood Escabeche

Escabeche is a dish of Spanish origin, fried fish marinated in a vinegary sauce and served cold. In the Caribbean, where it appears with the variant spellings of "escovitch" and "escaveach," it is more typically a dish of freshly fried fish—small whole fish or fillets—dressed with a tart sauce elaborated with sweet and hot peppers, lime juice, and cilantro. It can be served warm or at room temperature.

1 pound fish fillets (e.g., red snapper, cod, pompano, grouper)
Flour for dredging
2 to 3 tablespoons vegetable oil or olive oil, or more if needed
Salt
Freshly ground black pepper
1 large onion, cut in half and thinly sliced
1 medium red bell pepper, seeded and cut into thin strips
1 medium green bell pepper, seeded and cut into thin strips

2 teaspoons finely minced gingerroot
3 or 4 cloves garlic, minced
2 to 3 fresh hot chiles, seeded and minced
1 bay leaf
½ teaspoon salt
⅓ cup white wine vinegar
6 to 8 ounces medium shrimp, peeled and deveined
Juice of 1 lime
Small handful of fresh cilantro leaves, coarsely chopped
Tomato wedges and avocado slices for serving (optional)

1. Dredge the fish fillets lightly in flour. Heat the 2 to 3 tablespoons oil in a skillet over moderate to high heat. Fry the fish, turning once, until golden brown on both sides. Salt and pepper the fish lightly, remove from the pan, and set aside.

2. Add the onion, bell pepper, gingerroot, garlic, and chiles to the oil in the pan, adding another tablespoon or so of oil if necessary. Sauté, stirring, over moderate heat until the onion and the pepper are wilted and the mixture is aromatic.

3. Add the bay leaf, salt, and vinegar and simmer for a few minutes. Stir in the shrimp and cook just until the shrimp turn pink. Stir in the lime juice and remove from the heat.

4. Pour the pan mixture over the reserved fish fillets; sprinkle with the chopped cilantro. Serve warm or at room temperature, with tomato wedges and avocado slices if desired.

Serves 4 to 6

Spiced Shrimp and Pineapple with Cashews

East and West, the Old World and the New, come together in this intriguing piquant mixture: The peppers, tomato, pineapple, and cashews are all native American ingredients, while the seasoning is an eclectic Asian blend. I like it best in small portions as an appetizer or first course, served with plain rice or spooned into the pitted halves of small avocados.

2 tablespoons vegetable oil
1 medium onion, finely chopped
2 teaspoons finely minced gingerroot
2 or 3 cloves garlic, minced
2 to 3 small fresh hot chiles (jalapeño or serrano), seeded and minced (if you prefer a hotter profile, try a Scotch bonnet or habañero chile)
1 medium green or red bell pepper, seeded and diced

2 teaspoons curry powder (preferably Jamaican or West Indian)
1 medium tomato, coarsely chopped
2 large slices fresh pineapple, peeled, cored, and diced (about 1½ cups diced)
1 tablespoon soy sauce
Good squeeze of fresh lime juice
8 ounces medium shrimp, peeled and deveined
¼ cup roasted cashews, halves or coarsely chopped

1. Heat the oil in a skillet and sauté the onion, gingerroot, garlic, chiles, and bell pepper over moderate heat, stirring, until the onion wilts and just begins to turn golden and the mixture becomes aromatic. Add the curry powder and cook, stirring, for a few minutes.

2. Add the tomato, pineapple, and soy sauce. Mix well, then cook over moderate heat, stirring occasionally, for 5 to 10 minutes, until the mixture is thick and most of the liquid has cooked away.

3. Add the lime juice and the shrimp and cook, stirring, just until the shrimp turn pink. Stir in the cashews; taste for salt and spice; add a bit of cayenne or hot pepper sauce, if desired.

4. Serve with plain rice or spoon into pitted avocado halves.

Serves 6

Curried Chicken Pilau with Pigeon Peas

A number of different mixed rice dishes met at the crossroads of the Caribbean, from such diverse traditions as Spain, India, and West Africa. Although this one is most clearly modeled on the Indian pilau, it cannot resist the addition of Spanish bacon and African pigeon peas. The result is neither African, nor Indian, nor Spanish, but wholly Jamaican—and good!

4 to 5 slices thick-sliced bacon, diced
2 to 2½ pounds chicken thighs (skin removed, if desired)
1 large onion, coarsely chopped
1 medium red or green bell pepper, seeded and diced
3 or 4 large cloves garlic, crushed
2 to 3 small fresh hot chiles, seeded and minced, or 1 habañero or Scotch bonnet, seeded and minced, or ½ to 1 teaspoon crushed dried hot pepper

½ teaspoon salt
Several good grinds of black pepper
1 tablespoon plus 1 teaspoon curry powder (preferably Jamaican or West Indian)
2 medium tomatoes, coarsely chopped
2 cups chicken broth
1 cup rice
2 cups cooked, canned, or frozen green pigeon peas (gandules), drained

1. In a heavy pot or Dutch oven, fry the diced bacon until it is crisp. Pour off and discard all but about 2 tablespoons of the fat, or enough to generously film the bottom of the pot.

2. Add the chicken and brown slowly over moderate heat, turning the thighs to brown evenly. While the chicken is browning, add the onion, bell pepper, garlic, and chiles and sauté, stirring.

3. When the chicken is browned, sprinkle it with the salt and black pepper and stir in the curry powder. Add the tomatoes and broth, then cover and cook over low heat for about 50 to 60 minutes, or until the chicken is tender.

4. Stir in the rice, then cover and cook again over low heat for about 20 minutes, until all the liquid has been absorbed and the rice is tender. About 10 minutes before the rice is done, stir in the peas.

Serves 4 to 6

Shredded Pork with Onions and Peppers

This flavorful dish is one of many shredded meat preparations popular throughout Latin America, frequently called *ropa vieja*, "old clothes," because of the shredded, tattered appearance. This Cuban version is often served with fried plantains and stewed black beans, but it also makes an excellent filling for tacos.

1 pound boneless pork, not too lean, cut in large cubes or pieces

1 small onion, stuck with 3 or 4 whole cloves

2 or 3 whole cloves garlic, bruised

2 to 3 cups water

2 to 3 tablespoons olive oil

1 teaspoon ground annatto (achiote)

1 large onion, cut in half and thinly sliced

1 large green bell pepper, seeded and cut into thin strips

1 large red bell pepper, seeded and cut into thin strips

3 or 4 cloves garlic, minced

2 teaspoons ground cumin

1 teaspoon salt

¼ teaspoon freshly ground black pepper

1. In a medium saucepan, combine the pork, onion, and bruised garlic in the water. Cover and cook over low heat for about 1 hour, until the pork is becoming tender. Uncover and continue to cook for another hour or so, until the pork is very tender and almost all the liquid has cooked away. If too much liquid cooks away before the meat is tender, add a bit of water.

2. Drain the pork, let cool slightly, then shred coarsely with a knife and fork.

3. Heat the oil in a skillet over moderate heat, then stir in the achiote and the reserved shredded pork. Cook, stirring from time to time, for about 15 minutes, until the pork is becoming slightly browned and crisp.

4. Add the onion, bell peppers, crushed garlic, cumin, salt, and black pepper. Continue to cook, stirring occasionally, until the vegetables are soft and the meat is slightly crisp. Taste for salt.

Serves 4

Spicy Beef and Plantain Hash (Picadillo)

Picadillo, a spiced ground-meat mixture, is found in dozens of varieties throughout Latin America, showing its Spanish origins with such typical ingredients as olives, capers, and almonds. In this flavorful version, with its gingerroot, curry, and plantain, the focus shifts from Spain to a heavier influence from Asia and Africa. For best results, make the dish early in the day or a few hours before serving, so that the flavors have a chance to develop and come together.

1 pound lean ground beef
2 tablespoons vegetable oil
1 medium onion, finely chopped
1 tablespoon finely minced gingerroot
2 cloves garlic, minced
2 or 3 small fresh hot chiles, seeded and minced, or ½ to 1 teaspoon crushed dried hot pepper
1 medium red or green bell pepper, seeded and diced

1 tablespoon curry powder (preferably West Indian or Jamaican)
1 teaspoon salt
Several good grinds of black pepper
1 large medium-ripe plantain, peeled and diced (see NOTE on page 237)
⅓ cup dark raisins
1 cup tomato sauce
½ cup water

1. In a large skillet, brown the ground meat, crumbling it as it browns. When it is completely browned, remove it from the pan with a slotted spoon and set aside. Pour off and discard all the fat from the pan.

2. Add the oil to the pan, then the onion, gingerroot, garlic, chiles, and bell pepper. Sauté, stirring, over moderate heat until the onion wilts and the mixture becomes aromatic.

3. Add the curry powder and cook, stirring, for a minute or so.

4. Return the browned meat to the pan; add the salt, black pepper, plantain, raisins, tomato sauce, and water and mix well. Bring to a simmer, then cook, uncovered, over low heat for about 20 minutes, stirring occasionally, until the mixture is thick.

5. Remove from the heat, cover, and let stand for a couple of hours or until ready to serve. The picadillo can be reheated—if the mixture is very thick, you can add ¼ cup or so of water when you reheat. Taste for salt and hotness.

6. Serve with plain rice or with rice and peas, or as a filling for tacos, empanadas, or stuffed peppers.

Serves 4

Curry Goat

In a dish that has become emblematic of Jamaican cuisine, African, Asian, and Spanish elements combine in that lively blend so characteristic of the region. Except for the chile peppers, all the ingredients have been introduced from traditions outside the Americas. If you wish, you can add some chunks of sweet potato, zucchini, or yellow squash to the stew for the last part of the cooking.

2 tablespoons vegetable oil
1 large onion, coarsely chopped
3 or 4 large cloves garlic, minced

1 tablespoon finely minced gingerroot
1 habañero or Scotch bonnet chile, seeded and minced, or 2 to 3 other fresh hot chiles, seeded and minced

2 to 3 pounds shoulder or leg
of goat, on the bone,
chopped into largish
pieces (have your butcher
do this)
Salt
Freshly ground black pepper

2 carrots, sliced
1 tablespoon curry powder
(preferably Jamaican or
West Indian)
1 teaspoon turmeric
2 bay leaves
2 cups chicken stock

1. Heat the oil in a heavy pot or Dutch oven and sauté the onion, garlic, gingerroot, and chiles over moderate heat, until the onion becomes soft and the mixture is aromatic.

2. Add the goat and brown lightly on all sides, turning the pieces to brown evenly.

3. Sprinkle the meat lightly with salt and pepper, then add the carrots and stir in the curry powder and turmeric.

4. Add the bay leaves and stock, bring to a simmer, then cover and cook over low heat for 1 hour. If using sweet potato, zucchini, or squash, add them now.

5. Uncover and continue to cook, stirring from time to time, for another 1 to 1½ hours, until the meat is very tender and the sauce has become fairly thick. Remove the bay leaves. Taste for salt. Serve with plain rice or with rice and peas.

Serves 4 to 6

Spiced Fresh Corn with Tomato, Peppers, and Coconut

Fresh sweet corn in a creamy spiced coconut sauce seasoned with a typically eclectic Creole blend of ingredients. Serve this as a rather festive vegetable side dish at a barbecue or picnic supper, or as a nice change of pace from plain old creamed corn.

1 tablespoon vegetable oil
4 to 5 scallions, coarsely chopped
2 to 3 small fresh hot chiles, seeded and minced
2 cloves garlic, minced
1 large tomato, coarsely chopped
1 medium green or red bell pepper, seeded and diced
½ teaspoon salt

Several good grinds of black pepper
½ teaspoon dried thyme
1 tablespoon Worcestershire sauce
2½ cups fresh corn kernels (3 to 4 ears)
1 can (5 to 6 ounces) unsweetened coconut milk

1. Heat the oil in a medium, heavy saucepan and sauté the scallions, chiles, and garlic over moderate heat, stirring, until the scallions wilt.

2. Add the tomato, bell pepper, salt, and black pepper and cook, stirring, until the vegetables are soft and most of the liquid has cooked away.

3. Add the thyme, Worcestershire, corn, and coconut milk. Bring to a simmer, then cook, uncovered, over low to moderate heat for about 10 to 15 minutes, stirring occasionally, until the mixture is thick. Taste for salt and chile. Add a bit of cayenne, if desired.

Serves 4

Garlic Plantain Fritters

A popular legacy from the African kitchen, plantains are enjoyed constantly throughout the Caribbean in a variety of forms—sliced and fried, in fritters and chips, salted and sweetened. These crisp little fritters are delicious by themselves or as a savory accompaniment to almost any food.

1 large, very ripe plantain
    (see NOTE)
2 cloves garlic, crushed
¼ teaspoon salt

1 egg, lightly beaten
3 tablespoons vegetable oil
Coarse salt to taste

1. Peel the plantain, then cut it into chunks and mash with a potato masher or a heavy fork. Add the garlic, salt, and egg to the mashed plantain and mix well.

2. Heat the oil in a heavy skillet over moderately high heat. Drop the plantain mixture by heaping tablespoons into the hot oil. Fry for a few minutes, until nicely browned on one side, then turn the fritters to brown on the other side.

3. Drain the fritters on paper towels, then sprinkle lightly with coarse salt. Serve hot.

Makes about 8 fritters

NOTE: Like bananas, unripe plantains are green; ripe plantains are yellow; very ripe plantains are yellow with a good deal of black; and overripe are almost completely black and fairly soft to the touch. The ripest plantains are the sweetest.

Gratin of Rice and Hearts of Palm

"Spanish" rice—rice cooked in tomato sauce with onions and olive oil—is a dish that developed in the Americas and is in fact more typical of Spanish cooking in the New World than in Spain itself. It shows up in dozens of varieties throughout Latin America, embellished with seafood, chicken, ham, vegetables, and beans. This gratin pairs a Spanish-style rice with Brazilian hearts of palm in a rich cream-and-cheese sauce.

2 tablespoons olive oil
1 medium onion, finely
    chopped
1 cup long-grain rice
2 cups water
1 cup tomato sauce
½ teaspoon salt
1 jar or can (14 to 15 ounces)
    hearts of palm (plain, not
    marinated)

¼ teaspoon freshly ground
    black pepper
½ cup fresh or frozen green
    peas
½ cup heavy cream
1 cup shredded mild cheddar
    or Monterey Jack cheese

1. Heat the oil in a medium, heavy saucepan and sauté the onion over moderate heat, until the onion is soft and golden.

2. Stir in the rice, then add the water, tomato sauce, and salt. Mix well, bring to a simmer, then cover and cook over low heat for about 20 minutes, until all the liquid is absorbed. Remove from the heat and let stand, covered.

3. Drain the hearts of palm and rinse very thoroughly in cold water. Cut into ½-inch slices. Add the black pepper, hearts of palm, and peas to the rice mixture and mix well. Preheat the oven to 350°F.

4. Turn the rice mixture into a buttered 1½-quart shallow casserole or gratin dish. Drizzle the cream all over the rice, then top with the shredded cheese.

5. Bake for about 30 to 35 minutes, until bubbly.

Serves 4 to 6

Hearts of Palm, Avocado, and Orange Salad

This is a very pretty salad with a variety of contrasting colors, textures, and flavors and a wonderfully eclectic mix of ingredients in both the dressing and the components. Arrange the fruit and vegetables in an attractive pattern on the serving plate, then watch as the salad disappears in short order!

1 large blood or navel orange
1 jar or can (14 to 15 ounces) hearts of palm (plain, not marinated)
1 Haas avocado, pitted and peeled
Coarsely torn greens, with some radicchio or shredded red cabbage for color

1 tablespoon fresh lime juice
1 tablespoon seasoned rice vinegar (see Note)
1 tablespoon mayonnaise
2 tablespoons olive oil
Good dash of hot pepper sauce
Several good grinds of black pepper

1. Grate the orange for 1 teaspoon of zest and set the zest aside. Peel the orange, cut crosswise into 4 or 5 slices, then cut the slices in half.

2. Drain the hearts of palm and rinse very thoroughly in cold water. Cut into ½-inch slices. Cut each avocado half into 4 or 5 slices.

3. Place the greens on a serving platter; arrange the sliced orange, hearts of palm, and avocado in an attractive pattern on the greens.

4. Combine the orange zest, lime juice, vinegar, mayonnaise, olive oil, hot pepper sauce, and black pepper. Whisk until smoothly blended.

5. Drizzle the dressing over the salad.

Serves 4 to 6

NOTE: Seasoned rice vinegar is an import from Japan, a low-acid vinegar to which salt and sugar have been added. It is a very useful seasoning ingredient, widely available in most supermarkets and Asian groceries.

Guava Barbecue Sauce

The native tropical American guava has a distinctive sweet and tangy flavor that accommodates gracefully to Asian-style spicy sweet barbecue sauces. This easy sauce is excellent with spareribs, roast pork, chicken, or baked ham.

½ cup guava jelly
3 or 4 cloves garlic, crushed
1 tablespoon soy sauce
1 teaspoon ground ginger
½ to 1 teaspoon crushed dried
    hot pepper

1 tablespoon firmly packed
    brown sugar
1 teaspoon malt or cider
    vinegar

Combine all the ingredients in a small saucepan. Bring to a simmer and cook, stirring, over low heat for about 5 minutes.

Makes about ⅔ cup

Plantain Coconut Bread

Banana, plantain, and coconut breads are a common feature throughout the Caribbean, produced in a number of forms from rather dry, breadlike loaves, best toasted and served with butter or jam, to moister, more cakelike varieties, like this one. Except for the native Jamaican allspice, all the ingredients are post-Columbian imports; these breads show the assimilation of African and Asian foods into a European baking tradition.

2 large overripe plantains (see
    NOTE on page 237)
¼ cup fresh orange juice
1 teaspoon vanilla

½ cup firmly packed dark
    brown sugar
½ cup white sugar
1 cup vegetable oil

2 eggs	½ teaspoon ginger
2 cups flour	1½ teaspoons baking soda
½ teaspoon salt	1 cup dried shredded
1 teaspoon cinnamon	sweetened coconut
½ teaspoon allspice	

1. In a small bowl, mash the plantains thoroughly; combine with the orange juice and vanilla and mix well.

2. In a mixing bowl, combine the brown sugar, white sugar, oil, and eggs. Beat until thick and smooth. Preheat the oven to 350°F.

3. Combine the flour, salt, cinnamon, allspice, ginger, and baking soda and mix well. Add the dry ingredients to the batter and mix until just well blended. Add the reserved mashed plantains and the coconut and mix thoroughly.

4. Spoon the batter into a buttered 10- x 5-inch or 9- x 5-inch loaf pan. Bake for 40 to 50 minutes, until browned and firm and a straw inserted in the center comes out clean. Let cool in the pan for 20 minutes, then remove from the pan and let cool completely on a wire rack.

Makes 1 loaf cake

Candied Pumpkin

A wide assortment of pumpkins and squashes, ancient natives of the Americas, are enjoyed throughout the islands and Latin America in both sweet and savory dishes. These richly glazed sweet pumpkin chunks are flavored with some typical Spanish ingredients—citrus, cinnamon, and anise. They are delicious served warm or cold with ice cream, as a topping for custard or cheesecake, or as a sweet complement to roast ham or turkey.

1 (2- to 2½-pound) sweet pie
   pumpkin
½ cup firmly packed brown
   sugar
½ teaspoon cinnamon

¼ teaspoon anise seeds
¼ cup orange juice
2 tablespoons water
1 tablespoon fresh lemon juice

1. Cut the pumpkin in half; scoop out the seeds and fibrous matter. Cut each half into 8 chunks and peel.

2. In a deep skillet or pot, combine the brown sugar, cinnamon, anise, orange juice, water, and lemon juice. Bring to a simmer, then add the pumpkin chunks. Cover and cook over low heat for 10 to 15 minutes, until the pumpkin is just tender (test with a small sharp knife).

3. Uncover the pan and continue to cook over moderate heat, turning the chunks from time to time, until the syrup is fairly thick and the pumpkin is richly glazed.

Serves 4 to 6

new orleans

The Creole cooking of southern Louisiana, centered in the old port city of New Orleans, where the Mississippi River empties into the Gulf of Mexico, is made up of many of the same elements as the Creole cooking of the Caribbean, an eclectic mix of Spanish, African, Native American, and Western European traditions. But the differences between the two, sometimes subtle, often striking, illustrate the powerful effects on style and substance that can occur with slight shifts of cultural emphasis.

New Orleans began life as a French city and has preserved throughout her history a fundamental sense of Frenchness. On these shores, however, classic French cuisine found itself in uncomfortable intimacy with some rather strange bedfellows: pungent hot chile peppers; juicy red tomatoes; such foreign exotics as okra, bananas, and coconut; and that bizarre American grain, maize. Drawing its ingredients from a rich variety of local game and seafood, and from the newly established sugar and rice industries, the New Orleans pot simmered with piquant gumbos, zesty sausages, and spicy rice and vegetable mixtures.

The French contributed their own ingredients to this fermentative mix—butter, cream, and cheese, wines and liqueurs, and the daily necessity of life, crusty bread with its tender crumb. But more important than the ingredients themselves were the sense of style and the well-honed culinary technique that provided shape and clarity. Well-made stocks and court bouillons, a host of classic sauces, a sure hand, and a sophisticated palate—these gentled and refined the tumult of New Orleans food into its characteristic contours.

But though the French brought a heightened awareness and expertise to the New Orleans experience, their food did not remain unchanged. French dishes were invigorated with spicy sauces, reinvented with flavors and ingredients that would have been unimaginable on their native soil. For all the people who make up the vibrant culture of this multiethnic city have had full expression in the culinary design, their tastes and traditions an integral part of the whole. New Orleans has always maintained a festive and celebratory approach to food, in a largely public tradition where restaurants and chefs vie for excellence. In recent years new traditions from Southeast Asia and Latin America have entered the mix. Who knows where the creative endeavor will lead them?

RECIPES

Matzo Ball Gumbo

Deviled Crab Casserole

Gratinéed Stuffed Mussels

Red Snapper Creole-Style

Jumbo Shrimp Stuffed with Corn and Pecans

Rice Dressing with Shrimp and Sausage

Buttermilk Cracklin' Corn Bread

Banana-Rum Squares

Pineapple Bread Pudding with Hot Rum Sauce

Bourbon Fudge Pecan Pie

Matzo Ball Gumbo

In the nineteenth century, many Jews settled in the American South, bringing with them the tastes and traditions of their European homelands, and adapting once again to a whole new set of culinary possibilities. In this dish, the vibrant spirit and flavor of the Louisiana gumbo—itself an amalgam of African, Spanish, and native traditions—are refashioned within the guidelines of the biblical dietary laws: The prohibited shellfish is omitted and the smoky flavors of ham and sausage are provided by smoked turkey. The traditional matzo ball, rather than rice, is the starchy base on which the soupy stew is served.

THE GUMBO:

2 tablespoons vegetable oil
1 medium onion, finely chopped
2 stalks celery, with leaves, coarsely chopped
2 carrots, sliced
1 medium green bell pepper, seeded and diced
4 or 5 cloves garlic, minced
1 cup okra, trimmed and cut into small pieces
2 pounds smoked turkey drumsticks

2 cups canned crushed or chopped tomatoes
3 cups water
1 teaspoon salt
¼ teaspoon freshly ground black pepper
1 teaspoon dried thyme
1 to 2 teaspoons liquid hot pepper sauce, or to taste
Good handful of finely chopped parsley leaves
1 cup fresh corn kernels (or frozen defrosted)

THE MATZO BALLS:

4 eggs
⅓ cup melted chicken fat (or margarine or vegetable shortening, if desired)
½ cup water

1 teaspoon salt
1 clove garlic, crushed
2 to 3 tablespoons finely chopped parsley leaves
1 cup matzo meal

To make the gumbo:

1. Heat the oil in a heavy pot or Dutch oven and sauté the onion, celery, carrots, bell pepper, and garlic over moderate heat, stirring, until the vegetables become soft.

2. Stir in the okra and sauté for a few minutes.

3. Add the turkey, tomatoes, water, salt, black pepper, and thyme. Bring to a simmer, then cover and cook over low heat for about 1¼ to 1½ hours, until the turkey is very tender. Remove the turkey from the pot, let cool slightly, then remove the meat from the bones and cut into small chunks.

4. Add hot pepper sauce to the pot to taste, along with the parsley, corn, and turkey meat. Bring to a simmer, then cook for a few minutes. Serve the mixture over the matzo balls.

To make the matzo balls:

5. In a medium bowl, whisk the eggs thoroughly, then stir in the chicken fat, water, salt, garlic, and parsley and mix well. Add the matzo meal, mix thoroughly, then cover and refrigerate for 1 to 2 hours.

6. Prepare a large pot of boiling salted water. Roll the matzo mixture into small balls about the size of a cherry tomato. Drop the balls into the boiling water and cook for about 20 minutes. Remove the cooked dumplings from the pot with a slotted spoon.

7. To serve, place 2 or 3 matzo balls into a soup bowl; ladle the gumbo over the matzo balls. Pass additional hot sauce to add to taste.

Serves 4 to 6

Deviled Crab Casserole

This rich and highly seasoned crab casserole is an excellent example of how a classic French sauce gives structure and substance to a number of diverse local and ethnic ingredients. In much of Creole cookery, the roux evolved as a slowly cooked, heavily browned mixture, used as much for seasoning as for thickening. The sauce for this dish is thickened with the traditional French roux of lightly cooked butter and flour.

5 tablespoons butter, plus additional for buttering casserole or ramekins
4 to 6 scallions, finely chopped (about ½ cup chopped)
1 large stalk celery, finely chopped (about ½ cup chopped)
½ medium red bell pepper, seeded and finely chopped
3 cloves garlic, minced
2 tablespoons flour
1 cup chicken stock
Several good grinds of black pepper
1 tablespoon cream sherry

2 tablespoons heavy cream
½ teaspoon dried thyme
¼ teaspoon cayenne pepper
1 teaspoon Worcestershire sauce
Few drops of hot pepper sauce
1 cup shredded Gruyère, Emmentaler, or other high-quality Swiss cheese
1 pound fresh crabmeat, picked over to remove any cartilage
⅓ cup soft bread crumbs
Salt
Freshly ground black pepper
Paprika

1. Heat 2 tablespoons of the butter in a medium, heavy saucepan and sauté the scallions, celery, and bell pepper over moderate heat, stirring, until the vegetables become soft. Add the garlic and cook for another minute or two.

2. Stir in the flour to make a roux. Cook, stirring, for 2 to 3 minutes.

3. Add the stock and whisk it in until the mixture is smooth. Add the black pepper and the sherry, cream, thyme, cayenne, Worcestershire, and hot pepper sauce. Cook, stirring, until the mixture just comes to a simmer and becomes thickened and smooth.

4. Remove the sauce from the heat and stir in the cheese until it is well blended and smooth. Taste for salt, then fold in the crabmeat. Preheat the oven to 350°F.

5. Melt the remaining 3 tablespoons of butter, then stir in the bread crumbs, a good dash of salt, and several grinds of pepper.

6. Spoon the crab mixture into a buttered shallow casserole or individual ramekins. Sprinkle the bread crumbs over the top, then dust some paprika over the bread crumbs.

7. Bake for 20 to 30 minutes, until the casserole is bubbly and the bread crumbs are lightly browned.

Serves 4 as a main course,
6 to 8 as an appetizer

Gratinéed Stuffed Mussels

The New Orleans kitchen is a seafood kitchen, and while the focus is most intensely on oysters, shrimp, and crab, other shellfish have their place. In this dish, sweet plump mussels are enfolded in a classic French wine-and-cream sauce, heightened with the characteristic seasonings of the Creole kitchen. Serve three or four of the stuffed shells as an appetizer or first course.

2 tablespoons butter
1 medium onion, minced
1 small red or green bell pepper, seeded and minced
1 stalk celery, with leaves, finely diced
3 or 4 cloves garlic, minced
½ cup finely chopped mushrooms
1 medium tomato, coarsely chopped
½ teaspoon salt
Several good grinds of black pepper

¼ teaspoon cayenne pepper
2 tablespoons dry white wine
¼ cup heavy cream
Good squeeze of lemon juice
2 tablespoons finely minced parsley leaves
2 pounds mussels, steamed and shucked, shells reserved
⅓ cup soft bread crumbs
2 to 3 tablespoons butter, melted
Sprigs of curly parsley, for garnish

1. Melt the 2 tablespoons of butter in a skillet and sauté the onion, bell pepper, celery, and garlic until the onion wilts and just begins to turn golden.

2. Add the mushrooms and tomato and cook over moderate heat, stirring occasionally, until the mixture is soft and all the liquid has cooked away. Stir in the salt, black pepper, and cayenne.

3. Add the wine and cream, then cook, stirring, until the mixture thickens and there is just enough liquid to hold the vegetables together. Add the lemon juice, parsley, and mussels. Mix well, then remove from the heat. Taste for salt. Preheat the oven to 425°F.

4. Combine the bread crumbs and the melted butter and mix well.

5. Select the largest of the mussel (half) shells to stuff. Spoon the pan mixture into the shells, making sure that each shell has 1 or 2 mussels. Place the stuffed shells on a baking sheet or shallow casserole.

6. Sprinkle the buttered bread crumbs over the stuffed shells. Bake for 5 to 7 minutes, just until the mixture is hot and the crumb topping is lightly browned. Serve hot, 3 or 4 to a plate, garnished with sprigs of curly parsley.

Serves 4 to 6

TIP: A very good cook who did this recipe suggests chopping up the mussels before mixing them in the sauce. It's up to you; I personally can't bring myself to chop up mussels because I so love them succulent and whole.

Red Snapper Creole-Style

This simple but delicious dish is reminiscent of the spicy tomato-sauced dishes of West Africa as well as the flavorful seafood recipes of the Mediterranean. The flavor is characteristic of the Creole cooking of southern Louisiana, with its zesty blend of sweet and hot peppers, thyme, and Worcestershire sauce. Catfish fillets can be substituted for the red snapper.

2 tablespoons olive oil
1 medium onion, finely chopped
1 medium green bell pepper, seeded and diced
2 stalks celery, finely sliced
3 cloves garlic, minced
2 cups (14- to 16-ounce can) Italian-style tomatoes, with juice, coarsely chopped
1 tablespoon Worcestershire sauce
½ teaspoon salt
½ teaspoon dried thyme
Several good grinds of black pepper
½ teaspoon hot pepper sauce
Good squeeze of lemon juice
Small handful of finely chopped parsley
1¼ to 1½ pounds red snapper fillets
Additional chopped parsley, for garnish

1. Heat the oil in a large skillet and sauté the onion, bell pepper, celery, and garlic over moderate heat, stirring, until the vegetables soften and the onion is just beginning to turn golden.

2. Add the tomatoes, Worcestershire, salt, thyme, black pepper, hot pepper sauce, lemon juice, and parsley. Mix well, then simmer over low to moderate heat, uncovered, for 15 to 20 minutes, until the sauce is fairly thick and most of the liquid has cooked away.

3. Preheat the oven to 400°F. Layer the fish fillets in a lightly oiled shallow casserole or Pyrex baking dish. Salt and pepper the fish lightly.

4. Spoon the sauce evenly over the fish. Cover the baking dish with foil, then bake for about 15 to 20 minutes, or just until the fish flakes easily with a fork.

5. Garnish the fish with the additional chopped parsley and serve hot. This is traditionally served with rice, but it is also good with pan-fried or roasted potatoes.

Serves 4 to 6

Jumbo Shrimp Stuffed with Corn and Pecans

These highly seasoned stuffed shrimp are fairly easy to prepare and make a festive appetizer or first course. The stuffing ingredients are typical of the Creole kitchen, with distinctive flavors and textures uniquely characteristic of the eclectic style of New Orleans.

2 tablespoons olive oil, plus additional for drizzling over the shrimp
3 scallions, finely chopped
1 small red bell pepper, finely chopped
3 cloves garlic, minced
1 medium tomato, finely chopped
½ teaspoon dried marjoram
½ teaspoon hot pepper sauce
½ teaspoon salt
Several good grinds of black pepper

½ cup fresh corn kernels (or frozen defrosted)
¼ cup freshly toasted, coarsely chopped pecans
2 tablespoons finely chopped parsley
About 2 tablespoons soft bread crumbs
1 pound jumbo shrimp (about 10 to 15 to the pound)
Butter for baking dish
Fresh lemon juice
Lemon wedges and parsley, for garnish

1. Heat the 2 tablespoons oil in a medium skillet and sauté the scallions, bell pepper, and garlic over moderate heat, stirring, until the scallions wilt.

2. Add the tomato, marjoram, hot pepper sauce, salt, and black pepper. Cook, stirring, until the mixture is soft and most of the liquid has cooked away.

3. Stir in the corn, pecans, and parsley, then add enough bread crumbs to give the mixture some cohesiveness. Remove from the heat.

4. Peel and devein the shrimp, leaving on only the tip of the tail. Along the deveining cut, slice through the shrimp almost to the back but not all the way through. Flatten out the shrimp to butterfly.

5. Preheat the oven to 450°F. Butter a shallow casserole, baking dish, or pie plate large enough to hold the butterflied shrimp in one layer. Place the shrimp in the baking dish and sprinkle lightly with the lemon juice.

6. Spoon the stuffing evenly over the shrimp. Drizzle a little olive oil over the stuffing. Bake for about 10 minutes, or just until the shrimp turn pink. Serve hot, 2 to 3 per portion, garnished with a wedge of lemon and some sprigs of parsley.

Serves 4 to 6

Rice Dressing with Shrimp and Sausage

"Dressing" is the Southern term for stuffing, savory mixtures made from rice or stale corn bread used to stuff roast chicken or turkey. The dressings are frequently served on their own as main-course dishes, and in this capacity they more closely reflect the Spanish and African originals that so clearly influenced them. Oysters are a popular alternative to the shrimp.

½ to 1 pound fresh andouille, or other spicy fresh pork sausage meat, removed from casings
1 medium onion, finely chopped
3 to 4 scallions, coarsely chopped
1 small red or green bell pepper, diced
2 stalks celery, with leaves, finely sliced
4 cloves garlic, minced
1 to 2 tablespoons olive oil, if necessary

¼ teaspoon freshly ground black pepper
2 medium tomatoes, coarsely chopped
1 cup long-grain rice
½ teaspoon dried thyme
2 cups chicken stock
Several good dashes (or more to taste) of hot pepper sauce
8 ounces shrimp, peeled and deveined, or
8 ounces shucked oysters, with their liquor
2 to 3 tablespoons finely chopped parsley leaves

1. In a deep skillet or heavy pot, brown the sausage meat over moderate heat, breaking it up coarsely as it browns.

2. While the sausage is browning, add the onion, scallions, bell pepper, celery, and garlic. If the sausage meat does not yield enough fat, add a tablespoon or so of oil to sauté the vegetables.

3. When the meat is browned and the onions are tender, stir in the black pepper and tomatoes and cook, stirring, for a few minutes.

4. Stir in the rice and thyme, then add the chicken stock and hot pepper sauce. Bring to a simmer, then cover and cook over low heat for about 20 minutes.

5. After about 10 minutes of cooking, add the shrimp (or the oysters and their liquor). Cover and continue to cook until the rice is tender and all the liquid has been absorbed.

6. Stir in the parsley, then let stand, covered, off the heat, for 5 to 10 minutes before serving.

Serves 4

Buttermilk Cracklin' Corn Bread

From South America up to Canada, Native Americans used corn in a variety of pones, cakes, and flat breads. When Europeans arrived, they refashioned these products into the lighter, more airy breads to which they were accustomed, using eggs, dairy products, and chemical leaveners, mixing the cornmeal with wheat flour and additional flavoring ingredients. This Southern corn bread, unlike other more highly sweetened varieties from other parts of the country, is distinctly savory. It is best warm from the oven; leftover, it makes an excellent basis for poultry stuffing.

6 slices bacon
1 cup stone-ground yellow
   cornmeal
1 cup flour
1 teaspoon baking soda
1 teaspoon salt
1 teaspoon sugar

2 cups buttermilk
1 egg, lightly beaten
2 tablespoons bacon drippings
   or vegetable oil, plus
   additional for greasing pan
1 small onion, finely chopped

1. Fry the bacon until it is brown and crisp. Drain on paper towels, then crumble and set aside. Preheat the oven to 450°F.

2. In a large bowl, combine the cornmeal, flour, baking soda, salt, and sugar and blend thoroughly.

3. In a medium bowl, combine the buttermilk, egg, and drippings and mix well. Pour the mixture into the dry ingredients, along with the crumbled bacon and the chopped onion. Mix just until the ingredients are well blended—do not overmix.

4. Pour the batter into a greased 9-inch round or square pan. Bake for 18 to 20 minutes, until firm to the touch and lightly browned. Cut into wedges or squares to serve.

Serves 6 to 8

Banana-Rum Squares

The traditional African taste for stiff mushes and porridges made from starchy fruits and tubers met up in the American South with the European sweet tooth and its passion for puddings, pies, custards, and cakes. Reinforced by the burgeoning sugar-and-rum industry in the Caribbean, the collaboration produced such classics as candied yams, corn pudding, and sweet potato pie. These rich, moist banana squares are set off by a chocolate glaze studded with chopped peanuts, two native American foods that drastically changed their patterns when they joined the European sweet tradition.

4 medium, very ripe bananas	1 cup sugar
3 tablespoons dark or golden rum	2 eggs
1 teaspoon vanilla	2 cups flour
½ pound (2 sticks) unsalted butter, at room temperature	1½ teaspoons baking soda
	½ teaspoon salt

GLAZE:

2 tablespoons unsalted butter	4 ounces semisweet chocolate
2 tablespoons dark or golden rum	½ cup finely chopped salted peanuts

1. In a small bowl, mash the bananas thoroughly. Stir in the rum and vanilla and set aside.

2. In a large bowl, cream the butter with the sugar until smooth. Add the eggs one at a time, beating well after each addition. Stir in the mashed bananas.

3. Combine the flour, baking soda, and salt and mix the dry ingredients into the batter until they are thoroughly blended in. Preheat the oven to 350°F.

4. Butter a 13x9x2-inch cake pan. Spread the batter evenly in the pan and bake for about 35 to 40 minutes, until the cake is nicely browned and firm to the touch. Remove from the oven and let cool on a rack.

5. While the cake is cooling, make the glaze: In a small saucepan, combine the butter and rum and heat, stirring, until the mixture comes to a simmer. Simmer for a minute or two, then remove from the heat and add the chocolate, stirring until the chocolate is melted and the mixture smooth.

6. Spread the chocolate over the cooled cake; sprinkle the chopped peanuts over the chocolate. Cut into squares to serve.

Makes one 13x9x2-inch cake (12 to 16 squares)

Pineapple Bread Pudding with Hot Rum Sauce

Most cultures that use bread as a daily staple recycle their stale and leftover bread into innovative dishes—stuffings, casseroles, croutons, crumbs—and the French are no exception. New Orleans is known for a number of stale-bread concoctions, including pain perdu (French toast) and a variety of puddings. This one is very appealing, with its typical Creole additions of pineapple, pecans, and rum; I like it just as is, but the hot rum sauce turns it into a very festive dessert.

3 cups milk
2 tablespoons unsalted butter, plus additional for baking dish
½ cup sugar
4 cups stale French bread cubes or sourdough bread cubes
½ cup golden raisins
3 eggs

1 cup canned crushed pineapple, drained
½ teaspoon salt
¼ teaspoon freshly grated nutmeg
2 teaspoons vanilla
2 tablespoons dark or golden rum
½ cup coarsely broken pecans

HOT RUM SAUCE:

2 tablespoons unsalted butter, at room temperature
2 tablespoons firmly packed brown sugar

½ cup heavy cream
¼ cup dark or golden rum
Good pinch of salt

1. In a saucepan, combine the milk, butter, and sugar. Heat just until small bubbles appear around the edge and the butter melts.

2. In a large bowl, combine the bread cubes and raisins. Pour the hot milk mixture over the bread, mix well, then let stand for 1 to 2 hours. Preheat the oven to 350°F.

3. Whisk the eggs thoroughly, then stir them into the bread mixture, along with the pineapple, salt, nutmeg, vanilla, and rum. Mix well, then stir in the pecans.

4. Butter a deep 2-quart casserole or soufflé dish. Pour the mixture into the dish and bake for 60 to 70 minutes, until puffed and lightly browned.

5. Let the pudding cool; it will shrink as it cools. Serve chilled or at room temperature, with the hot rum sauce, if desired.

6. To make the sauce: Cream together the butter and brown sugar, then cook, stirring, until the mixture is smooth and thick.

7. Add the cream, rum, and salt. Mix well and simmer, stirring, for about 5 minutes. Serve the sauce warm or hot over the pudding.

Serves 6 to 8

Bourbon Fudge Pecan Pie

The praline is said to be the invention of French nuns in a New Orleans convent who translated a European tradition of sugared almonds into a confection studded with pecans, the sweet nut native to the American South. Pecans have become a staple in the Creole dessert repertoire, an unabashed exercise in caloric overload. In this rich pie they join with chocolate and bourbon, America's own distilled whiskey made from corn mash.

¼ pound (1 stick) unsalted
    butter
4 ounces (4 squares)
    unsweetened chocolate
4 eggs
1 cup white sugar
½ cup firmly packed brown
    sugar

3 tablespoons bourbon whiskey
1 teaspoon vanilla
Pastry for a 9-inch pie
1 cup coarsely chopped pecans
Whipped cream or ice cream,
    for serving

1. In a small saucepan, melt the butter and chocolate over low heat, stirring, until smooth and well blended. Let cool slightly. Preheat the oven to 375°F.

2. In a mixing bowl, beat the eggs until frothy. Gradually add in the white sugar and brown sugar and beat until the mixture is thick and smooth.

3. Stir the chocolate into the egg mixture, then add the bourbon and vanilla and mix well.

4. Fit the pastry into a fluted 9-inch tart or pie pan. Sprinkle the pecans evenly over the bottom of the pastry. Pour the chocolate mixture into the pastry shell.

5. Bake the pie for 30 to 35 minutes, until just firm and beginning to crack slightly on the top. Remove and let cool completely. Serve in wedges with whipped cream or ice cream.

Serves 8

index

beef *(cont.)*
   spiced pepper, 23
   spicy fried steak strips, 57–58
   sweet-and-sour stuffed peppers, 138
   tiny spiced meatballs with pine nuts, 124
   and vegetable stew in spicy tomato sauce
      (caldereta), 98–99
beet, roasted, salad with yogurt and dill,
   186–87
biryani, vegetable, 37–38
black-eyed peas in coconut-peanut sauce,
   27–28
bourbon fudge pecan pie, 257–58
bread:
   buttermilk cracklin' corn, 253–54
   plantain coconut, 240–41
   pudding, pineapple, with hot rum sauce,
      256–57
buffalo and black bean chili, 215–16
bulgur, cabbage rolls with lamb, herbs and,
   122–23
Burma, 62–73
buttermilk cracklin' corn bread, 253–54

cabbage:
   and bacon salad, warm, 201
   cornmeal-stuffed, braised with sauerkraut,
      182–83
   rolls with bulgur, lamb, and herbs, 122–23
   Straits chicken salad, 55
cakes:
   banana-rum squares, 254–55
   chocolate hazelnut, 188–89
   Jewish apple, 148–49
   plantain coconut bread, 240–41
   rich chocolate macaroon, 147–48
caldereta (beef and vegetable stew in spicy
   tomato sauce), 98–99
calf's liver with apples, onions, and Riesling,
   195–96
caramel coconut flan, 101–2
caraway, mushroom-spinach roll with dill
   and, 180–81
Caribbean, 225–42
carrots, golden rice pilau with raisins,
   saffron and, 113–14
cashews:
   ginger chicken with, 83–84
   shrimp with, in spicy coconut sauce, 20
   spiced shrimp and pineapple with, 230
cheese:
   bacon, mushroom, and Muenster tart,
      198–99
   and chile corn cakes, 221
   gratin of rice and hearts of palm, 238

and leek pie, 127
potatoes with cream and, 200
red pepper caviar with, 185–86
ricotta cheesecake with macaroon crust,
   167–68
cherries:
   summer fruits in white-wine syrup, 187
   sweet rice with fruit and nuts, 117
chicken:
   appetizer rollups with hoisin dipping
      sauce, 78–79
   chile-fried rice with shrimp and, 54
   and corn soup, garlic, 91
   curry, fragrant, 66–67
   with eggplant in tomato-fennel sauce, 159
   ginger, with cashews, 83–84
   groundnut stew, 10
   and mango salad, 82–83
   noodles, 67–68
   with okra and corn, 11–12
   with olives and fennel, 178
   pilau with pigeon peas, curried, 231–32
   piripiri wings, 21
   roast, with spiced tomato glaze, 110–11
   salad, Straits, 55
   spicy, with potatoes and green chiles,
      34–35
   spicy, with tomatoes, coconut, and
      coriander, 22
   strips, chile-marinated (pollo adovado),
      212–13
chickpeas:
   braised lamb with, 125
   lentils, rice and, 139–40
chile pepper(s):
   almond, and garlic sauce, 223
   and cheese corn cakes, 221
   eggplant with basil and, 58–59
   fried plantains with peppery dipping
      sauce, 14–15
   -fried rice with chicken and shrimp, 54
   green, posole with lamb and, 218–19
   green, spicy chicken with potatoes and,
      34–35
   green, spoonbread, 222
   marinated rock shrimp with coconut and,
      93–94
   mixed peppers with eggplant and tahini,
      140
   red pepper, tomato, and garlic purée
      (ajvar), 184–85
   relish, spiced (zhoug), 144
   spiced fresh corn with tomato, peppers,
      and coconut, 236
   spiced pepper beef, 23

stuffed with pork and peanuts, 84–85
Texas caviar, 220
chile pepper, dried:
    -marinated chicken strips (pollo
      adovado), 212–13
    pasta with olives, garlic and, 162
    red pepper, tomato and garlic purée
      (ajvar), 184–85
chili:
    buffalo and black bean, 215–16
    mixed, with pork and pinto beans, 216–17
chocolate:
    banana-rum squares, 254–55
    bourbon fudge pecan pie, 257–58
    hazelnut cake, 188–89
    macaroon cake, rich, 147–48
chopped liver, meatless, 141
chorizo, Filipino paella with shrimp and,
    94–95
choucroute garni (sauerkraut with mixed
    sausages), 196–97
chutney:
    date and onion salad, 39
    fresh onion and coriander, 116
    peach, 40
ciorba, mushroom, 173–74
coconut:
    baked banana pudding with, 28–29
    basil sauce, salmon poached in, 81–82
    broth, seafood noodles in (laksa lemak),
      46–47
    caramel flan, 101–2
    marinated rock shrimp with chile and,
      93–94
    peanut dipping sauce, sweet-and-sour
      lamb satay with, 56–57
    peanut sauce, black-eyed peas in, 27–28
    plantain bread, 240–41
    rice, aromatic, 70–71
    sauce, fresh cod and spinach in, 19
    sauce, spicy, shrimp with cashews in, 20
    spiced fresh corn with tomato, peppers
      and, 236
    spicy chicken with tomatoes, coriander
      and, 22
cod, fresh, and spinach in coconut sauce, 19
collard greens and lentils, spiced, 26–27
condiments:
    date and onion salad, 39
    fresh onion and coriander chutney, 116
    fried plantains with peppery dipping
      sauce, 14–15
    mixed olive salad, 166
    peach chutney, 40
    spiced hot pepper relish (zhoug), 144

coriander:
    and onion chutney, fresh, 116
    spiced split pea soup with mint and, 32–33
    spicy chicken with tomatoes, coconut and,
      22
corn:
    and chicken soup, garlic, 91
    chicken with okra and, 11–12
    chowder, creamy double, 210
    green chile spoonbread, 222
    jumbo shrimp stuffed with pecans and,
      251–52
    posole with lamb and green chile, 218–19
    roasted, and banana fritters, 15–16
    spiced fresh, with tomato, peppers, and
      coconut, 236
    sweet, and pumpkin custard, frozen, 61
cornmeal:
    buttermilk cracklin' corn bread, 253–54
    cheese and chile corn cakes, 221
    green chile spoonbread, 222
    -stuffed cabbage braised with sauerkraut,
      182–83
crab:
    casserole, deviled, 247–48
    and pork balls, crispy, 80–81
    and sweet potato cakes, crispy, with
      tamarind dipping sauce, 51–52
crawfish, Jollof rice with, 8–9
cream:
    fresh raspberry, 204
    gratin of rice and hearts of palm, 238
    mango, with pineapple, 224
    potatoes with cheese and, 200
    smoky eggplant, 130–31
cucumber(s):
    chunky mixed salad, 143
    and pineapple salad (rojak), 60
curry(ied):
    chicken pilau with pigeon peas, 231–32
    eggplant and potatoes, 25–26
    fragrant chicken, 66–67
    goat, 234–35
    lamb, Burmese-style, 69–70
    lamb and bean stew, 35–36
    lamb and peanut, 24–25
    Masaman beef, with peanuts and potatoes,
      86–87
    potato, with spinach, 71–72
custard:
    caramel coconut flan, 101–2
    frozen pumpkin and sweet corn, 61

date(s):
    and onion salad, 39

date(s) *(cont.)*
　　Sephardic fruit and nut paste (haroseth),
　　　146
desserts:
　　apricot yogurt with hazelnuts, 131–32
　　baked banana pudding with coconut,
　　　28–29
　　banana-rum squares, 254–55
　　bourbon fudge pecan pie, 257–58
　　candied pumpkin, 242
　　caramel coconut flan, 101–2
　　chocolate hazelnut cake, 188–89
　　fresh raspberry cream, 204
　　frozen pumpkin and sweet corn custard,
　　　61
　　Jewish apple cake, 148–49
　　mango cream with pineapple, 224
　　pineapple bread pudding with hot rum
　　　sauce, 256–57
　　pistachio revani with saffron syrup,
　　　132–33
　　plantain coconut bread, 240–41
　　plum tart with almonds, 203
　　rich chocolate macaroon cake, 147–48
　　ricotta cheesecake with macaroon crust,
　　　167–68
　　Sephardic fruit and nut paste (haroseth),
　　　146
　　summer fruits in white-wine syrup, 187
　　sweet rice with fruit and nuts, 117
dill:
　　mushroom-spinach roll with caraway and,
　　　180–81
　　roasted beet salad with yogurt and, 186–87
dips, *see* spreads and dips
dressing, rice, with shrimp and sausage,
　　252–53
dumplings:
　　banana-shrimp, 47–48
　　meat, in broth (mantu), 109

East Africa, 17–29
eggplant:
　　and anchovy sauce for pasta, 161
　　with basil and chile, 58–59
　　chicken with, in tomato-fennel sauce, 159
　　cream, smoky, 130–31
　　layered casserole of pasta and, 163–64
　　marinated, with olive oil and tomatoes
　　　(imam bayeldi), 128–29
　　meatless chopped liver, 141
　　mixed peppers with tahini and, 140
　　and potatoes, curried, 25–26
　　savory, with yogurt, 114–15
　　with shrimp, sesame, 65–66

Texas caviar, 220
escabeche, seafood, 228–29
Europe, 151–204

fennel:
　　chicken with olives and, 178
　　tomato sauce, chicken with eggplant in,
　　　159
fish:
　　adobo of, with tomatoes, 96
　　baked marinated, 52–53
　　Dalmation marinated tuna, 175–76
　　eggplant and anchovy sauce for pasta, 161
　　fresh cod and spinach in coconut sauce,
　　　19
　　ragù of swordfish with tomatoes and mint,
　　　158
　　red snapper Creole-style, 250
　　roasted sea bass with spiced yogurt crust,
　　　137
　　salmon poached in coconut-basil sauce,
　　　81–82
　　sardine and olive spread, 157
　　savory herring spread, 174–75
　　seafood escabeche, 228–29
　　seafood noodles in coconut broth (laksa
　　　lemak), 46–47
　　Senegalese, with mixed vegetables, 7–8
　　spiced pickled, 33–34
　　sweet-and-sour salmon with raisins and
　　　mint, 136
　　walnut-crusted salmon with vegetables,
　　　176–77
　　see also seafood
flan, caramel coconut, 101–2
fritters:
　　garlic plantain, 237
　　roasted corn and banana, 15–16
　　tiny spiced shrimp, 64
fruit(s):
　　and nut paste, Sephardic (haroseth), 146
　　and nuts, sweet rice with, 117
　　summer, in white-wine syrup, 187
　　see also specific fruits

garlic:
　　almond, and chile sauce, 223
　　chicken and corn soup, 91
　　pasta with olives, hot pepper and, 162
　　plantain fritters, 237
　　red pepper, and tomato purée (ajvar),
　　　184–85
ginger chicken with cashews, 83–84
goat, curry, 234–35
gratin of rice and hearts of palm, 238

nut(s) *(cont.)*
chocolate hazelnut cake, 188–89
ginger chicken with cashews, 83–84
jumbo shrimp stuffed with corn and
pecans, 251–52
pine, tiny spiced meatballs with, 124
pine, zucchini with raisins and, 164–65
pistachio revani with saffron syrup,
132–33
shrimp with cashews in spicy coconut
sauce, 20
spiced shrimp and pineapple with
cashews, 230
summer fruits in white-wine syrup, 187
sweet rice with fruit and, 117
walnut-crusted salmon with vegetables,
176–77
see also almond; peanut

okra, chicken with corn and, 11–12
olive(s):
braised lamb with rosemary, tomatoes
and, 160
chicken with fennel and, 178
lemony leeks with tomatoes and, 142
mixed, salad, 166
pasta with garlic, hot pepper and, 162
and sardine spread, 157
onion(s):
calf's liver with apples, Riesling and,
195–96
and coriander chutney, fresh, 116
and date salad, 39
shredded pork with peppers and, 232–33
soup with beer, 192
orange(s):
hearts of palm, and avocado salad, 239
salad, double, with honey and mint, 145
Sephardic fruit and nut paste (haroseth),
146

paella, Filipino, with shrimp and chorizo,
94–95
pasta:
hearty vegetable and sausage soup, 156
layered casserole of eggplant and, 163–64
with olives, garlic, and hot pepper, 162
see also noodles
pasta sauces:
eggplant and anchovy, 161
ragù of swordfish with tomatoes and mint,
158
sardine and olive, 157
pea, split, spiced soup with mint and
coriander, 32–33

peach chutney, 40
peanut(s):
banana-rum squares, 254–55
chicken groundnut stew, 10
chiles stuffed with pork and, 84–85
coconut dipping sauce, sweet-and-sour
lamb satay with, 56–57
coconut sauce, black-eyed peas in, 27–28
and lamb curry, 24–25
Masaman beef curry with potatoes and,
86–87
mixed vegetable mafé, 12–13
pan-fried spring rolls with shrimp and
(lumpia), 92–93
sauce, beef braised with vegetables in
(kari kari), 99–100
shrimp, spicy grilled, 6
and spinach sauce, 13–14
sweet-and-spicy bean curd with, 87–88
pecan(s):
jumbo shrimp stuffed with corn and,
251–52
pie, bourbon fudge, 257–58
pepper(s), bell:
chunky mixed salad, 143
fried plantains with peppery dipping
sauce, 14–15
mixed peppers with eggplant and tahini,
140
pork cutlets with wine, sour cream and,
179–80
red, caviar with cheese, 185–86
red, tomato and garlic purée (ajvar),
184–85
shredded pork with onions and, 232–33
spiced fresh corn with tomato, peppers,
and coconut, 236
spiced pepper beef, 23
sweet-and-sour stuffed, 138
Texas caviar, 220
pepper, chile, *see* chile pepper; chile pepper,
dried
Philippines, 89–102
picadillo (spicy beef and plantain hash),
233–34
pies:
bourbon fudge pecan, 257–58
leek and cheese, 127
pigeon peas, curried chicken pilau with,
231–32
pilaf, Ali Pasha rice, 126
pilau:
curried chicken, with pigeon peas, 231–32
golden rice, with carrots, raisins, and
saffron, 113–14

pineapple:
  bread pudding with hot rum sauce, 256–57
  and cucumber salad (rojak), 60
  mango cream with, 224
  spiced shrimp and, with cashews, 230
pine nuts:
  tiny spiced meatballs with, 124
  zucchini with raisins and, 164–65
piripiri wings, 21
pistachio(s):
  revani with saffron syrup, 132–33
  sweet rice with fruit and nuts, 117
plantain(s):
  and beef hash, spicy (picadillo), 233–34
  braised sweet pork with, 97–98
  coconut bread, 240–41
  fried, with peppery dipping sauce, 14–15
  garlic fritters, 237
plum(s):
  spiced lamb with, 112–13
  summer fruits in white-wine syrup, 187
  tart with almonds, 203
pollo adovado (chile-marinated chicken strips), 212–13
pork:
  braised sweet, with plantains, 97–98
  chiles stuffed with peanuts and, 84–85
  coins, golden, 68–69
  and crab balls, crispy, 80–81
  cutlets with peppers, wine, and sour cream, 179–80
  mixed chili with pinto beans and, 216–17
  shredded, with onions and peppers, 232–33
  smoked, with vegetables in wine sauce, 197–98
posole:
  creamy double corn chowder, 210
  with lamb and green chile, 218–19
potato(es):
  with cream and cheese, 200
  curried eggplant and, 25–26
  curry with spinach, 71–72
  Masaman beef curry with peanuts and, 86–87
  spicy chicken with green chiles and, 34–35
poultry, *see* chicken; turkey
pudding:
  baked banana, with coconut, 28–29
  green chile spoonbread, 222
  pineapple bread, with hot rum sauce, 256–57
  sweet rice with fruit and nuts, 117

pumpkin:
  and bean soup, creamy spiced, 227–28
  candied, 242
  soup, Thai, 76–77
  and sweet corn custard, frozen, 61
raisins:
  golden rice pilau with carrots, saffron and, 113–14
  Sephardic fruit and nut paste (haroseth), 146
  sweet-and-sour salmon with mint and, 136
  sweet rice with fruit and nuts, 117
  zucchini with pine nuts and, 164–65
raspberry cream, fresh, 204
red snapper Creole-style, 250
relishes:
  date and onion salad, 39
  fresh onion and coriander chutney, 116
  fried plantains with peppery dipping sauce, 14–15
  peach chutney, 40
  spiced hot pepper (zhoug), 144
revani, pistachio, with saffron syrup, 132–33
rice:
  aromatic coconut, 70–71
  chile-fried, with chicken and shrimp, 54
  Filipino paella with shrimp and chorizo, 94–95
  gratin of hearts of palm and, 238
  Jollof, with crawfish, 8–9
  lentils, and chickpeas, 139–40
  pilaf, Ali Pasha, 126
  pilau with carrots, raisins, and saffron, golden, 113–14
  sweet, with fruit and nuts, 117
  sweet-and-sour stuffed peppers, 138
  vegetable biryani, 37–38
rojak (pineapple and cucumber salad), 60
rosemary, braised lamb with olives, tomatoes and, 160
rum:
  banana squares, 254–55
  sauce, hot, pineapple bread pudding with, 256–57
saffron:
  golden rice pilau with carrots, raisins and, 113–14
  syrup, pistachio revani with, 132–33
salads:
  chunky mixed, 143
  double orange, with honey and mint, 145
  hearts of palm, avocado, and orange, 239

potato curry with, 71–72
split pea soup with mint and coriander, spiced, 32–33
spoonbread, green chile, 222
spreads and dips:
  lemony leeks with olives and tomatoes, 142
  meatless chopped liver, 141
  mixed peppers with eggplant and tahini, 140
  red pepper, tomato, and garlic purée (ajvar), 184–85
  red pepper caviar with cheese, 185–86
  sardine and olive spread, 157
  savory herring spread, 174–75
  spiced hot pepper relish (zhoug), 144
  Texas caviar, 220
spring rolls with peanuts and shrimp, pan-fried (lumpia), 92–93
steak strips, spicy fried, 57–58
stews:
  beef and vegetable, in spicy tomato sauce (caldereta), 98–99
  braised lamb with chickpeas, 125
  braised lamb with rosemary, olives, and tomatoes, 160
  chicken groundnut, 10
  chicken with okra and corn, 11–12
  curried lamb and bean, 35–36
  matzo ball gumbo, 245–46
  mixed vegetable mafé, 12–13
  posole with lamb and green chile, 218–19
  ragù of swordfish with tomatoes and mint, 158
  spiced lentils and collard greens, 26–27
  spicy chicken with potatoes and green chiles, 34–35
sweet potato and crab cakes, crispy, with tamarind dipping sauce, 51–52
swordfish, ragù of, with tomatoes and mint, 158

tahini, mixed peppers with eggplant and, 140
tamale pie, turkey, 213–14
tamarind dipping sauce, crispy crab and sweet potato cakes with, 51–52
tarts:
  bacon, mushroom, and Muenster, 198–99
  plum, with almonds, 203
Tex-Mex, 208–24
Thailand, 74–88
tomato(es):
  adobo of fish with, 96
  baked "stuffed," 165–66
  braised lamb with rosemary, olives and, 160
  chunky mixed salad, 143
  fennel sauce, chicken with eggplant in, 159
  glaze, spiced, roast chicken with, 110–11
  lemony leeks with olives and, 142
  marinated eggplant with olive oil and (imam bayeldi), 128–29
  pasta with olives, garlic, and hot pepper, 162
  ragù of swordfish with mint and, 158
  red pepper, and garlic purée (ajvar), 184–85
  red snapper Creole-style, 250
  sauce, spicy, beef and vegetable stew in (caldereta), 98–99
  savory eggplant with yogurt, 114–15
  spiced fresh corn with peppers, coconut and, 236
  spicy chicken with coconut, coriander and, 22
  Texas caviar, 220
  zucchini with raisins and pine nuts, 164–65
tuna, Dalmation marinated, 175–76
Turkey, 118–33
turkey:
  braised with garden vegetables, 121–22
  matzo ball gumbo, 245–46
  tamale pie, 213–14

vegetable(s):
  adobo with noodles, 100–101
  beef braised with, in peanut sauce (kari kari), 99–100
  and beef stew in spicy tomato sauce (caldereta), 98–99
  biryani, 37–38
  garden, turkey braised with, 121–22
  mixed, mafé, 12–13
  mixed, marinated artichokes with, 129–30
  mixed, Senegalese fish with, 7–8
  root, korma of, 115–16
  and sausage soup, hearty, 156
  smoked pork with, in wine sauce, 197–98
  soup with yogurt and herbs, hearty, 172
  walnut-crusted salmon with, 176–77
  see also specific vegetables

walnut(s):
  -crusted salmon with vegetables, 176–77
  summer fruits in white-wine syrup, 187
West Africa, 4–16